THE POLITICS OF THE TRAIL

Each day, as Oded Löwenheim rides his mountain bike along dirt trails and wadis in the hills of Jerusalem to the Mt. Scopus campus of the Hebrew University, he feels a strong emotional connection to his surroundings. But for him this connection also generates, paradoxically, feelings and emotions of confusion and estrangement.

Löwenheim confronts this tension by focusing on his encounters with three places along the trail that represent the present, past, and possible future of this land: the separation fence between Israel and the Palestinians; the ruins of the Palestinian village of Qalunya, demolished in 1948; and the trail connecting the largest 9/11 memorial site outside the United States with a top-secret nuclear-proof bunker for the Israeli cabinet. He shares the stories of these places and the people he meets along the way and considers how his own subjectivity is shaped by the landscape and culture of conflict. Moreover, he deconstructs, challenges, and resists the concepts and institutions that constitute such a culture and invites dialogue about the idea of conflict as a culture.

The Politics of the Trail asks: Can one emancipate oneself from the grip of a culture of conflict and violence, and at what social and emotional cost? Through his daily, close, and physical interaction with the terrain and landscape of conflict, Löwenheim grapples with this question and ponders as well about the concept of authenticity. This autoethnographic study thus shows how the personal is intimately intertwined with the political. By bringing in the personal experience of himself as an IR academic who is literally in the field, Löwenheim leaves behind him the detached narrative of academia and develops, instead, an account that reminds readers the humanity of both the producers and the subjects of political research.

Oded Löwenheim is Senior Lecturer in the Department of International Relations at the Hebrew University of Jerusalem.

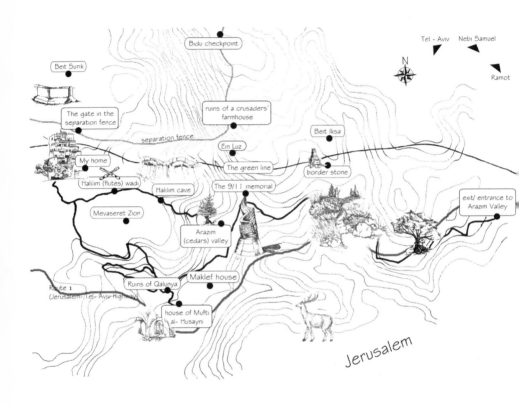

Tel - Aviv · Nebi Samuel

Ramot

Beit Surik

Bidu checkpoint

The gate in the separation fence

ruins of a crusaders' farmhouse

separation fence

Beit Iksa

Ein Luz

My home

The green line

border stone

Haliīm (flutes) wadi

Haliīm cave

The 9/11 memorial

exit/ entrance to Arazim Valley

Mevaseret Zion

Arazim (cedars) valley

Route 1 (Jerusalem-/Tel- Aviv-Highway)

Ruins of Qalunya

Maklef house

house of Mufti al- Husayni

Jerusalem

The Politics of the Trail

REFLEXIVE MOUNTAIN BIKING ALONG THE FRONTIER OF JERUSALEM

Oded Löwenheim

The University of Michigan Press
Ann Arbor

Published in the United States of America by
The University of Michigan Press
Manufactured in the United States of America
♾ Printed on acid-free paper

2017   2016   2015   2014   4   3   2   1

A CIP catalog record for this book is available from the British Library.

Library of Congress Cataloging-in-Publication Data

Löwenheim, Oded, 1970–
    The politics of the trail : reflexive mountain biking along the frontier of Jerusalem /
Oded Löwenheim.
        pages   cm
    Includes bibliographical references and index.
    ISBN 978-0-472-07212-5 (hardback) — ISBN 978-0-472-05212-7 (paperback) —
ISBN 978-0-472-12028-4 (e-book)
    1. Mountain biking—Jerusalem.   2. Mountain biking—Political aspects—Jerusalem.
3. Arab-Israeli conflict.   4. Löwenheim, Oded, 1970–   5. Jerusalem—Description and
travel.   I. Title.

GV1046.J47L68   2014
796.630956.94′42—dc23
                                                                                          2013050785

All photographs in this book are by Idit Wagner; used by permission.
The frontispiece map was created by Yael Wasyng-Fuchs and Yonatan Fialkoff.

ACKNOWLEDGMENTS

Melody Herr, my editor at the University of Michigan Press, was the best editor one can hope for—thoughtful, full of insights and ideas, and highly perceptive.

In Vancouver Island, Jerry Shulman was my first reader—he read this book while I still wrote the chapters, and implored me to finish it soon. I thank him for his keen interest. Peter Stein also read the entire manuscript and loved it. Thanks, Peter, for your big heart, humor, and optimism. Filipa Santos was kind enough to hear me read aloud great "chunks" of the manuscript. Thanks, Filipa, for your patience and for the cookies and the other goodies. Avigail Eisenberg invited me to present the book in her class at the University of Victoria, and it was a very positive experience. Thanks for all the people who listened to me talk about this book in Victoria, Vancouver, Nanaimo, Ottawa, Toronto, Fredericton, and, of course, Jerusalem.

Oren Barak, Yonatan Fialkoff, Hillel Cohen, Meron Benvenisti, Mira Sucharov, Amiram Oren, Shaul Arieli, and Rotem Mor walked and rode with me in the wadis and valleys in the frontier of Jerusalem, and helped me to see the landscape through eyes other than my own.

Idit, my wife, photographed the images for this book and helped me to look inside myself. The book is dedicated with love to her and to our children, Dror and Oshri.

CONTENTS

PROLOGUE

Losing Traction in the Hills of Jerusalem

It is an early morning hour at the beginning of May 2010. I am riding on my mountain bicycle on a single track, a narrow mountain-biking trail, that cuts through the Halilim (in Hebrew, "Flutes") dry riverbed. The days are getting warmer. In a few weeks, the scorching heat of summer will fall upon the hills and wadis (in Arabic, "valleys, dry riverbeds") around Jerusalem,[1] bringing with it the uniform yellows and browns of the long dry season, and a thin layer of white dust. But spring is still here, and for a few more precious days everything will still be green and colorful. The hill slopes on both sides of the trail are covered with green grass and patches of red buttercups. Here and there, a few violet-pink cyclamen still bloom. Yellow carpets of mustard flowers spread everywhere. The air is saturated with fresh and soft scents of blossoming flowers, wet soil, and lush grass.

Underneath the grass and the flowers, I see long rows of very old agricultural terraces made of countless blocks of limestone put carefully and accurately on each other in perfect order. In many parts, though, the terraces are slowly crumbling, stones gradually falling off, as no one amends the weathering caused by the elements. Innumerable terraces like these cover much of the Jerusalem and Judean hills. As I flow down with the single track toward the bottom of the wadi, I think, "Who built these terraces and when? They look ancient. It was an amazingly complex work, of many generations, to collect, pile up, and maintain all these numerous stones on each other in such accuracy, a work of perfect craftsmanship." I promise myself I'll read about the history of the terraces in the

Judean hills, and recall that I made this promise several times before but haven't found the time yet to explore the history of the landscape I pass through every day. This disturbs me. I find myself in recent years more and more yearning for the local landscape, for the real and authentic that I can feel with my senses; I crave the reachable, for what my eyes can see around me, for where my feet and the bike can take me. I need the things that I can sense and experience daily with my body: to breathe and smell the air of the hills, to feel the sun or the rain on my skin, to experience the terrain and the topography with my muscles. The physicality of mountain biking in these hills and wadis makes me feel I belong here, that I know the territory with my body.

But I'm coming from the "international"—I teach and study international politics. I think, not for the first time, how abstract and remote the international remains, a mostly imaginative realm that most people do not, cannot, physically experience or explore as such.[2] I wonder, "Could there be any international context to these terraces?" Immediately I realize how disciplined I am, literally. "I must let go a bit," I think.

I return my attention to the trail. Short almond trees, lush with green foliage, dot the terraces. Not too many weeks ago, the almonds were covered by a myriad of white flowers, blazing like ghosts in the night and glittering like snow during the day. The wind spread the sweet scent of the flowers throughout the wadi, making the hard climb on my way back home in the evenings a bit easier. Now, in this early May morning, on my way to the Mt. Scopus campus of the Hebrew University, in Jerusalem, I look around me and store in my memory— the cognitive, but also the physical—that of the muscles and the body—the coolness and beauty of spring. I will call upon these images and sensations in the coming long weeks of summer, cash them out to somewhat cool myself when working my way up in the hills in temperatures higher than 30 degrees Celsius (86 Fahrenheit), even in the morning and the evening.

Evergreen "Jerusalem pines," planted in the millions in the Jerusalem hills by the Jewish National Fund (JNF) during the 1950s and 1960s, dominate large swaths of the terraced landscape. The terraces transform the slopes into what looks like a giant's staircase. The staircases of terraces climb, on the wadi's northern and southern slopes, to the houses of my town: Mevasseret Zion (in Hebrew, Herald of Zion), a suburb of Jerusalem. White limestone-covered walls of large villas and houses at the top of the ridges shine in the morning's sun. All the houses on the northern ridge, the newly built neighborhood of Reches Halilim (in Hebrew, Flutes' Crest), have red tile, sloping roofs reminiscent of Swiss cottages in the Alps. Yet it hardly snows here, perhaps only once in a few years, and the red roofs are rather a manifestation of a petit bourgeois mentality, as well as a municipal bylaw that seeks to imbue the sleeping town of Mevasseret with "country" and "rural" authenticity.

The trail now turns a bit more rugged and technical (meaning challenging and requiring more attention and skill). Excitement and adrenaline surge through my body, and a pleasant sense of danger runs in me as I "clear" (namely, jump over obstacles to negotiate a trail successfully without crashing) half-a-meter-high drop-offs, hopping over rocks and roots. I constantly work with my body, standing on the pedals, bending my arms and leaning forward when I want to pull up the handlebar and hop over a rock, or stretching myself backward, positioning my body behind the saddle to move weight to the rear axle and thus lift the front wheel off the ground and prepare to jump over a descending "stair," landing on the rear wheel. I slow down as I near a switchback on the trail, trying not to wear down the track by skating in the curve and thus "bite" and undermine the soil with the outer knobs of the bike's tires. I care for the trail; I belong in it and own it by my daily passage through it. It is my trail. I feel I know every turn, every corner, rock, root, and stair in it. And I know all these elements both by quickly flowing in the trail and jumping over its obstacles in the descent and by slowly and patiently rolling over the trail in the ascent. I overcome this trail. The trail provides me with a sense of achievement and even intimacy.

The cold air of the morning fills my lungs; I shiver a bit because of the increasing chill as I descend further in the wadi. I feel alive, and as I clear another drop-off, I joyfully howl a long and loud "woo-hoo." I feel free and full of energy for the new day. The bicycle's shock absorbers cushion many of the blows and vibrations, but sometimes, in a sharp drop-off, the suspension reaches its maximal stroke and knacks. The blow is absorbed, uncushioned, by my body. I gasp, contain the pain, and continue the descent.

I am now about halfway down this trail. When I finish downhilling the Halilim wadi, I will enter the wider and less "technical" track of the Arazim (in Hebrew, Cedars) Valley, which will lead me, eventually, to Mt. Scopus. There I will change clothes, and put my bicycle in my office, and will often find myself during the day looking at the bike and yearning for the open spaces of the wadis. Mt. Scopus: the citadel campus, towering over Palestinian East Jerusalem and the Dead Sea.[3] Endless concrete corridors and labyrinths, buildings connected

The Halilim Cave (Cave of Flutes). *In the background*, the Har Nof neighborhood, Jerusalem. (Photograph by Idit Wagner.)

to each other by long concrete passageways (at the education building there are even narrow windows in the corridor, mimicking firing loopholes), huge underground parking levels, and high metal fences surrounding the heavily guarded compound. Open space is so rare here, found mainly on the older part of the campus. I need space, I need space, I keep thinking during the day.

Now I approach the deepest part of the Halilim wadi, where the opposing slopes turn into walls of a relatively high canyon. The dolomite walls of the canyon are dotted here, on both sides, with elongated and relatively low karst caves, created over the millennia by water permeating the sedimentary rock and dissolving it. The caves are divided into many small chambers and cavities, and the longest cave among the five is known as the Cave of Flutes. The cave gave its name to the whole wadi, says an explanatory sign at the trail's head at the top of the hill, amid the houses of Mevasseret, for it resembles a flute with its holes.

At the flutes cave the trail splits, and the southern part of the "fork" leads directly into the southern cave, making it a popular attraction for day hikers and groups of school students on a trip. As I roll farther down the trail, proud of smoothly crossing a narrow crevice between two rocks, I notice that about thirty Israel Defense Forces (IDF) soldiers are sitting within the cavities of the cave, their green-khaki uniforms blending with the brown dolomite rock of the cliff. The soldiers are intently looking at a young female soldier guide, probably from the education corps, who tells them about the region and the cave. This is probably a "knowing the land" tour, I think to myself.

Interlude: Masada Shall Not Fall Again

Seeing the soldiers in the cave immediately reminds me of a dream I had last night. I have often had this dream in the last few years: I ride my bicycle in the Judean Desert, on the eastern side of the Judean hills watershed, in some unknown location ("Why am I here?" I keep thinking in the dream's "director's comments" track. I really don't like the desert). Slowly, I ascend a rugged and winding single track along the side of the mountain, a deep chasm beneath me. It is an afternoon hour, and the heat is still almost unbearable. I pant heavily, and sweat is running down from my forehead. I literally feel the heat as a heavy blanket that covers me, and I struggle through. The switchbacks of the trail demand enormous concentration, especially because of the gravel that covers the trail, which causes the rear wheel of the bike to flutter when I lean forward to pass my weight to the front part for better climbing. I feel very tense—bodily and emotionally. Yet despite the temptation to get off the bike and walk it beside me until the mountain's top, thus reducing the physical effort and also minimizing the risk of slipping into the chasm in case I lose traction with the trail, I continue riding. I focus hard on the sharp curves, and, while dreaming, I realize, again in the director's comments track of the dream, that I probably have this recurrent vision due to those semitraumatic tours in the Judean Desert during elementary school. Then, in the late 1970s and early 1980s, perhaps as a part of some educational program of "knowing the land" combined with a desire to forge the spirits of the schoolchildren in preparation for their recruitment to the military one day, they used to take us to hike in the formidable steep and deep wadis of the Judean Desert.

I hated these trips, with their fast pace of walking along the narrow and high trails, with no rail to hold on to. The teachers' and guides' warnings not to play tricks while on the trail, because "just a few months ago a schoolchild died here after falling into the chasm," did not add to my confidence. I especially hated the long, never-ending climb to the rock of Masada, along the winding "snake path." The place itself gave me the creeps. Masada, a citadel fortified by Judea's King Herod the Great (74–4 BCE) on the plateau of a formidable isolated rock in the Judean Desert watching over the Dead Sea, was taken over by the fundamentalist Sicarii sect during the Jewish revolt against the Romans (66–73 CE). After laying siege to the fortress for a few months, the Romans stormed the rock in April 73, only to find the 960 Sicarii and their wives and children dead after committing mass suicide just before the collapse of the defensive walls.

I abhorred the desert. The strong sulfur odor of the Dead Sea on the way to Masada was repugnant. The desert frightened me with its deep wadis, and the endless winding paths on the exposed and sun-beaten hills and the edges of the high and sharp cliffs. The desert was, for me, filled with the scars of Roman imperialism and cruelty (Masada, for example, is encircled by a Roman siege system and military camps) and the remnants of Jewish mystical sects. The story of the "zeal for freedom" of Masada's defenders and their mass suicide especially frightened me, not least because of the somber and fatalistic tone in which we studied it.[4] The desert reminded me of death, violence, and cruelty. I was always afraid that some Roman horseman was chasing me along these narrow desert lanes. Eventually, I managed to avoid the school trips by claiming to be sick precisely on the day of the trip. "It is a pity that you chose not to join your class during our desert trips," my teacher wrote, disappointed, in my graduation report card. She, of course, knew about my "bluffs."

Back in my dream, after several occasions of nearly losing traction and falling into the abyss, my knees and arms trembling from unrelenting fear (unlike the pleasurable fear of jumping in the Halilim wadi), I eventually finish climbing this "snake path." Sweat drips into my eyes and blurs my vision. I sip some water from my water bag, take off my right-hand glove, and wet my fingers in the precious fresh water. I then wipe away the sweat with the water, and see more clearly: instead of reaching the top of Masada, the path ends at a long and dark tunnel in the mountain's side. I turn on my flashlight torch and slowly pedal into the tunnel. I suddenly feel coolness surrounding me. I stop to take a rest and hesitate whether to go farther in. It is very quiet, and the air is still. The tunnel smells of old age. Reluctantly, I decide to continue, just to explore a bit farther—after all, I can always downhill back. The tunnel's floor is a plane, covered with a thick bed of white powder. As I roll quietly into the tunnel, the bike's wheels toss the white powder into the air, and I ride inside a cloud of dust.

Then, not too far inside the tunnel, I see through the dust a desk and three IDF officers sitting behind it, looking straight at me. I stop, somewhat surprised, and the dust slowly sinks down. The torch's beam cuts through the falling dust, and I notice that behind the desk the blue, white, and golden flag of the IDF is hoisted on a flag stand. But along with the IDF flag, there is a crimson flag with the figure of a Roman eagle and a Hebrew inscription: "The Israeli Legion." Between the folds of the crimson flag, I recognize parts of the Latin adage *Si vis pacem, para bellum* (If you wish for peace, prepare for war). "What is the Israeli Legion," I wonder, feeling that this is not a good sign. None of the officers even blinks when the blazing light of my torch hits him. They look pale, ghostly, in the artificial light of the torch. Looking straight into the bright, bright light, the youngest officer (he looks like one of my students in the large class Introduction to International Relations [IR]), an ensign, utters slowly, "Masada shall not . . ." He then pauses in didactic expectation. As I remain silent and confused, the left-seated officer, a grave-looking captain, wearing the unit tag of the Israeli Legion, completes the sentence with the appropriate solemn and dramatic ending: ". . . fall again."

I remain silent, not sure where I am and when. Is this a parallel universe? Have I gone back in time? The ensign then says, "Excellent climbing job, soldier, good that you have reported to duty." I look around and behind me, and see no soldier, and then I realize he is talking to me. "Oh, you must have made a mistake here. I was released from the army many years ago," I reply. "Aren't you in my 'intro to IR' class?" I add, more reassured and trying to assert authority, some authority, at least. The ensign ignores this question, but the grave-looking captain says, disbelievingly, "Really, were you indeed discharged?" "Show us your discharge documents if you want us to believe you," adds the third officer, a lieutenant colonel, who slowly lifts his eyes from a copy of Oscar Wilde's *The Canterville Ghost*, issued by the Ministry of Defense's "Backpack Library." He is smiling like a Cheshire cat to the two others, who smile back at him, as if sharing a secret. "But it's ridiculous, I don't have the documents with me, I did not know you should carry them with you all the time, and, besides, I just went out for a bike ride," I exclaim. The officers remain silent and just stare at me. When I calm down a bit I say, "I can show you my university employee card, if that's a proof." "No, that does not prove you were indeed discharged," the ensign/student(?) replies.

Then the three officers begin to discuss my "case" among them. Sometimes they eventually believe me, reluctantly, and let me continue the ride. The tunnel goes on deep into the mountain, and finally it magically turns into the "Mt. Scopus Tunnel," a tunnel dug at the foot of the campus of the Hebrew University, shortening the road to Jerusalem from the Judean Desert (it also bypasses the Palestinian towns and neighborhoods of Anata and Isawiya). I enter the Hebrew University and ride to the older, eastern part of the campus. There, in the serenity of the well-groomed lawns and lanes of the Institute for Contemporary Jewry, amid aged pine trees and the old buildings of the Hebrew University (these are real buildings, separated and distanced from each other and not connected with concrete passageways), I relax. I view the blue Dead Sea and the white and round hills of the Judean Desert. From far away, the saline lake looks beautiful (one cannot smell it from here), and the hills seem so serene and peaceful, the violence inherent in this landscape hidden from the eye. I feel calm, at home. But sometimes the officers send me to ride back home, dozens of kilometers away (with no shortcuts in magical tunnels), through an excruciating ascent of more than twelve hundred meters, from the "lowest place on the surface of the earth" (the Dead Sea) to Jerusalem, to bring them the discharge documents or "produce" for them a replacement—"your son, for example," the officer from the "Israeli Legion" says dryly. And occasionally they physically take hold of me, remove me from the bicycle, and send me to a military prison for not carrying my discharge documents with me (in other versions of the dream I am "only" being fined the sum of a hundred shekels (roughly twenty-five US dollars) for not shaving and polishing my shoes that day ("But it's from the dust in *this* tunnel," I exclaim, to no avail). Whatever the "verdict" is, I always wake up from this dream shivering, realizing that even though I was discharged from the military, I never truly became free. I need open space, my body tells me, and I need to go out riding.

The Legend of the Flute

When my recollection of the night's dream fades away, I realize that I stand, my feet on the ground and the bicycle between them, in the shadow of an old almond tree, a few dozen meters on the trail farther down from the fork that leads into the Halilim Cave cliff. I want to continue biking, ride away from the soldiers and my dream. Then I hear the instructor: "... So we're sitting now in the flutes' cave, the cave which gave its name to the whole wadi." The guide sounds as if she recites a lesson plan bequeathed to her by many generations of field guides. I smile to myself when I recall how I, too, was bequeathed the lesson plans of the Introduction to IR course that I have taught for four years, and how restless and uncomfortable the students in my class become when I "deviate" from the "official" handouts. I decide to stay a bit and hear her out. Perhaps by staying and listening of my own free will, "eavesdropping" on them, I can reverse the imposing and coercive experience of the dream, of my life?

The guide then tells the soldiers about the geology of the cave and the hills that surround it ("... the Kissalon rock formation ..."). I am about to mount the bike again when I hear the guide saying, "And now, would you like to hear the legend of the flute?" The soldiers, who would probably do almost anything to continue sitting and lying idly, vocally respond, "Yes, yes." "Ok," the guide says. I, too, want to hear the legend. I never heard the "flute's legend," and I love legends—after all, I teach a course called Science Fiction, Fantasy, and (International) Politics. And to tell the truth, something of the idleness-seeking of the soldier remains in me until this day.

"Once upon a time," the soldier-guide begins, theatrically, and the soldiers giggle. "Once upon a time, there was a young and beautiful daughter of the mukhtar [chieftain] of the Arab village of Kolonia,[5] which stood right here on the ridge, where present-day Mevasseret is." "The village of Kolonia?" I think. I did not know such a village existed. I thought Mevasseret was built on "virgin" soil, not land conquered away from the Palestinians. I know about the "Battle of the Kastel" in 1948, not too far away from here. But I never saw any ruins of Palestinian houses in Mevasseret itself. And there are no "Arab Houses" in Mevasseret.[6] I hold back this new information and question, in the meantime. None of the soldiers makes any comment regarding the mention of the "village of Kolonia." I hear the guide continuing: "And the time came when the mukhtar wanted to marry off his daughter. 'Listen, Fatma,' the Mukhtar said to his daughter [some soldiers giggle at the stereotypical Arab name, Fatma]. 'It is about time for you to marry. I have chosen a groom for you—Ahmed [again, giggles], the son of the rich mukhtar of our neighboring village, Abu G'osh.' 'But ya Baba [Oh, Daddy],' cries Fatma [the guide overdramatically mimics a weeping girl's tone], 'I don't want to marry Ahmed, he is too ugly! I want to marry Jamil, the sheep herder from our village. I love him.' 'Love?!' exclaims the mukhtar. 'What has love to do with marriage? And besides, he is too poor to marry you.' But Fatma refused to marry Ahmed and cried for days. Eventually, her father felt pity for her. 'Listen, Fatma,' he told her. 'I will announce a contest—whoever succeeds in taking my bewitched herd of sheep out to pasture in the morning and returns the entire herd in the evening, without a single sheep missing, shall marry you. But whoever loses even one sheep—I will personally behead him with my sharp sword.' [The guide mimics a dreadful laughter.] Fatma agreed to her father's proposal, and thus many potential grooms came to Kolonia, hearing about the challenge and the beautiful and rich bride. But none of them managed to take the herd out and return all the sheep.

"Many heads were taken off by the cruel mukhtar's sword. Eventually, Jamil, the poor herder from Kolonia, reported to the mukhtar. 'I accept the challenge. I will take out your sheep and return all of them by the evening.' 'As you wish,' replied the mukhtar, smugly, happy to be able to get rid of this disturbance when the evening comes. Fatma tried to persuade her loved one not to accept the challenge, but to no avail. He took out the herd. Many hours passed, and as the sun was about to set, the villagers heard the sheep coming back, bleating and raising dust along the path. Jamil was marching behind them, playing his flute. 'Well, let's see how many sheep you bring back,' said the mukhtar, and he started to count them all. He then, disbelievingly, counted again, and again. To his dismay, all the sheep were there. 'How did you do that?' he demanded, but Jamil stayed silent. Reluctantly, the mukhtar married the young couple . . . They lived happily ever after."

The guide finishes her story, but then one of the soldiers cries from within the cave, "But how did he do that? How did he manage to return all the bewitched sheep?" "Oh," the guide says, expecting this question. "When they were grazing in this wadi, some of the sheep went astray and disappeared. But then Jamil took out a flute he once found in this very cave. Jamil went up into cave and started to play the flute, and the cave, with its magical powers, amplified the flute's tune, which was carried by the wind all over the wadi. The charming tune drew back all the recalcitrant sheep." The guide pauses for a moment. "And they say that until this very day, you can hear the tune of that magic flute here, in the cave, when the wind blows through its many cavities."

A Thin Layer of Soil over Sharp Rocks

The legend ends, and the soldiers pick up their backpacks and M16s and return to the trail to continue their tour. I get on the bicycle too. I try to recall whether I have ever heard the cave playing like a flute, and can think of no such case. I then think, "Perhaps the concrete sheep statues in the roundabouts of the Reches Halilim neighborhood belong to the bewitched herd from the legend?" And then, "Quite a stereotypical tale and representation of the 'Arab.' Sounds more like a distasteful *chizbat* than an authentic Arab legend,[7] but who knows . . . I should check out its source when I reach my office." ("And the history of the terraces too," I remind myself. "And also, I should look for information about the village of Kolonia. It can't be that Mevasseret stands on the ruins of a Palestinian village . . .").

Busy with these thoughts on Israeli concrete sheep and a Palestinian ruined village, I continue riding down, and suddenly I miss a curve. Or, more accurately, the trail is simply not there anymore. Instead, the trail abruptly turns into a network of deep crevices and cracks. Much of the trail is now exposed, revealing sharp rocks that lay beneath the thin layer of soil that was carried away with the flood that raged here a few days ago. The upper layer of soil is so thin in these mountains, like the layer of political normalcy that is also so slim in this country. A major rainstorm (more than 200 mm of rain fell in a couple of days, about 40 percent of the average annual rainfall in Jerusalem) had transformed the lower part of the trail into a tricky "rock garden." Engaged with the thoughts about the flute's legend, Kolonia, and the military, I forget this and immediately pay the price: I lose traction and crash into a thorny bush, the bicycle falling on my side. I hear the branches crack under my body's weight and the thorns brush against my sunglasses and helmet. Luckily, I wear gloves and elbow and knee guards. My initial response is "Well, a little adventure on the way to work today." Then I think, Star Trek–like, "damage control," and slowly lift the bicycle and myself. Except for a few scratches and bruises, I am intact. My protective gear worked fine. The bicycle, too, thank goodness, is not damaged. Just a bit of mud on the frame. "Resume your positions," the "captain" in my mind is saying.

As I stand up, I notice that three men, roughly the age of sixty, are staring at me. I brush off the mud and dirt from my riding jacket and look at them more carefully. I recognize them: I sometimes see them climbing up the wadi during the morning, when I descend it. We usually pass each other with just a short "good morning" greeting or nods. They always seem to me like three retired friends from Mevasseret who have gone out for a morning walk in the wadi. Now I take a closer look at them. I notice that one of them holds a long wooden staff, and that his and the others' clothes are quite old, matted. I also notice that two of the three men are not shaved, their faces covered with four or five days of growth.[8] They smile at me, and the one with the wooden staff says, "Are you all right? You should be more careful with this bicycle." When he speaks, I see that some of his upper incisors are missing. He speaks Hebrew, but there is a trace of an Arab accent in his voice. "Yes, thanks, I'm ok," I reply with a smile, moving my tongue over my front teeth, making sure they are intact. I am a bit embarrassed that they saw me crash. Am I frightened by these people, who I now realize are Palestinians? Should I be worried? No, they're not young, not the "typical" terrorist type. Also, we've seen each other many times and they did not harm me. "But that was when I was riding, on the bicycle, and could have escaped quickly," I say to myself. "All the more so," I reply to myself, "This man could have easily knocked me off the bicycle with the staff..." "Are you from Mevasseret?" the staff holder intervenes in my deliberations. "Yes, I'm riding to work, through the Halilim wadi and then in the Arazim Valley." As I talk, I think, should I tell them where I work? Was that a good idea to tell them about my route? They might pass the "intelligence" to some Palestinian armed band ... there were so many murders of lonely hikers in the hills around Jerusalem. "Where are you from?" I ask, casually. The men seem a bit reluctant to answer, but eventually the staff holder says, "I'm from Beit Iksa, there." (He points with the staff at the Palestinian village of Beit Iksa, farther up on the trail, above the Arazim Valley.) "And we're from Beit Surik and Biddu," the two others say.

I am surprised—and my response is very untactful, I guess: "But how do you cross the fence?" (meaning the separation fence between Israel and the Palestinians). "Oh, don't worry, we've got permits," the man from Beit Surik says, his face becoming serious. He reaches in his pocket and pulls out a carefully folded piece of paper and presents it to me. I can't see exactly what's written there—I don't take the paper from him—but I manage to see the menorah symbol of the State of Israel and the IDF's Civil Administration unit logo on the top of the permit, and inscriptions in Hebrew and Arabic. "Oh, no, I did not mean this," I say, and wave it away with my hand. But even though I am uncomfortable with him showing me the permit, I also feel somewhat reassured: I know that the Israeli Shin Bet (General Security Service—the country's secret police) is- sues these permits only to "trustworthy" Palestinians (for example, collaborators with the Israeli authorities) or "low-risk" persons. The man puts the paper back in his pocket, carefully refolding it. "We just come to work here in Mevasseret, we're doing gardening jobs." "We don't come to steal or commit any crime, you know. We work here for more than twenty-eight years now. I built many houses in Mevasseret," adds the man with the staff, solemnly but also humbly—his look lowered a bit to the ground.

I do not know how to reply to what he just said, and how to respond to their self-justification/fear. Did I give them the impression that I think they come to steal? Perhaps they sensed my hesitation when I told about my route? Why did he "show me his papers," did I look in any sense "official"? Unconsciously, I grope for my bicycle jacket's upper pocket. What am I looking for there, I ask myself when I suddenly notice what I'm doing. Am I searching for my military discharge documents? Perhaps I look for a letter of recommendation from my dead father, who these elder men suddenly remind me of?[9]

I respond by saying, "Wallah [an Arabic exclamation], no, I did not think you are thieves," and immediately notice an orientalist, somewhat condescend- ing tone creeping into my words. I, a Jewish Ashkenazi (that is, with Central Eastern European origins) university professor, riding an expensive mountain bike and my face unrecognizable behind my sunglasses and helmet, covered by three medical insurances (calculated risk . . .), coming down from affluent Mevasseret, enjoying political rights and freedoms these men so obviously lack, tell them, with an attempted Arab authenticity, that I trust them to say the truth . . . We then talk about how we all pray for peace in our times. All the "problems," the men say, stem from bad governments and not from "good, regu- lar people, who have no trouble living and working together." Finally, after a few minutes, they say they have to continue their climb because they're late for work. We part with good day wishes. I continue riding and think about these men. Were they indeed honest in their hopes for peace or did they just want to placate me? What do they mean by "peace"? I wonder what they said to each other about me after our parting. Did I look honest to them? Did they ridicule my look and fall from the bicycle? Shall we talk again the next time we meet on the trail?

The Wars of the Jews

About an hour later I arrive at Mt. Scopus campus. After I change clothes and store my bike in my office, I talk with my colleague Oren Barak about the meeting at the Halilim wadi. Oren says how sad it is that even the very mundane social interactions between Jews and Palestinians are immediately framed within the security/occupation context. I recall the men's concept of "bad governments," and think that if I understand *government* in Michel Foucault's terms as "the conduct of conduct,"[10] then indeed they were right. There is a lot of bad "government" in this land.

I'm reading today the new Hebrew translation (from the Greek) of Yossef Ben Matityahu's (known also in Latin as Titus Flavius Josephus) *The Wars of the Jews* (with the Romans), which tells the story of the First Jewish-Roman War (The Great Rebellion) in 66–73 CE. Yossef, who was at the beginning of the revolt the commander of the Jewish rebels in the Galilee, surrendered to the Romans after realizing that there was no hope of avoiding defeat by them. Later he became known as Flavius Josephus, a court historian of the Roman emperor Vespasian. I think about Josephus's frustration with Jewish stubbornness, as he saw it, and about his pessimism and bleak outlook for the Jewish future and destiny in light of the horrible destruction that the Romans inflicted upon the Jews as they crushed their revolt (even though Josephus, as a court historian, is very apologetic as to Rome's brutality and cruelty). According to his narration, Josephus personally tried to warn the rebels that the Romans were too mighty and it would be better to surrender instead of being defeated and destroyed. The Jews did not surrender, and the Romans destroyed Jerusalem and Judea.

While reading this book, I think: indeed, throughout the centuries, it was Rome that disappeared and the Jews, as a people, and Judaism, as a religion and culture, survived. But was the price worth it? And perhaps the Jews would have survived even if the rebels had surrendered to the Romans? Yossef is also the single historical source for the story of the Roman siege of Masada and the mass suicide of the Sicarii rebels there. I cannot avoid thinking about Masada when I ride every day in the Arazim Valley near the construction site of a huge nuclear-proof bunker that the Israeli government is digging there. The daily witnessing of the preparation of the bunker horrifies me. I think about self-fulfilling prophecies, fearing that when our government (without quotation marks, this time) shelters itself there, the rest of the people in this country will be doomed. It is a Masada in reverse.

Busy with these not so cheerful thoughts, I remember, before I leave campus, to Google "Kolonia and Mevasseret" (in Hebrew and English). The search soon takes me to the Wikipedia entry on the 1948 destroyed Palestinian village of Qalunya (this is the "official" transliteration). The Hebrew Wikipedia entry discusses Qalunya mainly in the Jewish context: it mentions that Flavius Josephus tells about the founding of the village as a colony for the veterans of the Tenth Roman Legion, which destroyed the Temple in Jerusalem during the Great Revolt, and that in the 1860s Jews purchased some of the village's lands and established the colony of Motza there. In 1929, the Wikipedia entry continues, Palestinians from Qalunya attacked the Jewish colony and murdered almost all the members of the Maklef family. Finally, on April 11, 1948, the Jewish militia Palmach attacked and conquered the village, which dominated the highway to Jerusalem, and destroyed more than fifty houses (and this was not a *chizbat*). The English version of the entry repeats much of the information of the Hebrew entry but also adds something about the Palestinianess of the village: "In the late nineteenth century, Qalunya was described as a moderate-sized village perched on the slope of a hill, 300 feet (91m) above a valley. Travelers reported that it had a 'modern' restaurant. The villagers tended orange and lemon trees that were planted around a spring in the valley." There is also an Arabic entry, much longer and more detailed than the previous two, but I do not read Arabic that well.

In the English entry I find a link to a website called Palestine Remembered. There I spend much time viewing old pictures from Qalunya. In one picture, two little Palestinian children, a girl and a boy, stand with two goats amid flowering almond trees in a well-cared-for and cultivated field on the mountainside.[11] Another picture that draws my attention is a depiction of the village on April 10, 1948, so the title of the picture says, a day before its conquest and destruction by the Palmach.[12] I recognize the outlines of the hills and wadis in the pictures, and the flowering almonds look so familiar. But the place is nonetheless foreign to me. I feel sorrow and confusion. I wonder what happened to the two children in that picture. Then I think, do I really want to know more about this village? About why and how it was destroyed? I feel I am beginning a tricky journey.

When the day at campus finally ends, I return to Mevasseret through the Arazim Valley (and see the bunker's work site for the second time that day) and the

Halilim wadi. Climbing the single track, I recollect the morning's events. Thick darkness now covers the wadi. I light up the trail with my helmet flashlight. As I turn my gaze up to the cavities of the Halilim Cave, the flow of bright light from the torch is reflected in the shining eyes of a jackal, which quickly disappears in the pressing darkness. I hear other jackals howl in the distance. Their howling reminds me now of the legend of the flute. There is no one on the trail and in the wadi. No sign of the three Palestinian men or the soldiers. "Did the men meet the soldiers up on the trail? They must have had," a thought crosses my mind. "Should I have warned them about the soldiers? No, the soldiers probably did not harm or harass them: they were not on active duty and were busy with their trip," I find myself hoping. Yet I also understand now that I was so focused on my own fears and thoughts that morning that I did not even think to tell (warn?) the men about the soldiers who were just a few minutes up the trail. "You know what, perhaps warning them would have insulted them. After all, they said they were not 'thieves,' offended by my question about how they cross the separation fence. There was nothing that they should have been worried about—they had entry permits to Israel. And if I told them about the soldiers, they might have hidden or escaped, and if caught they would immediately become 'suspects.' It's better that I did not say anything. It's like the 'Prime Directive' from *Star Trek*," I try to reassure myself.[13] At the same time, I feel that I should have said something that would at least have informed them about the soldiers. On the other hand, "why should I 'warn' someone about soldiers of my own country?"

Strange shadows reach toward me, as my torch throws light on trees, bushes, and rocks in the wadi. Despite the rational knowledge that there is nothing to be afraid of, I become somewhat anxious. I should have returned while there was still daylight and not lingered on campus reading about Qalunya. The darkness, the slow progression on the hard ascending trail, and the loneliness of this ride bring out my basic fears. "But it's good," I say to myself. "Thus I get to confront those fears, to articulate them." In the distance I imagine that I hear the hooves of a Roman war-horse pursuing me. ("He probably comes from the 'Masada' bunker or the Tenth Legion's colony in Qalunya . . ." I try to joke with myself.) No, I calm myself, there is no Roman horseman. The Romans are long gone from this land. The only Romans left here are ancient olive trees, which the Palestinian fellaheen (peasants) call Roman to signify their antiquity. The clatter of hooves is just my heart pumping in the climb. I then start singing, quietly, the hymn that my wife, Idit, taught me a few days ago: "Even though I walk through the darkest valley, I will fear no evil, for you are with me" [Psalms 23:4]. The ancient words encourage and comfort me. "And there is no such thing as the 'Israeli Legion.' And even if there were, they cannot recruit me again, cannot enslave me again. I'm almost forty now," I say to myself. "But they can recruit my children—in the dream, they wanted me to send a replacement, did they not?" I answer myself. I then think again about the Palestinian man from Beit Surik, who showed me his military-issued "entry permit" this morning. Although he never was a soldier like me, he had lived most of his life under military rule. And while I only dream of being required to "produce" military-issued documents, he really has to carry these papers all the time. I know I am much better off than he is in many, many ways. And I know that the comparison is unfair and infuriating in many respects, but I feel that both of us are under military, imperial, rule. This realization saddens me immensely. I feel deep empathy toward him and his friends, not the least because we also share this trail on a daily basis.

As I continue to work my way up the rugged trail, the lights of Mevasseret's houses and streets become visible on the top of the ridges above me. The trail is not that dark anymore. I think about the village of Qalunya, which disappeared from these hills sixty-two years ago, when my father was seven years old, like my son now. "Could Mevasseret be erased from the face of the land like that too one day?" I wonder. Almost inevitably I then think about the doomsday bunker in the Arazim Valley. I feel I live in a delusional and dreamlike reality: an army that does not release me, even in my dreams, and demands a replacement; fabricated legends about a living village that was here and now is simply erased; men the age of my dead father humbled, disciplined, and desperately seeking a day's living; a new Masada dug underneath a mountain. I know that all this is "for real," but I strongly feel I must wake up. And I want to awaken others. I then decide to write this book.

Introduction

MOUNTAIN BIKING IN THE FRONTIER OF JERUSALEM

An Exploration of External and Internal Landscapes of Conflict

On Personal Stories and Subjective Writing:
The Merits and Shortcomings of Using the Self
as a Source of Political Knowledge and Interpretation

This book is the story of my daily mountain bicycle rides along the northwestern frontier of Jerusalem, Israel. I ride, back and forth, from my home in Mevasseret Zion, a suburb of the capital city,[1] to the Mt. Scopus campus of the Hebrew University, in Jerusalem, where I am a faculty member in the Department of International Relations (IR). It is usually a one-hour ride (if I don't stop along the trail or deviate from the path—but I often do, thus prolonging the ride), totaling eleven kilometers in each direction. For the great part of the ride, I bike along the frontier between Israel and the Occupied Palestinian Territories.[2] The mountain bicycle, with its high maneuverability, off-road capabilities, and direct contact with the terrain (more on these aspects below), creates for me a unique sensory and bodily experience of connecting with the geographical space I cross every day. The bicycle also serves, literally, as a research tool that provides many opportunities to reach and observe places and spaces that are usually out of the daily ambit or interest of many Israelis. Yet despite the relative seclusion of parts of my trail, during the rides I also often interact with diverse people I meet along the trail and witness spaces and locations that are shaped and influenced by the Israeli-Palestinian and the broader Israeli-Arab conflict(s) (the "Masada" nuclear bunker is even related to the Israeli-Iranian conflict).

In their turn, these people and places become atoms or elementary particles that *make up* this conflict.[3] The bicycle ride is actually the story of my exposure *to* and exposure *of* these landscapes and human realities that are wrought by the conflict and that, in turn, reproduce it. I tell about my interplay with the landscape and the people that inhabit it or pass through it (the "exposure to" element) and about the process of understanding and giving meaning to these interactions (the "exposure of" element in my journey). It is a story of revelation, reflection, and evaluation, and of personal transformation. An account of belonging and strangeness, of emotional closeness and distance, and mainly of confusion: the more I get to know the trail I ride on, the more I become perplexed about my personal road and the place where it takes me. The book is an invitation to readers to join me along the bike trails and share (but not necessarily accept or condone) my insights and feelings during the ride and its aftermath. I invite readers to open up to my experience and being, to get to know a piece of the "Israeli condition" through my experience. Hence, my relation is an offer of and request for companionship.

Why would one want to read such a book, which is composed mainly of personal stories, experiences, and interpretations? Is companionship a legitimate goal in an academic book? And what does this "detailed account of so many trivial circumstances and insignificant happenings," these "descriptions of ordinary travels, seeing, imagining, and remembering have to do with anything?"[4] What will readers learn from such stories, and what is the general conceptual or theoretical lesson that can be drawn from them? After all, this is a subjective account, and, in addition, many factual aspects I discuss in the book, especially those related to the history of the Israeli-Palestinian conflict, are already known to scholars of this quarrel.[5] Nonetheless, I believe there are several reasons to read this book.

First, my text is a form of ethnography, and as such, it literally provides a view from the field of the conflict in Israel and Palestine. My stories about places and people I meet along the trail are connected to each other not only by the fact that they take place along a continuous physical geographical route or space but also because they run parallel to each other by being thick descriptions of various aspects of the culture of conflict that imbues the Israeli being.[6] Thus, the stories could help in diagnosing this culture and plunging into it.[7] Through my gaze as a wandering, sometimes "loitering" and "idling," mountain bicycle rider, various real-life manifestations of conceptual categories such as "security," "conflict," "war," "deterrence," "terrorism," "borders," "refugees," and "ethnic cleansing" are witnessed on the ground and interpreted, and some of the human implications that they entail are brought to light.

In addition, and especially in the Israeli context, the ethnographic process of documenting and interpreting is so important because of the increasing tendency of the Israeli state to eradicate and hide its contested history and controversial present conduct. Especially since the early 2000s, after the collapse of the Oslo peace process and three wars (the second Palestinian uprising, the second Lebanon war [2006], and the Gaza war [2008–9]), a mentality of self-righteousness, siege, and victimhood has taken hold over Israeli politics and society more than ever before. Consequently, Israel's state institutions and political system are trying to reduce the "resolution" of the political gaze of internal and external critical observers alike. These hindrances and restrictions on the critical gaze manifest themselves in many occasions and contexts, some of which I will discuss in the various stories of the book. Specifically, I will relate my personal experiences of critically gazing at the landscape through which I pass every day, and the responses I receive from colleagues, students, family members, friends, and various officials about the questions that arise in me due to these observations. Many of these responses, though definitely not all of them, are negative or even scolding. They expose a society that is not only more and more sanctifying a culture of ignorance and silence, as it did for many decades, but also developing a culture of *active silencing*. In this manner, my ride stories serve as an amplification of the critical gaze's resolution in one of the most contested political territories in the world. And this witnessing-recording-interpreting project is also an invitation to readers to reflect on how *their* daily environment is constructed and how politics plays a role in shaping their immediate surroundings, as well as politics' input in their proclivity and ability to even observe and interpret these surroundings from the outset. This project is, therefore, a methodological, epistemological, and theoretical exercise in opening one's political eyes.

It follows, then, that this book is not only an ethnographic study but also an *auto*ethnographic one. Initially a method and a way of writing that originated in anthropology and interpersonal communication studies, autoethnography has made inroads into various other social science disciplines, including IR and political science, geography, and even business.[8] In autoethnography, authors first "look through an ethnographic wide angle lens, focusing outward on social and cultural aspects of their personal experience; then, they look inward, exposing a vulnerable self that is moved by and may move through, refract, and resist cultural interpretations."[9] Employing various modes of textual expression, such as short stories, poetry, fiction, novels, photographic essays, journals, fragmented and layered writing, and social science prose,[10] autoethnographers use their own experiences in a culture to look deeply and reflexively at self-other interactions.[11] Thus, several authors see autoethnography as a method that provides, through the personal perspective and narrative of the autoethnographer, new knowledge and understanding of general social structures and conditions.[12] For example, Eric Mykhalovskiy argues that "to write individual experience is, at the same time, to write social experience." This is because "a whole social organization is needed to create each unique experience."[13]

Accordingly, the stories I tell here are strongly grounded in my own daily practices and experiences, my sensory sensations, my dilemmas and difficulties, my personal transformations, and my range of emotional responses to realities I encounter. As personal knowledge and experience, these stories are recalled by me in minute and multiple dimensions, which are not always accessible in other forms of ethnographic research. By telling these stories in an honest and open manner, I hope to identify and expose the way the subtleties of power manifest themselves.[14] The personal point of view could flesh out the abstract notion of the Israeli culture of conflict into something more concrete and graspable because it contains unmediated "data" that in an account about the experience of others might get lost or even not be discovered/disclosed.

Indeed, some readers might argue that even if a person tries his best to be attentive and sensitive to the details of the reality he experiences and is involved in, and to be honest and disclosing in his narration, such "true accounts" are never complete and unbiased. Another objection could be that telling one's story can never come from the point of view of an author, only that of an agent. This is because the narrator is not the one who began the story, which, as a political reality, was there before he entered the plot and will continue to develop after his leaving.[15] I agree that there are biases and "blind spots" in my narration, and, of course, I do not pretend to monopolize the story of the Israeli culture of conflict in the sense of being its initial or single author. Yet I do want my story to be added to the broader story of the conflict, and I want this story to make a difference, for the better, in this conflict.

Also, it is precisely the subjectivity of my narrative that could teach readers more about this culture of conflict and its structures of power. This is because in many respects I am a product of this culture of conflict, and my subjectivity was constituted by it in various layers and by all sorts of technologies of power. Therefore, by identifying the *limits* of my reflexivity in this subjective account, one could learn more about the reality I describe. Things that remain hidden from my eyes or underappreciated by me might be very visible and important to other readers, whose physical location, personal identity, and emotional involvement in this conflict are different from my own. Furthermore, my grappling with how to tell these stories (for example, what to include in the main text and what to put in the notes, or which "tone" to use) could be revealing in similar senses. Such grapplings are actually opportunities that help to illuminate the way the conflict as a culture and mechanism of control, and the metastructures that inform it, constitute my own agency and subjectivity, thereby shedding light on both the benefits and shortcomings of using the self as a source of political knowledge and interpretation.

There is also an ethical issue in reading one's own account of a conflict that one is a "native" of; as Elizabeth Dauphinee admits, IR, as well as probably other social science disciplines that study conflict and war, "is a discipline built on the deaths and losses of others, and these are deaths and losses that we never personally experience. It is a discipline built on the lives of people that most of us never even meet and, if we do meet them, we certainly never get to know them. We don't invite them to our homes. We don't meet them for coffee. We don't attend their weddings. We don't attend their funerals. We don't love them. If we do, we do it secretly and we never, ever admit it."[16] I do not think that scholars and students from another country or culture should avoid, in principle, researching other people's conflicts. Also, I acknowledge the scholarly value of such lack of involvement. But there is also much truth in Dauphinee's critique that people make a career out of conflicts that do not pertain to them directly. Reading an account of a person who suffers the consequences of a conflict on his own body and soul is more ethical in this sense. Of course, insiders in a conflict can also "profit" from it in the manner Dauphinee describes. But still, there is a principled difference between such a profit (in my case, I admit that I would be very glad to have written about the culture of violence in Israel as a historical phenomenon, one belonging to the past and not to the present) made by a local and by an external: the insider pays various prices for making this (supposed) profit, prices that the outsider will never pay. I turn now to discussing some of these costs as a second reason to read this book.

A second reason to read this personal and subjective account is that through this author-reader interaction I hope to contribute to a grassroots or people-to-people process of mutual understanding, recognition, and dedemonization concerning the conflict in Israel-Palestine. Moreover, I wish to encourage interdisciplinary social science research that will consider the personal implications of conflicts such as the Israeli-Palestinian one for people's daily lives and subjectivities. In this vein, one of my goals here is to share the burden of my experience with a broad and diverse readership. This process of sharing is also a distinguishing factor between this book and many other ethnographic works on the conflict in Israel-Palestine.[17] The burden I carry, and wish to share here, stems from revealing and witnessing the actual deployment of violence and coercion (both Israeli directed and Palestinian directed) and feeling the intensity of negation and exclusion that such violence and coercion breed and serve at once. The burden intensifies when I uncover the debris of past violence, within myself and in the outer landscape, and when I see the preparations for future violence along my trail. The burden becomes heavier when I realize how lonely and secluded I am becoming, due to even paying attention to this pervasiveness of violence and coercion, in a society that rapidly moves from ignorance and silence to organized silencing.[18]

Writing in order to share the personal pain and burden generated by this culture of conflict and violence is not a narcissistic act of navel gazing or confessional self-pity as some readers might consider. First, and more generally, sharing is a form of resistance to loneliness. We increasingly live in a world of "lonely people," as the Beatles said. Politically, it is much easier to govern—or even dominate—lonely people than people who maintain strong communal and human/cosmopolitan connections. Autoethnography, in this regard, is an attempt to maintain such connections between an author and his readers, between a researcher and his students. Political science, if it wants to adhere to an ethic of freedom and peace, had better, in my view, open itself up to writings that are aimed at strengthening a sense of *human*—not only professional—community.

Second, and more specifically in the context of this book, autoethnography is also a work of deconstruction and resistance to dominant mechanisms of reification and reproduction of violent conflicts. Sharing in this manner reflects the tensions that exist in living in a world that is both of our making and not.[19] When I share here with you some of the emotions and thoughts I develop as a result of being embedded in this culture of conflict and governed by it, I want to cast doubt on what is considered in this culture as "sacred," "important," "self-evident," and "natural." I also want to problematize what is understood in this culture to be things that are best not taken out and discussed with the "gentiles."[20]

Too often we internalize as parts of our identities the cultural truisms we grew with. Political structures and practices instill in us various feelings and values that constitute our subjectivity and thus might limit to a great extent our personal freedom.[21] When I reveal my grappling with the culture of conflict and the burden it places on my mind and soul, I do not intend to demean the experience of others or to say that what I feel and experience is the only way to understand this culture. I only wish to show how pervasive and engulfing this culture is and to suggest an alternative to the dominant narratives. At times my writing might seem to some readers to border on the cliché. Perhaps. I indeed have a tendency to be too emotional sometimes. But even this can be useful from a theoretical point of view, for what is "war" or "conflict" if not clichés in certain respects too? Perhaps my clichés will remind readers that the so-called objective, serious, and scientific concepts we use so much in the social sciences entail many clichés within them too . . .

Viewed from the microperspective of an individual "elementary particle" within this conflict, a mountain biker riding on the trails, things might seem different from the familiar status they have at the macrolevel: sometimes tragic and outrageous, sometimes ridiculous, and sometimes boring or merely nuisances (my recurring dream of "losing" my military discharge papers exemplifies all these aspects). I want readers to realize that the conflict produces people in it as persons who carry its violence and pain in multiple manners and different geographic and bodily sites. Such understanding—which I strive to achieve by evocatively sharing my own burden—could be an important step in liberating people from it.

We, Israelis, and I believe that also the Palestinians have become so accustomed to violence, conflict, and victimhood that they have become part of our identities. And many people and even governments around the world have become accustomed to this protracted conflict to the extent that increasingly they lose interest in it. The sharing of my burden is, therefore, meant to remind those who see this conflict as a granted or unavoidable "fact" that a way to start thinking about how to end it (and of course, there are those who, in effect, have become addicted to the conflict and do not want or cannot think to end it) is to resist it on its most mundane and daily levels.

More broadly, and not only in the context of the conflict in Israel-Palestine, I want to argue that writing in an individualist orientation such as this could help writers understand themselves better. Identifying to yourself what bothers and hurts you in the world, and why so, is an essential step in understanding how your subjectivity was constructed, and, consequently, a prerequisite for acquiring a more agentive role in the world. Sharing this self-understanding in published writing can, in turn, humanize our writings—and no less important, our oral teachings—as social and political scientists.[22]

We often write and teach in an objective and detached style, in a realistic and authoritative omniscient voice. This is why so many social science academic texts and university courses look and sound so similar to each other and, naturally, generate distance between author and reader or between professor and student.[23] While such a distance has its many known benefits, it also has several shortcomings. One of them is sometimes boredom. Another is the instillment of cynicism in the reader/student or the breeding of, in effect, indifference to the fate of other human beings, who become "actors" in a "case study" and not human beings in real-life situations. This is not a necessary outcome, but it is a plausible one. And, based on my personal experience, a common one. Added to this is the tendency of many political scientists to adopt a statecentric approach, which treats the state and its institutions and practices not as a means (for achieving human well-being, prosperity, and happiness, for example) but, practically, as an end in itself or, at least, as given social facts that cannot be transformed by academics, merely analyzed as phenomena that present to us interesting intellectual puzzles.

Furthermore, when we refuse to write or read, to teach and learn, about the personal effect—on us or on other people as specific individuals—of the violence inherent in the political, we not only reify this violence as a given phenomenon that takes place on the remote and abstract "international level" or in the barbaric context of "civil strife," for example. What we do by such an evasion or refusal is to avoid a more comprehensive discussion of the different facets and workings of violence and conflict. In *Placing Autobiography in Geography*, Pamela Moss encourages geographers to use autobiography in their research: "We need to accept what we do and scrutinize its meaning."[24] While I agree with Moss's call, I also believe that we should also scrutinize the meaning of what is being done to *us*, personally—and to others—and contemplate whether we are willing to accept this or change it. Autoethnography is a way to probe our subjectivity and thus at least try to emancipate ourselves. Autoethnography, therefore, offers companionship and an ethic of care.

Thus, by sharing the personal experiences and emotions that political conflict infuses and inspires in us, we admit to being human and involved in the world about which we write and teach. By this we inevitably also add a novel aspect to the understanding of the political and the social. Sharing with others our political experiences and stories that take place in the actual world of the living—in evocative terms—opens them to our subjectivity and encourages them to think about how social and political constructs constitute *their* own subjectivity. While such understandings and sharing might sharpen differences and conflicting interests, I believe that ultimately they can help people transcend conflicts and disagreements by revealing all of us as humans who suffer, rejoice, have doubts, and seek dignity and recognition. This is not a naive representation of politics itself as an "artificial" obstacle for human fellowship and friendship. My political autoethnography only shows how *specific* political phenomena, practices, institutions, and situations take a toll that can perhaps be reduced or avoided altogether once we recognize the personal price they exact from us and other people.

In the context of the Israel-Palestine condition, it was especially Meron Benvenisti's candid writings that made me aware of the benefits of one's public sharing of his personal sorrow. This, despite, paradoxically, Benvenisti's overall pessimism. He thus writes at the end of his *Sacred Landscape: The Buried History of the Holy Land since 1948*,[25] "I began this work as a mea culpa, an attempt to offer an apology for those wrongdoings that my research would reveal to me. But having completed the book, I realized that the personal part was the easiest." He then implies that in the absence of an apology for past wrongdoing by the Israeli state and this state's lack of willingness to alter its present conduct, there can be almost no positive change.[26] Seven years later Benvenisti writes at the end of his autobiographical book, *Son of the Cypresses: Memories, Reflections, and Regrets from a Political Life* that because of the absence of solutions to the Israeli-Palestinian conflict (in his view), "I am today a sad and pessimistic person, beset by a profound sense of brokenness.... I fear for my grandchildren. How will they live here? What am I leaving them?" Yet despite Benvenisti's overall pessimism, he nonetheless opens a small window of hope, an optimism that I wish to use as the starting point and rationale for my book: "I seize on this faint hope that maybe, after all, something shared [between Israelis and Palestinians] will evolve instead. That maybe, despite everything, we shall learn to live together. Maybe we shall come to understand that the Others are not demonic, that they, too, are part of this place."[27]

Sharing the burden of my experience is not identical to Benvenisti's search for personal and national forgiveness in his *Sacred Landscape*. Although I believe in the positive and therapeutic effects of apologies and requests for forgiveness, I think that forgiveness—on both sides of the conflict—must be preceded by much hard work of self-reflection and introspection, personal and national. Otherwise, it might be hollow or too early and will only create more grievances. I wish that through the open and frank sharing of my experiences, my grappling with identity questions, and my emotional burdens I will contribute to the process of mutual recognition that Benvenisti considers as the hope for the common future of Israelis and Palestinians. By revealing and sharing a wide array of feelings and reflections that arise in me while riding along the symbols of conflict and violence in this land, I hope to transmit a more complex and humane picture of the reality on the ground, to deconstruct the conflict and violence from the level of the ordinary citizen. Furthermore, the sharing of these pains is also an invitation to a frank and open dialogue, a declaration that I wish to talk with whoever read this text, and not hide behind the thick walls of the Mt. Scopus campus.

For Benvenisti, really belonging in this country means to be native, authentic, like himself. "Natives," he continues, "don't question their identity."[28] By this he means that he does not need affirmation from anyone of his rights and place in this land, for he was born here and he knows it in the most intimate ways—physically, geographically, historically, and politically. This strong and unmovable sense of belonging not only enables him to acknowledge the rights of the Palestinians and take part in salvaging their "buried history" but, in fact, necessitates this: the other is a part of him.[29] For him it was much easier than for me to see the Palestinian Arab as part of this land. This, I believe, is to a great extent due to the personal circumstances of his youth (he was born in 1934 Jerusalem, in British Mandatory Palestine), which included traveling across the land that was shared then, even if very reluctantly, by Jews and Arabs under external British rule, without one side actually governing the other: "[T]he Arab landscape . . . gave rise to images, smells, and a sense of human warmth so powerful that their mark has not been erased after half a century."[30] And "[T]his is a land that has always had Arabs in it; it is a land where the Arabs are the human landscape, the natives. Hence, I do not fear them. I cannot see myself living here without them. To me, Eretz Israel [the Land of Israel] without Arabs is a barren land."[31]

My own biography is different altogether. Although I was born and raised in the same city as Benvenisti, in Jerusalem, this city was already the capital of the State of Israel,[32] with all the implications of such a change. While Benvenisti toured and traveled the *living* Palestinian villages and interacted with the Arabs as equals,[33] I saw the sites of *ruined and deserted* villages around Jerusalem and grew up under the impression that this was always their condition, if I ever bothered to think about these places in historical terms.[34] In addition, when I learned or thought about the "War of Independence" (the 1948 war), I was taught that the "Arabs" brought their defeat on themselves by refusing to recognize the 1947 UN partition plan for Palestine and by declaring war on the Jewish "Yishuv" (pre-state political community). Thus, whereas for Benvenisti the Palestinian was a constant presence and an insider, native, like himself, for me, as a youth and a grown-up, the Arab, in general, was an external invader, a source of constant threat, and, no less important, a dominated person almost by definition. The mental separation between Palestinians and Jews, even in the "unified Jerusalem" into which I was born,[35] was already a concrete reality long before the erection of the "separation wall/fence." My sense of nativity was extremely different from Meron's and, I believe, much more permeated by fears of the other and by negating and externalizing him.

My journey, then, is not only an effort to see whether I am capable of stripping off such fears and perceptions from myself but also, in its basis, an inquiry into whether I *want* to go through this process. Can I, should I, change my basic identity, my sense of nativeness? For me the answer is yes: I want to be able to say, like Benvenisti, "I do not fear [the Palestinians]. I cannot see myself living here without them." However, this positive answer was the result of an intensive process of internal and external observation, inquiry, and reflection, which in itself was painful and is not completed yet. Nonetheless, by posing these queries to myself and by discussing the process I went through, I hope that readers of this book will reflect on similar questions and issues regarding themselves too.

Riding to Mt. Scopus: From Commuting to [the Department of] IR to Autoethnographic Decommuting

I started riding the trail from Mevasseret Zion to Mt. Scopus at the end of 2005, after our family moved to that suburban town. When we first moved into our apartment at Mevasseret, I thought that I would be able to work most of the time at home. Little did I know that my children had other plans for me while at home ... I had to commute to campus if I wanted a quiet work space. Mevasseret is relatively close to the city, but I did not dare use public transportation, as the horrors of busses exploded by Palestinian suicide bombers were too fresh in my mind (in the early 2000s, with the eruption of the second Palestinian uprising, dozens of suicide bombers exploded themselves in busses, malls, and other public locations in Israel, and Jerusalem suffered heavily). As our family car served Idit and the children (for practical and security reasons) and we were unable to bear the costs of owning and servi(ci)ng a second car, I had to settle for the bicycle (I knew very little then about the condition known as *upgraditis*—the insatiable desire to upgrade the bike, its components, and the rider's equipment).[36] Thus, my riding began due to practical and political constraints (that is, living in a country where you're afraid to use the bus due to terrorism).[37] At least, I thought then, I could save on gas, help the planet, and get some exercise on the road.[38]

While afraid of riding a bus, I was also reluctant to cycle on the highway to Jerusalem (Highway 1)—Israeli drivers are not very patient toward cyclists, to say the least. I decided to look for alternative routes. Riding a mountain bike (instead of a faster and lighter road bike) on dirt roads and single tracks thus became the preferable option. Consequently, mountain biking, which is for most riders a leisure recreational activity, became for me a daily practice that grew out of necessity. As we will see below, choosing this specific type of bicycle had important implications for what I was able to see along my road. After much trial and error, the Halilim wadi and Arazim Valley route turned out to be the best path for me—no cars on most of its parts and a relatively direct course

to Mt. Scopus, though with long climbs and sometimes technically challenging sections. An hour's ride in each direction was not that time consuming, I
thought, and increasingly I enjoyed the physical exercise, the open spaces, and
the freedom that the bicycle offered. I rejoiced in the incognito of the bicycle:[39]
no license plates, no need to carry a driving permit, and no annual insurance and
taxes to pay. I was also pleased with the bike's ability to escape "much of the dis-
ciplining that other forms of mobility are subjected to."[40] After all, you cannot
fly with your car, but you can gain some "airtime" when you "clear" drop-offs . . .

However, as the years passed, I noticed that my biking in the hills turned
from a practice of somewhat adventurous and sportive commuting to work to
a work(out) of experiential and explorative decommuting:[41] I was still riding
in order to get to campus, eventually, but I discovered that a great deal of my
thoughts and observations actually took place on the trail and in its surroundings.[42] Furthermore, I hadn't only thought while on the trail; I also thought
about the trail. Increasingly I strayed from the track to new places and locations and pondered and reflected on the meaning of what I saw. The move from
commuting to decommuting was a gradual process. The things I saw, and the
meanings I ascribed to them, in 2007 or 2008, for example, were not the same
things I perceived in 2010, when I finally realized that there is an important
political story to be told about my ride. What I was able, and willing, to observe,
both literally as seeing and metaphorically as perceiving and understanding
myself and others, was determined by material/physical, cognitive/intellectual,
and emotional factors and processes. Each dimension had its own independent
input in my ability to see the space I ride through and to reveal to me the burden I carry, but the three features of cognition, emotion, and materiality also
mutually constituted each other. Here it is important to note that the burden
I am talking about in this book was partially with me before I started riding to
Mt. Scopus, and also partially accumulated during these rides. Before I started
these rides, the burden was composed mainly of fear of the other and anger and
even hatred toward him (and, in fact, during the second Palestinian uprising/
intifada of 2000–2005(?)—there was no official end), also toward Palestinian
women, as there were several cases of female suicide bombers). It is difficult to
live in a state of mind of constant fear, anger, and hate. During the rides, the
burden became the explicit realization that indeed I was immersed in such a
state of mind, and the resultant resentment about the political conditions that
had constructed me in such a manner. I also developed a rejection of the ideolo-

gies, institutions, and structures that (seek to) maintain other Israelis in such a state of mind. Furthermore, the burden also evolved to include the exposure of some of the pain, anger, fear, humiliation, and bitterness that Palestinians carry with them. By becoming exposed to the other's pain and burden, I became more aware of the mutual constitution of pain by both sides, and this, of course, only intensified my own personal sorrow and sense of being locked in a nightmare.

Let me expand a bit about these mutually constitutive dimensions below. I think they are important in tracing the process of how I woke up to see that I live in what I call in the prologue to this book a "delusional and dreamlike reality." Or, at the very least, how I woke up from one layer of this dream.[43]

Mountain Biking as a Material and Embodied Practice of Seeing

Mountain biking is primarily a material and embodied experience and practice.[44] This is true for many disciplines of cycling in general, but it is especially relevant for mountain biking. In material terms, mountain and off-road biking are much different from road biking. For example, "cross-country"/trail mountain biking, the most common style of mountain biking and the one I practice too, is usually considerably slower than road or street riding because of the rugged terrain and the heavier and sturdier structure of the bicycle itself. While decreasing the mountain bike's speed, the strong and durable materials and components of such a machine allow riders to negotiate a wide array of obstacles along the trail, to experiment with various kinds of tracks (in terms of soil type, incline, ruggedness, curviness, etc.), and to maintain a high level of control over the bicycle in changing path conditions.

Moreover, the mountain bicycle offers a much more intimate, embodied, and unmediated contact with the terrain and the outside environment than other vehicles do. This engenders a unique travel experience, which is usually absent when using more "normative" forms of mobility. The intimacy and connectedness, literally, generated by mountain biking also create a more nuanced perception of the places and spaces I pass along and through. As Tim Ingold argues, "[A] place owes its character to the experiences it affords to those who spend time there—to the sights, sounds and indeed smells that constitute its specific ambience. And these, in turn, depend on the kind of activities in which inhabitants engage."[45] Thus, especially compared to the driver or passenger of a car and other forms of motorized commuting transportation, and even compared to the road cyclist or to riders of motorized off-road vehicles (such as motorcycles, all-terrain vehicles [ATVs], and pickup trucks), the mountain biker is much more "in" the environment.

While using motorized transportation or vehicle, you are usually shielded and separated from the "outside." The passenger cabin of a car or bus becomes a space in itself, often air-conditioned, from which one looks outward to the space crossed (a "reversed aquarium" on the move . . .). In other cases, the outside is not even being noticed, as commuters are busy in talking with each other, listening to music, reading, or dealing with some electronic gadget, for example.[46] Alternatively, endless advertisement posts and signs, often electronic and digitized, on highways and increasingly even residential streets, create a disoriented experience.

Yet on the mountain bike you are *in* the outside. Because the rider is the "engine" of the machine, the physical effort of mountain biking in off-road conditions is much greater than driving or riding any motorized vehicle. Being the engine of the bicycle means that there is a limit to the rider's ability to insulate herself/himself from the environment (too much insulation and shielding will cause overheating and discomfort). Thus, on the mountain bike, the rider feels the imposing weight of a summer day's heat or the stab of a winter night's chill, tastes the dust of the path, struggles with headwinds, and smells the various odors and scents of the world. The rider's bones and muscles absorb vibrations and blows from rocks and roots on the trail, and her/his skin is often bruised or cut if one loses traction and falls on some "element" along the trail. The lesser ability to insulate oneself physically from the environment also arouses a completely different spectrum of emotional reactions and sensory experiences than those felt by motorists, who are usually much more materially protected than the rider of a mountain bike. Imagine that you are driving in your car, alone, on a lonely dirt road at night in a remote wadi when you suddenly see in front of you a pack of wild dogs. You would probably feel much safer than being there with a bicycle, exposed . . .

Yet, despite such feelings of exposure, which sometimes might indeed become unpleasant, the physical effort and bodily experience during the ride connect me (and I believe many other riders as well) much more and in a direct and close manner to the space I ride in. The close connection among me, the bicycle, and the terrain generates not only a perception of the bike, the machine, as an extension of my body,[47] but creates an emotional connection with the space by producing a sense of achievement, overcoming, and satisfaction during and after each ride. Geography becomes a much more felt constraint (uphill, rugged, or technical terrain, for instance) or a source of excitement and joy (during, for example, a fast and challenging downhill ride). In the medium and long run, geographic space even shapes and transforms the bodily "geography" of the rider. The daily trial of the ascents and technical trails builds certain muscle groups in my body, and sometimes leaves bruises, wounds, and scars on my skin. Thus, geographic space blends with my body, materially and emotionally. As Justin Spinney argues, "[T]he character of a place is dependent upon *how* we are in a place, and how we perceive and organize sensory input. . . . While technologies are often considered simply as means to meet practical demands, the character of a place depends on 'how things are made' or experienced, and is consequently determined by the technical realization of a place. Ultimately then, our perceptions of our environment are informed by the goals, skills and technologies available to us."[48]

In this sense, an important material characteristic of a mountain bike is its being an extremely maneuverable a machine that can cross almost any terrain. Where it cannot roll, you can lift it on your shoulder or walk and pull it alongside you. There is no necessary element of "path dependence" in riding a mountain bike. For me this maneuverability translates into many detours and excursions from my regular path into places that I would not have discovered otherwise. Thus, my ride line often looks like a zigzag or a tree with many branches. In such excursions, I often not only see and experience new places and spaces but also get to talk and interact with "marginal" people who seek or are pressed to seek the privacy and loneliness that the dirt paths around Jerusalem can offer. Such conversations and discoveries of new locations, small as they may be, largely constitute my sense of place.

Another material aspect of the blended mountain biking/commuting I practice is that it usually takes much more time than driving. This longer duration enables a close familiarity and knowledge of the trail and the surroundings, as I become an "expert" on the trail: I intimately know its various elements (specific rocks, roots, trees, bushes, curves, etc.) and even recognize specific animals that live in the space I cross. The usual slowness of the ride also highlights the fact that our world, which we increasingly see as a small and connected place, is, in fact, very big. It takes me, as a skilled, well-equipped, and fit rider, almost an hour to complete the eleven-kilometer ride from home to campus. In this manner, I get a more concrete, direct, and, in fact, corporeal sense of distances in larger scale. Because I know in my body how difficult it is to complete these eleven kilometers, I appreciate much more the efforts of passengers and travelers of previous historical eras who used their legs and nonmotorized vehicles to get from place to place.[49] I also understand the vulnerability of modern society in the sense of its high dependence on fast and comfortable mobility.

As I pass along or under highways and main roads, I also think about how much physical space the infrastructures of modern mobility occupy—roads, highways, bridges, intersections, junctions, parking lots, and so on. Compared to these dimensions, I feel dwarfed on the bike, which hardly occupies any physical space. I think about how much space we could have saved in a small and condensed state such as Israel, in which territory is the most contested "product," had more people used bicycles instead of motorized transportation.

The relatively long duration of my ride and the freedom from car violence along most of my route to campus also allow me considerable time to think and muse, quietly. While commuting in a car or on public transportation, one can, of course, think and ruminate as well. But there are many structural obstructions against thinking on such occasions: for instance, when driving, one has to be constantly alert to the fast and changing conditions of the road, and many commuters—passengers and drivers alike—keep thinking about how to shorten the time spent on the road in order to "get there" as quickly as possible. Being stuck in a traffic jam or caught up in busy traffic often leads one to grumpy thoughts, not to constructive and positive ones.[50] And beyond providing more quality time for thinking, the off-road trail as a space also enables much flexibility in terms of deviating from the track, riding against the "direction of traffic," or simply stopping wherever and whenever you want. Stopping or lingering in a spot off the trail for a moment or two, and sometimes more, enables you to examine your surroundings in a more thorough manner, without anyone scolding and honking at you for delaying the traffic or blocking the road.[51]

Often, when I tell people that I cycle to work, their immediate question is "And how much time does it take you, with or without the stopping and lingering?" I sometimes reply. Others' focus on the duration of the ride shows me how our society wires us to think in terms of "efficiency."[52] Indeed, I am a tenured faculty member who enjoys job security. As such, it could be argued, I am less given to time pressures. I also don't have to sign an attendance card, and I enjoy much freedom of movement in the sense that, in principle at least, I can do my research work almost wherever I choose. Yet often it is precisely my tenured colleagues, my peers, who wonder about or mock my "waste of time." I don't want to open a Pandora's box here, but against this criticism of my supposed waste of time, I must ask, in our day, how much time do we actually have to think in academia? Not much, I fear. A great deal of the current structure of incentives and constraints in academia reproduces and enhances an anti-intellectual climate in universities. Great emphasis on "publishing by the kilo," for example, often leads to replicating one's own work in countless manners and titles or to petty debates on marginal and inconsequential issues among experts belonging to very small and often impenetrable and/or inaccessible research communities. This and other practices (for example, the constant chasing of research grants) are immensely time consuming, but they are considered necessary parts of the production of knowledge. For me, on the other hand, the longer the ride takes, the more time I have to actually do my job: open my eyes to what is around me and reflect on what I see *in the world*.

In these senses and others, my cycling experience of place and space is much more diverse and nuanced than other commuters' and builds a tight connection to place. As opposed to the sense of a nonplace that the remoteness and seclusion of motorized transportation produce, cycling creates a complex set of sensory feelings and emotional experiences, a more tangible and intensive, bodily, and direct one. It also provides the rider with more opportunities to communicate in various manners with other people who also walk or cycle along the trail. Several such conversations and encounters that I had during my rides opened my eyes to political aspects I would not have noticed otherwise.

Intellectually and Emotionally Opening Up to the Politics of the Trail

As an international relations researcher, I have always been interested in the concept of power and in the actual workings of power in the international system. But for many years, as a student and as a scholar, I was mainly attracted to the more traditional and conventional aspects of power. As a student, I was very much intrigued by the concept of the "Great Powers" in IR. The Great Powers, the militarily and economically leading states in the world, represented to me nostalgic images of nineteenth-century diplomacy, congresses, and pomp. "High politics," the study of peace and war between the Great Powers according to many IR specialists,[53] enabled me to connect with some bigger and allegedly important reality. Note the capitalization of the words *great powers* in many IR works—a capitalization that denotes importance and perhaps also seriousness and solemnity. This connection to the world of the powerful also made it possible for me to clarify to myself many of the dynamics of the regional conflicts in the Middle East. But the study of high politics and the Great Powers and their "Great Game" (what a sad and terrible term, I now realize, to denote intervention in other countries' matters and concerns, often not by peaceful means), also enabled me to *unexplain* most of the realities of "regional" conflicts I witnessed and experienced in Israel and the Middle East. International relations theory— which for many years meant for me the debates about how the international "system" works and what the international "structure" is composed of—helped me reduce and take control over my deep fears of war and violence. War, and especially war or conflict between the Great Powers or even between the Great Powers and smaller states or nonstate networks and groups, is always rationalized and modeled theoretically and conceptually in the discipline of IR.

Moreover, war and violent conflict in the IR that I knew, even if taking place among "regional" states or within states themselves, were often a function of Great Power politics. In the context of either "wars by proxy," decolonization and the creation of "weak states," or the inhibiting role the Great Powers play with regard to their regional "clients" or allies,[54] I preferred to see local war and conflict in my country as greatly shaped and influenced by the Great Powers. I knew, of course, that the Israeli-Palestinian and Israeli-Arab conflicts have many "internal" and local causes and dynamics, but those seemed to me too messy and difficult to understand. Moreover, they seemed too *painful* to deal with because, and this I can formulate to myself more clearly only in retrospect, their study from the inside can lead to critically questioning one's own identity and conduct. And, at any rate, I thought, the "parties" to these conflicts eventually abide, or at least are considerably restricted and constrained, by the interests and pressures of the United States and other "major" states.

For a time, this restricting influence of the Great Powers indeed permitted me to avoid thinking seriously about the situation of protracted conflict in my country. "America will fix it," I used to think whenever the "peace process" between Israel and the Palestinians ran aground. But during the second Palestinian intifada, with its countless suicide bombing attacks, I realized that America, by itself, cannot fix it. Something was really broken here, and the bloody intifada and its brutal oppression by Israel only crushed my hopes for peace into smaller pieces. At the same time, the Bush administration's "war on terror" and the 2003 Iraq war also highlighted for me the limits of "fixing" things through further breaking them. (A quick thought: why do we capitalize wars' and conflicts' names? For that matter, why do we even call wars by specific names? Yes, there are considerations of speech and writing convenience and uniformity that encourage such a practice. And of course, there are psychological and political inputs and interests in the naming of specific wars. Most important, however, naming wars softens and masks, to some degree, the horror and absurdity of mass murder and killing. It also honors the dead and gives meaning to the violence. But naming and capitalizing wars also naturalizes war by treating it as a thing that, like other real objects, entities, and beings, has a name. Therefore, due to considerations of convenience and uniformity, let me from now on in this book refer to wars and conflicts by their commonly known names, but without capitalizing them. This is not meant to underrate or dishonor the sacrifices of the victims of the war, on the contrary. It is part of my desire to denaturalize war as a human practice.)

Perceiving the limits of great power ability—and even inclination and interest—to end or at least to restrict violent conflict where I live forced me to think more seriously about the internal motivations of this conflict. The 2006 Lebanon war and the war in Gaza in 2008–9—in which the international community did play a certain restrictive role but at the same time tolerated Israel's wielding of destructive force against Hizb'allah and Hamas and vice versa (as well as many "collateral" damages inflicted on innocent people)—opened my mind to think about the part played by emotion in violent conflict. It was one thing to write about emotion in the US-led war on terror and the war in Iraq, as I did in my 2007 book, and another thing to witness at close hand a whole society infused with what I saw as emotions of revenge and self-righteousness.

I always knew, and been told since childhood and in the education system, the media, and even Israeli academia, that Israel's enemies are led by their emotions of hatred and revenge against Israel, whereas Israel is an "advanced, liberal and Western democracy" that "extends its hand for peace but is rejected time and again." Or "The Palestinians never miss an opportunity to miss an opportunity."[55] I thus wanted to think that Israel is a rational, just, and enlightened state (if such a thing exists at all in this world . . .), or at least seeks to be one. But the jubilation of many, too many, of my students, my *students*—my supposed partners in the pursuit of knowledge and understanding—during the Lebanon war, and especially during the Gaza war ("it's high time that we show them once and for all," etc.), as well as the deeply satisfied and ranting reactions of the general public and the media to these bursts of terrible violence, saddened me a great deal. I could not stay blind to the discrepancy between the images I endeared and the reality I perceived. I wrote (with Gadi Heimann) "Revenge in International Politics" partially as a way to deal with the sad realization that I live in a society that is not only overtly militaristic but also openly vengeful (of course, Gadi may have had other motivations. I refer here solely to my own views). The writing of this article took two years of exhaustive work, which involved several submissions to different journals and extensive reading on emotion and revenge from various academic disciplines, such as drama and theater studies, political psychology, comparative literature, and sociology. When we finished this project (published in *Security Studies* in 2008–9), I knew that I had taken a big step toward looking into myself and the society that I am a part of. But I still adhered to the conventional academic formula of distanced and detached analysis.

Writing "Revenge in International Politics" made me contemplate such aspects along my trail. I thought much more about the role of emotion in politics, and about my own emotions toward politics. The long duration of the rides and the opportunity to think and observe during this time also brought ever more to my attention the traces and marks of violent conflict alongside my trail. The bike ride that was initially an "evasive maneuver" a la *Star Trek* to avoid exploding busses, and which developed into a physical and emotional practice of connecting with the terrain and the landscape, now prompted me to look around more carefully.

Especially, I became aware of how much I experience fear and anger when I ride next to the government's nuclear bunker. The bunker came to symbolize for me a combination of governmental and state arrogance and duplicity,[56] existential fear and anxiety, selfishness, fatalism, and a readiness (though, perhaps, not a willingness) to sacrifice the lives of millions while saving the lives of a few. Moreover, while I knew there were rational and supposedly objective reasons to build it, the bunker also signified for me the cementing—literally and metaphorically—of the violent and conflict-prone state of mind that condemns me and Israeli society to keep carrying the burden of war and violence.

I began more and more to encircle the work site of the bunker with my bicycle, going up the surrounding hills to get new vantage points on it. I wanted to see what was going on inside the site, beyond the fences that enclosed it. The secrecy and securitization that surrounded the place, which before the wars of 2006 and 2008–9 did not bother me much, now angered and depressed me ever more. I was distressed by the presence of the "security state" in the middle of my bike trail and felt estranged from the state, which had dug a big hole in "my" territory to conduct wars from within. It frustrated and frightened me to see "war," as an entity in itself, so to speak, brought so close to me despite my best efforts to evade it by riding the bicycle off the road on isolated trails. The bunker imposed on me the "strategic" element of the conflict: it clarified to me that my government is preparing itself for cataclysmic events. I feared the self-fulfilling nature of such preparations. I also felt that the bunker, as a protective site against a national catastrophe, symbolizes the degree to which Israel feels hated and unwanted in this region. It hurt me to see this desperate conviction literally entrenching itself in the beautiful hills of Jerusalem. I felt the pain of the land. My conversations with other people about the bunker revealed to me that many regular Israelis not only justify the project on rational grounds (the need for "continuity of government" in case of national disaster) but also tap into the emotional image it transmits: that hatred toward Israel in the Middle East is inevitable and independent of Israeli policies and actions, and that such hatred might indeed bring one day a cataclysmic war. Many of my interlocutors were even proud that such a site was under construction and treated it as a symbol of power to be revered. These responses and realizations drove me to understand that I should do my best to desanctify this site and cast doubt on its underlying rationale: that hatred is inevitable and independent of what my state is doing.

Parallel to my developing awareness of the symbols of violence and conflict I witnessed and experienced along my trail, my father's Parkinson's disease worsened, until he was hospitalized in August 2008. He never returned home and died in a nursing home in September 2009. His disease and death, as well as the long period of hospitalization, increased my awareness of the transitory and fragile nature of life. Of course, almost any mortal is conscious of this truth. But when I saw my beloved father dying, I internalized this fact on a much deeper level than before. But more than this: the intense experience of his hospitalization left me existentially sad. It was not only his suffering and long and painful dying that saddened me so. It was also the knowledge that a whole world would die with him.

My father was born in 1941 in Budapest. In 1944, while my grandfather was taken to be a slave laborer in the SS "labor platoons," my father and his mother escaped the transports to Auschwitz by hiding in the basement of the Jewish Hospital in the Budapest Ghetto. After the war, during his school years, he suffered anti-Semitism and was often involved in street fights with anti-Semite bullies in the streets of Budapest. He witnessed with his own eyes the Soviet tanks shelling residential buildings in Budapest in 1956. Those experiences eventually turned him from a Hungarian patriot and a follower of communism into a Zionist (that is, inasmuch as a fifteen-year-old can truly understand these various identities), and he convinced his parents to immigrate to Israel. Yet once in Israel he increasingly longed for Budapest and in many cultural and emotional senses continued to "live" in Budapest and Hungary while in Jerusalem. His Zionism soon faded away, as he found himself in the sands of the Sinai Desert, fighting the Egyptian army in the 1967 and 1973 wars (and, also, during long months of reserve service at the Suez Canal during the 1969–70 war of attrition. My name, Oded, a biblical name (2 Chron. 28:9), which in Hebrew means "the one who encouraged," was given to me when my father returned from that war just upon my birth).

Indeed, my parents' home was a Hungarian one: my mother was born in Transylvania, the Hungarian-speaking part of Romania, and my parents spoke Hungarian among themselves and with my sister and me. My grandparents, too, spoke only Hungarian, except my father's father, who was an orthodox rabbi and was fluent in Hebrew even when in Hungary. Interestingly, my other grandparents could read Hebrew, but they hardly understood what they were reading—in the Diaspora, Ivris (Hebrew, in Yiddish pronunciation) was the holy tongue, which served for prayer at the synagogue, and Jews learned to read it so they would be able to read the Holy Scriptures and prayers, yet without fully understanding them. In Israel, my grandparents barely learned any Ivrit (Hebrew, in Israeli-Hebrew pronunciation), as almost all their neighbors were Hungarian Jews like themselves, living in a relatively closed community of immigrants (hundreds of Hungarian Jews were housed in huge industrially built residential blocks in Brazil Street in the Kiryat Yovel neighborhood in southwestern Jerusalem. Even today, when almost all these people have died, you can still hear there Hungarian).

In fact, Hungarian, not Hebrew, was the first language I learned, from my parents and grandparents. Only when I started going to kindergarten, in 1973, did I begin speaking Hebrew. In this manner, I, too, was an immigrant, and perhaps in many ways I retain this identity of a latecomer in Israeli society. This sense of partial strangeness—and the deriding and intolerant responses I received from other children due to my Hungarian background—pushed me away from this identity. I wanted to be a "real" Israeli, to shed the Hungarian-ness.

Thus, as an adolescent and a young man, I refused to share and understand my father's longings for the world he left at the age of sixteen. I wanted to hear about his life in Israel as an "Oleh Hadash" (Hebrew, "a newcomer"), but his longings for Budapest and Hungary created in me an emotional antagonism. I felt his longings represented a Diaspora and immigrant mentality, something that the proud Sabra (that is, the "authentic" Israeli, born in Israel and not in the Diaspora) that I wanted to be should reject. I thought of all the Hungarians as complicit in the Holocaust and as inherently anti-Semites, and could not see why he missed their culture and country. As I grew up, though, my attitude changed, perhaps became more nuanced and mature, especially as I became a father myself. I understood the value of the simple daily stories and experiences, of the humor, the culture, the food, and the memories. When I took my children to see the playground where I used to play as a child; my grandparents' building in Brazil Street and in Nissan Street; the falafel diner where we used to stand in a long line with all the rest of the people from the neighborhood on the first night after Passover, when it was permitted to eat leavened bread again; my old tree house; or the bench on which I kissed my first girlfriend, I realized how central is my childhood landscape in my sense of self, and how important it is for me that my children will know and see these places.

But with my father it was too late now: the more I wanted to know about his childhood and youth, the more his dementia and cognitive problems worsened, and we could not talk about these things in a meaningful way. I saw how many aspects we had failed to realize in our relationship. As my children kept asking me every night at bedtime to tell them about my childhood, I was happy and thankful for their interest and desire to link their lives to mine. Yet I saw how much the politics of state and nation building in Israel, with its negation of the Diaspora as an experience of Jewish life worthy in itself (and not only as a necessary prelude to Jewish revival in Israel) and with its identification of the "gentiles" as inherently anti-Semites and hostile, was a major cause in my rejection of my Jewish Hungarian roots. Although my father wrote a doctorate and many articles on the history of the Hungarian Jewry,[57] I felt that his passing away meant that a great part of the history that now mattered to me most, the personal and private one, would disappear too, fixating that rootless part of my identity.

Added to these feelings of missed opportunities were the alienation and loneliness of the hospital. My father lay in the internal medicine departments of two general hospitals in Jerusalem for more than four months, and in a nursing home during the rest of the time. There he also died. What saddened me so much was that hardly anyone from the medical and nursing staff in these institutions really seemed to care about him. Yes, they usually treated his body reasonably—most of the time he was clean and well fed. They administered his medications properly. But barely anyone was ever interested in who he was (he lost the speech ability a few days after his initial hospitalization in August 2008), what he did in his life, what he liked, and so on. He was always treated as an object among other objects in his condition, a present/missing person.[58] I know there are multiple reasons for this, and that none of the staff meant anything wrong. In Israel, medical staffs are overburdened with hard work in crowded wards, they are often underpaid, and the underlying mentality of the medical profession is of scientific detachment, of authoritative and rational examination. The disparity between my father's (and the other members of my family's) physical and emotional pain and distress due to the disease and the hospitalization, the building mourning and the knowledge of coming death, on the one hand, and the cold professional or simply tired remoteness of the medical staffs, on the other hand, was stark. This coldness and professionalism with which human life was treated in the hospital could not fail to remind me of the similar attitude and mentality in which human life is often treated in the academic discipline of IR. It made me contemplate further the question of why I study international politics, and forced me to think more seriously about the human dimension of politics. The sense of fragile existence and lack of solidarity and deep empathy led me to recognize that any analytical framework that does not incorporate in it empathy and care, in evocative terms, might take part in reproducing the cruel practices it studies (see the discussion above). I felt an urge to be *in* the world, to write from an involved and subjective, not detached and objectivist, place. I wanted to hear and tell stories, people's and places' stories. This brought me, eventually, to autoethnography.

Thus, I understood that I want to go to the world outside campus, feel and be nourished by its reality, and at the same time write about it and participate in the complex process of imagining the world in an empathetic and caring manner. I will write an *experiential* autoethnography. I will use the bicycle, the machine with its material parts (which, in some senses is also a work of ideas and imagination—see Robert M. Pirsig's *Zen and the Art of Motorcycle Maintenance*) and my bodily experiences and sensations while riding it, to engage with the world of politics and history. I had no orderly plan of action, and no research program. In fact, from day to day I was pulled toward this project by dreams at night, by the sights I saw on my trail, and by the incidental meetings and rendezvous with people on this path. Nevertheless, I felt that there was a story here, on my trail, which must be told, of places and people. I was not sure yet what exactly the story was, but I felt an urge to look for its meaning. I thus wrote down my experiences, thoughts, emotions, insights, and conversations with others in field notes (I carried a notebook in my bicycle backpack, and often found myself stopping every few minutes to write); I read historical and geographic literature on the specific places along my trail and often wandered off to reading about broader (hi)stories of the Israeli-Palestinian/Arab conflict. I also rode to other locations that seemed to me related to the space of my daily trail.

Gradually, toward the summer of 2011, after more than a year of intensive riding, investigations, interviews, conversations, and readings, I realized that what I was actually writing was not only the story of how I exposed the human and physical landscape I ride along every day and what prompted me to this endeavor. Rather, I understood that the underlying story in my ride was that of the daily process of creating intimacy and closeness with the landscape, and of the emotional price that comes with such intimacy.[59] I also realized that while "[a]ll sorrows can be borne if you can put them into a story or tell a story about them,"[60] the very telling of this story might create in itself new sorrows and burdens.

A Note on the Problem of "Noblesse Oblige," or on "Shooting and Crying"

Writing an autoethnography involves, by definition, a vulnerability of revealing yourself. On the face of it, this could be an incentive for prudence in what one discloses about oneself. Some could argue that this might even lead to various manipulations or calculated and strategic representations of oneself. For example, critics from the political Right in Israel could say that by sympathizing and identifying not only/mainly with Israeli-Jewish suffering and pain caused by the conflict but also with the Palestinian predicament and hurting, I aim to present myself as a "good Jew," one that distinguishes himself from his fellow so-called colonialist Zionist Israelis, in order to please the "world." Such an image would then enable me to gain international recognition as an intellectual that opposes the "oppression" and "occupation" of the Palestinians (the Israeli Right denies that there is a condition of occupation in the West Bank and Gaza and considers these territories as either "liberated" or, at most, "disputed"). Consequently, the argument could further go, I might receive various material honors (for example, invitations to lecture abroad or research funds from the European Union and other "anti-Semitic" or "anti-Israel" organizations like the Ford Foundation). Such claims against critical Israeli academics have increasingly been made in Israel in recent years not only within universities but also in the mass media and the Knesset (Israel's parliament), to the extent that some professors feel their freedom of expression, as well as their academic freedom, is under siege.[61]

Such accusations can hurt me to a considerable degree. First, it is insulting to be accused of being an ideological opportunist. Second, such an image might increase student discontent with my teaching and become manifested in their teaching evaluations, which bear some weight in my future promotion procedures. Third, there is a risk of being physically attacked. During the 1940s, there were several incidents of violent attacks by revisionist (extreme nationalist) activists against Hebrew University professors that were seen by them as "traitors,"[62] and in September 2008, Professor Zeev Sternhell from Hebrew University's Political Science Department was injured after a bomb exploded at the entrance to his house in Jerusalem. The suspected perpetrator, who was later arrested by the police, was a fundamentalist Jewish settler who was also accused of the murder of two Palestinians in 1997. Talkbackists on various websites often also call for violence against "disloyal" professors.[63] The rector of Ben Gurion University of the Negev, Professor Zvi Hacohen, wrote in a letter to the faculty of the university, upon assuming the office of the rector in September 2010, that "several faculty members [of BGU] received threats of death and the Internet is filled with incitement against them and with calls to harm them. The road from here to actual physical harm is short, and eventually there might be some deviant who will act [upon this incitement]."[64] Personally, I have received hate e-mails from utter strangers (my name already appears in the "Isra campus" list of "fifth-column" Israeli academics), as well as responses from family members in dinner talks who believe that "anti-Zionist" and other "disloyal" professors should be fired (that is, from their jobs . . .) or even put before a firing squad (the person who told me this was completely serious).

On the other hand, critics from the political Left might argue that my narration is nothing more than a sophisticated exercise in Israeli propaganda (*hasbarah*).[65] By showing my doubts and identity struggles, by exposing my fears and sorrows, the argument could go, I not only try to depict a more complex picture of the reality of conflict but also seek to exact undeserved sympathy and identification while remaining on the more powerful and even victimizing side of the conflict.[66] Such extreme postcolonialist critiques might argue that unless I embrace the "one state solution" as a way to get out of the essentially colonial situation in "Israel/Palestine," my work remains an act of "shooting and crying" or "noblesse oblige" by a privileged member of an elite group within what is in their eyes a colonial and racist regime.[67]

To that critique I respond by saying that, first, I want the shooting to stop from all directions. Personally, I never shot anyone, and I am doing the best I can to see that my government, on its part, will stop shooting too. And this leads me to my second response: there is a difference between crying and *whining*. Yes, I often cry because of the situation in my country. But I do not whine: my crying comes from a place of a desire for change, not out of self-pity and "addiction" to the conflict.[68] I am not exactly sure what is the change I want to see in Israel-Palestine in terms of political and institutional structure—two states for two peoples, one state for two peoples, some sort of con/federation, several Jewish-Arab city leagues/networks,[69] or even an international protectorate, for example. I am also not sure that any of these "solutions" is feasible at this moment in history. But I do know that I don't want to see a country in which people will grudgingly live with each other due to the lack of alternatives, or worse still, will fantasize (and occasionally try to act on their fantasies) in order to expel/destroy the other. I hope that one day Jews and Palestinians in this land will be able to accept and *welcome* each other as people with legitimate and equal rights to share this small piece of land.

For this to happen, much has to change yet. In parallel with the implementation of any politico-institutional solution, an emotional and perceptual change has to take place. Of course, the two things may be, in reality, interdependent.

Yet this does not preclude in principle the fact that we should seek each of them independently. In this regard, I believe that my "relative advantage" lies in showing in a personal and evocative manner how I face my fears, sorrows, pains, and uncertainties, and try to share them in order to deconstruct the realities that generate them. The ride, in itself and also in the stories and insights that emanate from it, eventually seeks to open up a space for emotional sharing and empathy. In the current situation in Israel-Palestine, this is not something that can be easily underestimated. Into this space I invite the readers of this book.

Now, I do not mean to say that people—Israelis and Palestinians—are blind to sites like those I investigate and visit in this book (memorials, ruined villages, the separation fence, etc.). In fact, in many cases, such sites and spaces are even sanctified by one "side" or become objects of resistance and hate by the other "side." But while for Palestinians the ruins of a depopulated village from the 1948 war, for example, are seen as almost a holy place, for Israelis such sites represent exotic and "natural" ruins or a testimony to the inferiority of the Palestinians and the fate they "deserved" due to their "refusal" to accept the 1947 UN partition plan for Palestine. *In this respect, my journey is a process of realizing that one "side's" pain is necessarily the source of the other's pain too.* I think that most Israelis and Palestinians know this, on this or that level. But many do their best to ignore this simple truth and focus only on their own pain, while denying or underestimating the other's pain, or worse still, taking satisfaction from the other's pain. By opening up to the pain and sorrow that violence and conflict produce for *both* Israelis and Palestinians, or at least by earnestly trying to open up to this, I seek to show how we are all—Israelis and Palestinians, victors and defeated, conquerors and conquered—victims of the conflict.[70] I wish not to enshrine this victimhood as such, but rather to use it to create a sense of revulsion at the vicious status quo, a revulsion that, in its turn, will help to subvert this status quo and open our minds to seek "solutions" based on mutual acceptance.

Victimhood in the Israeli-Palestinian conflict is not symmetrical—in many respects the Palestinians' degree of victimhood is much higher than the Israelis'. But in other respects, the supposedly more powerful Israelis are no less victims of the conflict, and I am not referring here just to the obvious aspects of terrorism and bereavement that Israelis have suffered throughout the years too. Namely, the very ignoring or silencing of history, as well as the shutting of our eyes in the present to avoid seeing the suffering and pain that we inflict on the

Palestinians (and no matter whether there is a specific "security" or "military" justification for each case of anti-Palestinian measures), produces many Israelis as foreigners, or perpetual "immigrants" as Meron Benvenisti once told me, in their own country. Hence, my crying—which emanates from the inherent pain of this landscape and the people who live in it—is an act of connecting with it, of becoming a native who not only owns the land but also owns up to its "fractured, agonized appearance."[71]

On the Methodology of The Politics of the Trail

In this subsection, I elaborate on some methodological issues that relate to the writing of this book. First, let me say something about the *density of the layers of information* in this book. As you may have noticed, there are in my text various departures from the main story line. In addition, I have a tendency to write long footnotes with more stories in them. Part of this stems from the explorative nature of the bike ride itself, with its many excursions from the trail. But in a more profound sense, these many layers of information are a testimony to the heavy emotional burden that I and others along this trail carry. The various memories, dreams, associations, and details are the raw material, the components, of this pain and burden. If the aim of this book is to show the complexity of the Israeli culture of conflict and to share this burden, then the details have importance in themselves, even if sometimes they seem unrelated to each other. Thus, while I do not want to distract the reader's attention from the story, I want the reader to know that the story here is actually the multitude of stories themselves.

The veracity of most of my stories and descriptions cannot be validated through traditional scientific methods. This, in fact, pertains to a great part of the auto- and ethnographic literature in general. Indeed, throughout the period of the "official" research I conducted between May 2010 and July 2011 (when I left Israel for a sabbatical leave on Vancouver Island), I kept journals and field notes. I also had several tours along my bike trail with colleagues and friends, whose impressions and ideas are sometimes intertwined in the chapters.

However, it is important to keep in mind that the object of this book is not to present a truth in the positivist sense but to convey feelings and emotions, experiences and insights. The human and social condition is much richer and broader than the segment of it that can be observed and examined in positivist methods. Social science must broaden its borders in order to include in it more dimensions of social life. How, then, will a reader "know if I am telling the truth, when no one 'knows what is going on in a person except the human spirit which is within'?"[72] Much like this pondering of Saint Augustine, I can only hope that readers will believe my sincerity and will open their hearts to my relation. In autoethnography, writes Dauphinee, a space is opened "for the reader to see the intentions—and not just the theories and methodologies—of the researcher. It opens us to a deeper form of judgment. That is the core of its ethics."[73]

Having trust in the autoethnographer's honesty and truthfulness is not such a unique and extraordinary request in the context of the social sciences. First, much of the data and information we have in the social sciences are unverifiable, or we do not bother to verify it. Second, because all theory is value laden, even if not consciously written as such or explicitly mentioned in the text, and values cannot be verified scientifically, all theories contain an element of faith and trust, Dauphinee further writes.[74] Instead of trying to refute my arguments (and become frustrated by the innate inability to do so), I ask the reader to use Ellis's criteria to appraise the value of this work: has it made you contemplate in a complex manner your own experience? Did you think that I maintained high ethical standards when presenting the reality of the conflict? Did I manage to make my inner world reachable to you and to merge you into the story?[75] Was the story written aesthetically? Did it raise curiosity? What was in your eyes the normative worthiness of the story? Does it have the potential to stimulate social action?[76]

The Geographical Boundaries of the Research

As said above, my bicycle route goes through Mevasseret Zion, the Halilim (Flutes) Wadi, and the Arazim (Cedars) Valley. The Arazim Valley is municipally a part of Jerusalem, but it is a "metropolitan park" and not an inhabited area. It is, at least at a first glance, seen by many people as a piece of nature or a "green lung" along the edge of the city, containing open spaces of fields and hill slopes, groves and woods, hiking and cycling trails, and picnic spots. It is not conceived as a political space per se, as opposed to much of Jerusalem's space. People view it as a space for recreation and leisure, as well as a corridor for critical infrastructure leading to the city (water lines, electro-optic cables, railway and motorway bridges and tunnels, etc.). Mevasseret Zion, though not a natural or outdoor space in this manner, is also often seen by many people in Jerusalem, and in the town itself, as a "normal" place, in which politics mainly concerns the affairs of the Local Council of the town, and the tensions between old residents and newcomers. The secular-religious intra-Jewish conflicts of Jerusalem, as well as the Israeli-Palestinian conflict in the city, are not a major perceived characteristic of Mevasseret. This perhaps explains the influx of secular, middle-class Jewish residents from Jerusalem to Mevasseret. This apolitical image was also the way I perceived this town and the valleys that connect it to Jerusalem before I started my rides and research.

Yet, it is especially interesting to examine Mevasseret and the Halilim and Arazim area precisely because of their supposedly "normal" and apolitical nature. The political elements relating to the Israeli-Palestinian conflict within Mevasseret and these valleys are usually hidden from the eye of the average Jewish-Israeli observer, and this means that these elements have gone through a process of deep political naturalization. My journey entailed exactly the exposure, the uncovering, *of* these elements and dimensions, and my relation is about the various responses and processes I experienced after realizing what I was exposed *to*. To uncover these elements and dimensions, I also sometimes rode to places and areas outside my daily trail, to see related, similar, or opposite landscapes, phenomena, and geopolitical manifestations. In the same vein, I also read about such phenomena and places, in order to see the broader context of the things I encountered in my daily rides to Mt. Scopus. Seeing this broader context was important in understanding how what I see locally is constituted by the conflict in general, and how this local landscape also plays a role in the further construction of this struggle.

While my ride continued for another four kilometers within the city of Jerusalem itself after emerging out of the Arazim Valley, I believe that the more interesting part of the ride was exactly the allegedly apolitical segment of it and the "archaeological" work I performed there. While Jerusalem itself is political par excellence in so many aspects (for example, Intra-Jewish, Jewish-Palestinian), the Halilim-Arazim region is supposedly "natural space," a declared nature reserve and metropolitan park. The uncovering of the political in such an environment not only shows the manner in which mechanisms of power work in Israel-Palestine in the context of geographical space but also demonstrates how the inner landscape of people is constructed. I show this construction and deconstruction through my stories of connectedness and alienation with the terrain and the "natural" space.

Finally, my account stops at the end of the Arazim Valley not the least because the emotional burden had been already too heavy to continue the investigation: I could not continue this microscopic investigation along my route in the streets of Jerusalem itself because the load I carried from the previous parts of the trail was too heavy for a single book. The urban parts of my ride are perhaps the material for a future book.

Ethical Considerations in This Story

While this book is an autoethnography, it also contains information, stories, impressions, and thoughts of or about other people—people I met along the trail or people I talked with about the things I saw during my rides. Is it ethical to disclose information about others in the author's personal and/or professional life? Is it ethical to tell about my impressions of others, which sometimes are not positive? Furthermore, there is a tension between, on the one hand, providing an authentic and engaging autoethnographic account and, on the other, compromising the reputation, privacy, and trust of others.[77]

In light of these considerations, I weighed seriously whether the disclosure of private information about others is necessary for the argument or purpose of my text.[78]

Hence, I blurred personal and identifying details about several people who asked me to avoid mentioning them directly. I also blurred the identity of people whom I thought might have disapproved the context in which I embedded their disclosures to me. I used pseudonyms or composite characters in the case of vulnerable and disadvantages persons, who are, almost by definition, less able to defend their privacy.[79] Thus, for example, I changed the names and identifying details of the Palestinian men I met in the Halilim wadi, not least because they told me that they could not have any open relationship with me (for example, invite me to their villages) for the fear of being defined by their community as "collaborators with the occupation" and suffering dire consequences.

There were, however, several cases of short, but revealing, conversations with people who remained anonymous to me, and I to them. I sometimes chose to remain anonymous due to my own physical security considerations, or simply because of the fleeting nature of a specific encounter. In such cases, I see no problem with telling what people told me, because I do not know who they were and they did not know who I was. These encounters should be seen as occurring in the public sphere, and therefore they enjoy only a low level of privacy.[80]

More important, however, is to remember that this book is an *autoethnography*. When I tell about other people, I mainly *examine them in light of what I learned about myself*. I mainly examine *my* reactions and responses to these people, and through these responses, with their limits and intensity, I try to shed a light on the broader societal and cultural context. In other words, the focus here will not be on other people as such, but as persons who helped me understand something about myself as a product of a culture of conflict and violence. This understanding, then, is useful in enabling me to interpret and share this culture from a subjective and personal point of view. And this, after all, is the purpose of this book.

The Structure of This Book

Before ending this introductory chapter, let me present briefly in this section the chapters that will follow. These chapters are, aforesaid, storied investigations of various places, people, and spaces along my trail. At the basis of this investigation is my struggle to resist the violence that is imprinted on the landscape, the external and internal, perhaps cleanse myself of it, and not let it continue to constitute me. Ultimately, then, the book raises a question: can one lead a nonviolent life in a violent space and society, and at what price?

Chapter 1 and chapter 2 are called "Mortal Danger: Two Rides along the Separation Fence" and "A Fence behind a Fence behind a Fence: Riding after the Unknown Soldiers and Looking for a Breach in the Fence." They deal with the way I "discovered" the separation fence that winds just next to my street in Mevasseret Zion. Of course, I saw the fence from the moment I came to live in Mevasseret in 2005. However, like many Israelis, I did my best to ignore it.[81] Only during 2010 did I begin to explore the fence by riding along the paths and trails that parallel it in the Mevasseret region. This brought me to the story of the 2004 campaign by a group of residents from Mevasseret who struggled to change the route of the fence so that it would be diverted from the immediate vicinity of the houses of Beit Surik—Mevasseret's West Bank neighboring Palestinian village. The chapter investigates my changing attitude about and perception of the whole question of the separation fence. Through the description of my meetings and interactions with Mevasseret residents who helped to save much (but not all) of Beit Surik's agricultural lands from being cut off by the fence; by telling about my meetings with people from Beit Surik, at the village beyond the fence; by investigating specific sites along the fence itself; and by recounting the experiences and the dreams of my rides on the trails along the fence on the Israeli and Palestinian sides, I explore my own feelings toward the fence, as well as discussing the emotions of the people around me with regard to this structure. I relate the internal conflict I have between the sense of security from suicide bombers, a sense of security generated by the fence, on the one hand, and, on the other hand, my physical and emotional sense of suffocation because of the fence. I ask a question that I present to many other Israelis, and which despite my sense of suffocation remains (quite) unresolved for me: if you ride along the separation fence and see a hole or a breach in it, would you report it to the authorities? In this way, these chapters are a novel treatment of the fence, and, in fact, of the whole project of separation in Israel-Palestine (the fence is the largest infrastructure project in Israeli history) by examining the emotions that produce the physical process of separation in this country and, in turn, are generated by this process.

Chapter 3 and chapter 4, "Riding to Qalunya, Part I: Truing the Wheel of Time?" and "Riding to Qalunya, Part II: L'Hôte," are the story of yet another "discovery" of mine: my finding of the ruins of the 1948 demolished and depopulated Palestinian village of Qalunya. In these chapters, I present the process of my learning about Qalunya. I tell about how and where I discovered the origin of the "Legend of the Flute" that I presented in the prologue to this book (incidentally, the location of this episode is important) and how I met the grandson of the real mukhtar of the village. I also tell about my visits to the single remaining Palestinian house in Qalunya: the summerhouse of Mufti Amin al Husayni, the leader of the Palestinian national movement during the 1930s. In 1937, Husayni fled from British Mandate Palestine and eventually turned out to be a protégé of the Nazis in Berlin. Since then, he has become in Zionist historiography and Israeli public discourse what I call here "the Last Nazi." For while Israel, in effect, was willing to disregard the Nazi past of many West German officials during the 1950s onward (as well as the Nazi connections of officials from other states),[82] it never forgot the Nazi past of the Palestinian mufti. Often the 1948 Palestinian Nakba (literally, in Arabic, "disaster") is still interpreted in Israel through this perspective of the Last Nazi, namely, that the Palestinian defeat was morally justifiable not the least because of the Nazi fervor of the Palestinian leadership then.

Qalunya, the Husayni house, the system of agricultural terraces, the wells and springs of the village, and the rain drainage conduits that I found among the overgrown vegetation in the village are places for me to contemplate the Nakba and the 1948 war, a war that led to the establishment of the state of Israel (it is called in Hebrew "the war of independence"). How do I feel, personally, about the history that I revealed through my discovery of Qalunya? What do I feel when I stand within the house of the Last Nazi? Why am I so much attracted to that place? Did 1948 set a course that we, Israelis and Palestinians, have no choice but to continue to follow? Can I, should I, identify with the deep sorrow and pain of those who lived here and were displaced?

Thus, my ride to Qalunya is a depiction of my emotional response to discovering 1948 and the Nakba, an issue that basically was a terra incognita for me until 2010. The ride to Qalunya is a story of revealing a new, painful, historical space, and the struggling of what to do with this finding. In Qalunya I also realized that 1948 is still alive, literally, today: I tell in these chapters about my encounters and meetings, on the trails of Qalunya and elsewhere, with refugees from the village and their descendents, who regularly come to explore the ruins of the village. Thus, the chapters also discuss the question of connection to place, ownership, and belonging: in many of these random encounters and planned meetings in Qalunya, it was not entirely clear to me (and I believe to some degree to my Palestinian interlocutors too) who is the "real" owner of this place and who is the visitor. Who is the host and who is the guest? In fact, the best way to describe my feelings following these encounters is encapsulated in the French word *l'hôte*: it means, at the same time, both "the guest" and "the host," as in the 1957 story by Albert Camus by the same title.

Chapter 5, "The Last Ride (for the Meanwhile) in the Arazim Valley," is the story of riding the trail that connects two places: the "9/11 living memorial"—the largest 9/11 monument outside the United States—and the work site of the doomsday bunker. Whereas the previous chapters dealt with the process of my exposure of and exposure to the violence of the past (1948 and before) and the violence of the present (the occupation and the separation fence), this chapter tells about my thoughts and feelings with regard to the interplay between the violence of the present and that of the *future*. The 9/11 memorial, called in Hebrew the "Twins' Monument" (Andartat HaTëomim), is a political structure that reflects not only Israeli sympathy and identification with the American people following the terrible tragedy of 9/11 but also, I realized, Israel's need for

American approval and legitimacy for its own never-ending "war on terror." The chapter explores the monument's micropolitics, which is, in fact, emblematic of so much of the macropolitics of Israel. This highly visible memorial, which was built with a two-million-dollar donation to the Jewish National Fund by rich American Jews, was erected in late 2009 in the middle of the Arazim Valley, joining, even if inadvertently, the siege on a small neighboring Palestinian community just across the Green Line—the village of Beit Iksa. Yet at the same time, the monument calls for "peace among nations" and "tolerance." I examine my own reflections in the memorial's "reflection plaza" and my personal reactions to this monument, which towers over the course of "my" trail. I try to clarify to myself why the presence of this literally and metaphorically protruding and towering monument creates so much antagonism within me and ask myself whether I can be tolerant of it.

As opposed to the monument's physical protrusion and the conscious desire of its builders to make it highly visible, the site of the government bunker, which is situated not too far away from there, is a place of secrecy and concealment. Dug deep into the mountain and hidden away from the eyes of the wanderer in the Arazim Valley is the bunker. When approaching the place, one can only see a dark hole in the mountain, which is the entrance to the escape tunnel of the bunker, and fences surrounding a big quarrylike work site full of high piles of rocks that are ground by a huge machine into gravel for industrial use. Thus, the site tries to maintain secrecy as to its purpose, but it is a noticeable scar on the landscape: white dust from the excavation and grinding covers all the vegetation outside the site for great distances. Yellow signs on the site's fence, clearly visible in the general background of the dusty white fallout, announce, "A Security Installation—No Photographing." The wary looks on the faces of the armed security guards who constantly patrol the perimeter of the site indicate that one is not welcome even as a passerby on the trail. As opposed to my ability to linger in the reflection plaza of the 9/11 monument, here I cannot tarry too much, for the security guards will come almost immediately to see whether I need any "help."

But the very nature of the site demands lingering and reflection. First, visibly, the place corrupts the landscape. This in itself arouses anger at the destruction of the beautiful hill, which was strewn with a myriad of almond trees before the bunker was built. While the Ministry of Defense, so I was told, promised to carry out restoration works when the construction ends, this is yet to be seen . . . And at any rate, the construction works have already entered their tenth year there. But more than this: much like the strangeness and alienation I feel at the site of the 9/11 monument, a site that the residents of Provincia Judea built as an offering to the "emperor" (that is, the United States), at the bunker, too, I feel that this place was not built for me, the "common citizen," and also not for the likes of me. It is a shelter for a government whose members and officials will probably evade the fate of hundreds of thousands, if not millions, of other people in this country should the need to hide in this bunker arise.

What would be my fate in that war? Whereas for those inside the bunker the place is supposed to enable the "continuity of government" in a dark hour, for me the bunker represents the dark hour itself. And this dark hour might very well come precisely because of the never-ending war on terror that the Twins' Monument seeks to legitimize. (On the other hand, perhaps the trail between the monument and the bunker represents some hope: that the United States will restrain Israel from initiating wars that will require the use of this bunker [here comes the IR person in me again . . .], precisely due to the commitment and sympathy the United States has toward Israel, the commitment and sympathy the monument seeks to garner?) I explore these connections in the chapter and discuss my emotional responses to these two scars on the landscape I cross with the bike every day.

The final chapter, titled "Contradictions: Some Concluding Thoughts about *The Politics of the Trail*," tries to see whether there are points of light and hope within this bleak landscape of violence. First, I try to clarify to myself why I so much love this landscape, despite its saturation with violence. Perhaps I have reached the same conclusion as Robert Musil's Ulrich, the protagonist of *The Man without Qualities*: "that anyone who really loved his country must never regard it as the best country in the world."[83] Then I tell about my bike rides on Vancouver Island, British Columbia, where I spent a sabbatical and wrote this book, and how they compare to the rides along the frontier of Jerusalem. I think about my multilayered identity at the point of completing this book, and about my sense of belonging in this island too.

The chapter also reflects on the way I became a disorganized and incoherent, so to speak, expert on the Israeli-Palestinian conflict and especially the Israeli culture of conflict. I discuss the merits of such incomplete and disorganized expertise and show the bike ride's role in this development. I end with some thoughts about the importance of opening our eyes to what's around us, of exposing the sorrow and pain that are contained in the landscape and the structures, physical and social, that violence confines us to. The price of this "responsibility to know" might be high, as I discussed in the "Shooting and Crying" section. But in the long run, it is a price worth paying. For by exposing these sorrows and pain, we can strike the structures and idols of violence, "as Nietzsche put it, with a 'hammer as with a tuning fork,' so as not to smash them, but to make them sound, and resonate, divulge their own hollowness, and vomit out the human sacrifices they have demanded."[84]

Chapter One

MORTAL DANGER
Two Rides along the Separation Fence

February 2006: First Ride to the Fence

MORTAL DANGER—MILITARY ZONE
ANY PERSON WHO PASSES OR DAMAGES THE FENCE
ENDANGERS HIS LIFE

These words are printed in Hebrew, Arabic and English (in this order) on a plastic orange-colored sign. The sign carries the logos of the IDF (a Star of David within which a branch of olive interlaces a short, gladiatorlike sword), and the IDF's central command (a profile of a roaring lion) in its upper right and upper left corners, respectively. It is attached to a 2.5-meter-high, wire steel fence gate, and is wobbling and creaking in the wind. The gate stands half open on an asphalt road, which splits from Mevasseret Zion's northernmost street—Har Canaan [Mount Canaan] street. The road itself has no street name. It leads to the town's water tower, a 40-meter-high, naked concrete standing "finger," which overlooks Har Canaan Street and is the tallest (in meters) and highest (in elevation) structure in Mevasseret. My bicycle odometer indicates that I have ridden 417 meters from my apartment building to here.

I came today to this highest point in the town to observe and examine the space between Mevasseret and Mt. Scopus, to locate the trails that descend from Mevasseret to the Arazim Valley (Cedar Valley). I know that there should be a trail here—the local newspaper talked about a trail called the "Interlopers'

Path" (in Hebrew, Shvil Ha-Shabachim),[1] which goes around here, connecting Mevasseret and the Palestinian village that I can see from my home but have forgotten its name. The newspaper article mentioned that thanks to the separation fence, dozens of Palestinian interlopers who used the path every day—and thus "gave" it its name—disappeared from Mevasseret's streets. I am looking for that path, to see whether it is "ridable" and whether it connects to other trails on the northern edge of Mevasseret that might flow into the Arazim Valley.

Indeed, to my east, on the slope that falls down to the Reches Halilim neighborhood, I can see a narrow path that parallels the perimeter of the neighborhood. But the path disappears in the shrubbery and thistles below my line of sight; the gradient here is too steep for me to follow the route of the trail. A barbed wire fence, which frames the half-open gate, prevents me from approaching farther on the slope toward the east. While I prefer to ride on dirt paths, in order to avoid cars, I realize that with all this barbed wire, it will be quicker to go down through the streets of the town.

I turn my attention back to the half-open gate and the orange-colored sign. I stand on the ground, with the bicycle between my legs, and hesitate about whether to go through. I stare, somewhat puzzled, at the sign and listen to the creaking sounds. Another notice, a yellow signpost that stands by the gate, with the no-entry red and white symbol painted on it, says, "NO ENTRANCE EXCEPT SECURITY VEHICLES."

My gaze wanders beyond the half-open, half-closed gate. I see the asphalt road continuing and an olive grove on its eastern side. I also see the Palestinian village farther up the road. "Is this the separation fence?" I wonder. "No," I think, "the barbed wire fence here is too rusty and old, and the separation fence was erected just a year or two ago. It couldn't have worn down that much. Besides, it is so easy to cut this fence. This must be some 'service' road leading to the fence itself. But why is the gate open? Someone might slip in, nonetheless . . ."

It is noon. A clear winter day, the air is sharp and visibility is excellent. No one else is here, at the top of the hill. It is quite eerie here, even though I am only a few dozen meters from Har Canaan Street and the daily, mundane suburban normalcy of Mevasseret. Shall I continue my ride or shall I obey the yellow sign, refrain from entering this "military zone"? Is there really a mortal danger lurking here or is this just the usual "disclaimer"? Do I enter "the territories" if I pass in the gate? What will happen if someone comes and closes and locks the gate behind me? I will be locked behind the fence . . . I look worryingly around me.

But I don't see any Palestinian interlopers close by. Nor any soldiers. From the Palestinian village, perhaps one kilometer as the crow flies, I hear the muezzin calling for the noon prayer. "Allahu Akbar" (God is greatest), chants/calls the muezzin four times, summoning the people to the mosque. The hills echo the muezzin's call. This echoing makes me watchful and uneasy, somewhat reinforcing the feeling that this is indeed a "military zone" and the sign is not just a disclaimer. As the muezzin's call eventually ends and the echo subsides and fades away, the silence returns. I then hear children's laughter from the village. It is probably recess time at the village school. Somehow, the cheerful sounds of the children reassure me, and I mount the saddle of the bike and start pedaling through the gate. I decide to go just a bit farther, where I can still keep eye contact with the gate, and see what lies ahead. I ignore the orange and yellow signs and pass through the gate.

The bike is rolling softly over the paved road, which starts to gently decline. I look over my shoulder and can still see the gate. To the east of me, the olive grove continues, while to the west, all kinds of construction debris and waste (brick and concrete fragments, old and rusting pipes, electric cables, and an assortment of scrap metals) are randomly thrown at the side of the road. Who threw all this here? I feel in a liminal space. The grove looks attended, though— the soil is plowed and harrowed. The grove surely belongs to someone from the Palestinian village. I look nervously at the olive trees. If the grove is cultivated, I think discontentedly, someone might be there. Where am I—beyond the fence already? As I think this, I suddenly hear a dry branch cracking, and something is leaping and running away between the olive trees. My heart starts beating fast; blood drains from my skin, and my muscles become tense. My gaze sharply turns to examine the grove, and my fingers, almost automatically, squeeze the brake levers of the bike. I stop abruptly and quickly look around me, searching for a person's figure or shape—a Shabach (interloper) perhaps. I curse my impulsiveness—I should have stayed behind the gate. Then I see among the trees that it was just a deer. He was probably resting among the olive trees when I suddenly arrived and startled him. The deer gallops farther into the grove, disappearing from sight. I relax a bit and look behind me—the gate is not seen anymore, hidden by a curve of the road. Just a few more meters, I promise myself, somewhat enjoying the sense of danger and adventure (only a few seconds ago I was sure I was in "mortal danger," but now I am reassured and think I am in some game . . .).

The gate in the fence that stands before the separation fence. This fence "guards" the "real" fence. (Photograph by Idit Wagner.)

I begin riding again, and a few seconds afterward, as the road starts to descend more sharply, I reach what I now realize is the real separation fence. My initial reaction is a sigh of relief. Tension drains from my body. I understand that the area I just crossed was simply a corridor to the fence itself and that I am still on the "right" side of the fence. I take a close look at what is ahead of me. Before me, there is another steel wire gate, but this one is closed and locked with a heavy padlock. Long and high stacks of barbed wire edge the gate's framework from the sides and from above. On the other side of the gate, a two-lane patrol asphalt road runs from east to west. The road is then paralleled by a lighter fence, but with various electronic devices hooked to it—electric cables, short antennas, and sensors. A similar gate to the one I'm standing before now is fixed on that fence. A dirt road leads to that gate. "The interlopers' trail," I realize. Beyond that fence, I see another stack of high barbed wire and a meter-high steel railing, and behind the railing and throughout its entire length, a wide ditch is dug. This complex of fences and barriers stretches to the east and west as far as the eye can see.

My initial sense of relief is quick to disappear, though. There is something very threatening here. I feel a strong urge to leave. Even though I can see the fence's route from my bedroom's window, this is the first time I actually stand just in front of it and see how complex a system it is. I am reassured by the barrier's multilayered structure, and I am content with this separation, which stopped the terrible and traumatic suicide-bombing attacks. I understand that it would take a considerable effort to cut through this complex of fences and barbed wire, which is probably surveyed by electronic equipment. But the presence of the fence, while providing me with a sense of security, is, at the same time, also menacing and imposing. I feel that this is "Land's End," beyond which indeed "mortal danger" might lie. I hold the gate with one arm, wanting to remain seated in the bike's saddle so that I'll be able to dart away in case of trouble. A strong wind starts blowing, from the north. The locked gate is wobbling in the wind, just a little bit, but I shudder both from the sudden motion of what seemed just a moment ago a stable anchor and also from feeling how the fence transmits to my body the intense enmity that exists between Israelis and Palestinians.

As I look at this composite barrier, while holding on to the wobbling locked gate, I realize how similar this fence system is to the border between Israel and Lebanon. In a flash of a memory, I recall how, during my military service in the late 1980s, I managed to avoid being posted to that dreadful border only to be sent to serve ("serve who?") in the brigade headquarters in the occupied Palestinian city of Hebron. While the Lebanese border was fenced with a similar system of composite alarm and barbed fences with patrol roads between them, a sight that gave me the creeps on the single occasion I was there, the Hebron headquarters was a massive and thick, concrete, British-built Tegart fort from the time of the Mandate in Palestine, so different from the provisional, transient appearance of other military structures.[2] Located in the middle of a hostile and fanatical Palestinian city, so we soldiers were told by our officers (the education officer even drew a large "instructive" placard, which included that information and the biblical story of Hebron and Abraham the patriarch, and hung it in the fort's foyer), the compound was nonetheless fenced and guarded very lightly, with many breaches in the rusty fence. I spent almost three years in that fort, but never in that time did any Palestinian infiltrate the compound. We were so carefree, assured in our power and superiority, that we walked outside the fort in the courtyard, even at night, without our personal rifles, which we often left in our rooms inside (unlocked). We felt so superior to the Palestinians then.

In 1997, five years after I was released from the army, the building was handed over to the Palestinian Authority, as part of the Oslo peace process. But in June 2002, while laying siege to Palestinian "wanted" militants who had barricaded themselves in there during the second Palestinian intifada, the IDF bombed and destroyed the fort in Hebron. Reading about the bombing operation while I was a postdoc fellow at the University of Toronto saddened me much. You might expect that as a "peacenik leftist" I would be pleased by the destruction of this symbol of violence, occupation, and foreign rule (British, Jordanian, Israeli, and, to some degree, Palestinian Authority too). But I was part of that place for almost three years. And when I say that I was part of that place, I do not simply mean that I had just been there, physically, doing my military duty. Indeed, I witnessed coercion and humiliation taking place within the fort's walls, seeing how the whole place functioned as an integrated machine of occupation and oppression. I did not see torture or brutal violence, only "moderate physical pressure" in interrogations of detained Palestinian "disturbers of the public order" at the police station, which was housed in the fort. I saw humiliation and disrespect for defendants' and their families' rights in trials of those Palestinian teenagers held in the military court in the fort (I often used to evade my military jobs and instead go watch these trials—partially enjoying the "show" and partially abhorring it). I saw officers reveling in staff preparations for military raids or routine patrols of "displaying presence" (a synonym—and indeed, a euphemism—for small-scale, daily harassment operations undertaken by the army in the streets of Hebron). And I led Palestinian collaborators, doomed to eventual death or social ostracism by their own people, to the offices of smug Shin Bet (Israel's General Security Service) officers who traded intelligence from these people for all kinds of material benefits or promises to avoid doing harm or "causing problems." I was appalled by this elaborate apparatus of occupation, but I was also fascinated by it, enthralled with the sense of power that my petty and meaningless military jobs invested me with (thankfully, I never personally injured or killed anyone). I felt I intimately knew the Tegart fort. It was not my "home," as I used every opportunity to take a leave and go to my real home, in Jerusalem. And I did not return to the Tegart fort after my release from the military. Nonetheless, the fort was in some sense dear to me.

For I loved a woman, my commanding officer Yif'at (pseudonym), in that fort. Having a room of my own in what used to be the British officers' quarters (the Israeli officers were housed in a better, renovated part of the fort), I half secretly, half openly shared the room with her. Everybody knew about that, but no one said anything to the high-ranking officers. We spent many precious and sweet hours in that room, with Hebron's view seen from the window and the porch of my room on the third floor of the fort. How easy it would have been to sneak into the fort and kill us while we made love. Yet, no one ever even tried. Only stray "Palestinian" dogs crept into the compound to scavenge on the garbage of the fort's large kitchen. We both politically opposed the occupation (which we nonetheless were an integral part of), but we had no misgivings when we loved each other in the middle of an oppressed and occupied city, in the streets of which we could never stroll unarmed or sit in its cafés.

When the IDF destroyed the fort in 2002, I felt that something in me was destroyed too. I know that this might sound terrible, but this is how I felt and I cannot deny it. Love and passion, as well as the sense of power, might leave a nostalgic mark on one's heart even when occurring in the context of oppression, humiliation, and violence. It was a semiforbidden love (there were no strict rules then like in today's world with regard to superior-subordinate relations), which was intensified by the feeling of domination and "action" that the suppression of the first Palestinian intifada provided us. But it was also intense, genuine, and deep love. Looking now at the complex separation fence that spreads out before me, here at the very end of Mevasseret's last street, I realize that instead of the light, breached, fence of the Hebron brigade headquarters I am now surrounded by the "perimeter fence" of the Israeli-Lebanese border, that "Lebanon," that zone of chaos and danger, is here, on the brink of my home.

At the Lebanese border, the guarded and complex fence was breached many times. Over the years, people in the Israeli villages along that border were sometimes murdered in their beds, busses hijacked, farmers shot at, and soldiers killed in their posts and patrols. How can I live and raise my children here, in Mevasseret, when I see such a "Lebanese" fence so close to my home? Standing there with the bike, I feel deep hatred lurking behind that fence, such intense hatred and active will and daring to act on it that the "border" had to be fortified to this extent. As I watch over the other side, as I hold the gate in my hand, I paradoxically feel too close to the Palestinian enemy. Even though no one is on the other side, and even though I know that the territory behind this segment of

The water tower of Mevasseret Zion at Sheik Abdul Aziz. *Behind me*, the separation fence and the Palestinian village of Beit Surik. *In front of me*, Har Canaan Street, Mevasseret Zion. (Photograph by Idit Wagner.)

the fence is controlled by Israel's military, I feel that it would be better to leave. I mount the bike and turn around, back to Mevasseret.

March 24, 2011: *The Whole Border Police Chasing Me*

At the bottom of wadi Kissalon, just beneath my neighborhood in Mevasseret, exactly at the point at which this dry riverbed begins its winding path toward the coastal plain, there is a point in the separation fence where one can shake hands with someone from the other side, through the fence. Well, the fence complex is 50 to 75 meters wide, so you obviously cannot shake hands through it. But you can do this *under* the fence. Here the fence is built on a battery of

Fig. 4. The drainage pipe under the separation fence. I emerge from the pipe, after viewing the Palestinian territories at the other end. (Photograph by Idit Wagner.)

limestone rocks and concrete reinforcements that block the path of the wadi. On both sides of the battery, the fence climbs up, to the opposing U-shaped slopes of the wadi. In order to let the water flow in the riverbed during winter, the engineers of the fence installed a drainage pipe underneath the battery. About 1.8 meters in diameter, the concrete pipe goes under the entire width of the fence (roughly 50 meters here). On the Israeli side of the pipe, there are no bars or anything that prevents entrance. The pipe ends, at the Palestinian side, with a round gate that is made of thick, steel, vertical bars. A heavy padlock ensures that the gate remains closed. I wonder who has the keys to all the fence's gates? Small animals can slip through the bars, but not people (perhaps, just perhaps, very young children). However, you can easily extend your hand through the bars to the other side.

It is a morning hour. I am not riding to campus today, but rather I have gone in the opposite direction, to do some fieldwork and "patrol" the trails northwest of Mevasseret, along the separation fence in this region. The sun is already quite high in the sky. But the wadi is still shady. Pine trees that were planted here in the late 1950s and early 1960s cast their shadows on the wadi, preserving the coolness of the morning. The pines were planted on these hills to demarcate the Green Line (the 1949 armistice agreement line between Israel and Jordan) and as part of a program of "security afforestation." I learned this fact from my friend, the geographer Amiram (Ami) Oren. Ami, an expert in the "security landscape" of this country,[3] told me that the policy of security afforestation was designed to enable the military to camouflage soldiers among the trees and to hide military equipment and installations in the woods.[4] Such afforestation is no longer practiced, but more recently, along the separation fence of the Gaza Strip, the Ministry of Defense and the Honey Council (the organization of honey producers in Israel, for Pete's sake!) inaugurated a joint project to plant eucalyptus, carob, jujube, and avocado trees. The trees will hide the Israeli villages and towns behind them and will provide the bees with opportunities to collect high-quality honeydew.[5]

Here, at the edge of the security forest, the separation fence roughly follows the path of the Green Line. This overlap is not incidental: it is the result of a public and legal campaign led by residents and activists from Mevasseret in 2004, which brought the Israeli Supreme Court to intervene against the initial proposed route of the fence in this area. The original plan of the Ministry of Defense was to draw the fence line just fifty meters from the houses of Beit Surik (yes, this is the name of Mevasseret's neighboring Palestinian village). Without the intervention of the Mevasseret activists, almost all the agricultural lands of Beit Surik would have been severed from the village by the fence and become subjected to the infamous "permits regime"—the system of regulating (and often preventing) the entry of Palestinians to any of their agricultural land that lies beyond (west of) the separation fence. While I concentrate on the very steep and technical descent, I nonetheless find time to glance with content toward the other side of the fence, toward the carefully plowed and harrowed patches of land, where beautiful groves of grapevine, almond, olive, peach, and apple grow. I respect the activists from my town, regular people who managed to prevent a great harm to their neighbors.

The bike's wheels throw clods of earth and small stones as I come to a sharp stop at the bottom of the wadi. I look up to Mevasseret's water tower but can't see it. The surveillance cameras that are installed on its top are blind here, precisely at this weak spot in the fence complex: the pines and the sharp slope hide me. Indeed, I now realize, this is an unintended benefit of the policy of security afforestation. I steer the bike to a very narrow path, bordered by high, thorny thistles on both sides. I ride for thirty meters along the trail within the thistle "savannah." Finally, I reach the mouth of the drainage pipe. This is not the first time I have come here—I found the pipe a few months ago, while following the narrow "single track" that led to it. I look around me—there is no one here. I lean the bike on the rock battery, so that the front wheel can be seen from within the pipe—I feel I need this "anchor"—and peer into the cylinder. Perhaps some animal is inside this "cave." It is dark inside, only in the distance do I see the daylight shining from the other side. I pick up a stone and throw it into the pipe, to make sure there is no animal inside (a jackal, hyena, or stray dog). Silence. I go in.

The floor of the pipe is full of silt and mud. I spread my legs and walk above the layer of mud, like a spider, on the walls of the pipe. There is a heavy odor of dampness, as in a deep basement or cave. Had I wanted to be ironic, I think while I walk, I could have said that I am now, literally, exploring the roots or foundations of the conflict. Eventually, I arrive at the other end of the pipe. I hold the cold bars of the gate in my hand. The coldness of the metal passes through the glove I wear. I look at the padlock and wonder how much time it would take to tamper with it and open it, or just to cut it with a "parrot beak" cutter. I can almost hear the padlock snap. I extend my other hand through the bars. My hand is now in the "territories." I look at the agricultural slopes of Beit Surik. I appreciate the beauty of the terraces and the carefully cultivated groves.

Then, up on the hill, I can see the plot of olives that I helped plant last October, together with the members of the village's agricultural committee and a group of American Jews that came to the village with a nongovernmental organization (NGO) called Rabbis for Human Rights. It seems that the olive seedlings struck good roots in the rocky ground, despite the relatively dry winter that we have had this year. The seedlings are still green, and the protective plastic shields around their stems have prevented the deer from grazing on them. It turns out that the fence not only locked several Palestinian villages, Beit Surik the closest to Israel among them, in an enclave that has an opening in only one direction but also excluded a considerable number of deer from their grazing territories and split the deer population. The result was that while on the Israeli side the deer are a revered symbol of noble, biblical, nature (although there, too, the open spaces occupied by the deer are constantly shrinking), for the Palestinians, who lost their ability to earn their livelihoods in Israel once the fence was erected, and therefore had to return to agriculture or expand existing cultivations, the deer became a pest. I recall one of the farmers in Beit Surik, who told me he worked as a gardener in Israel for many years before the erection of the fence and now grows pears on his plot up on the hill, lamenting this. I become so sad—and angry—that the fence causes Israelis and Palestinians to develop diverging attitudes even regarding these magnificent animals.

The olive seedlings in Beit Surik are the first trees I have planted since I was a child. In elementary school, each year on Tu BiShvat, the Hebrew "New Year's Day of the Trees," which takes place around mid-February, we went out to plant pine or cypress seedlings on the hills around our neighborhood, Kiryat Yovel. We planted a whole wood on the hill of the 1948-depopulated Palestinian village of al-Maliha (I did not think about the place in these terms then ... In Hebrew it is usually referred to as Mal'ha, and during my childhood, it was considered just a poor Jewish neighborhood in Jerusalem). The pines grew quickly and covered the ancient agricultural terraces. Within a decade, the landscape seen from my parents' apartment was transformed. But in the late 1980s, most of the trees were knocked down and removed by bulldozers, which bit off great chunks of the hill to build on it a new luxurious neighborhood and a huge mall. I was amazed, as a youth, when I watched the bulldozers gobble the hill and the young trees. I could not imagine that this was possible. I was angry, and felt betrayed, that they had destroyed the trees, which we had so carefully and lovingly planted. Now that I know about the purposeful policy of planting trees in order to hide the remains of destroyed Palestinian villages, to blur the Green Line, or to prevent access to land,[6] I feel doubly frustrated about having been a pawn in this project of "making the desert bloom." Nonetheless, when I pass today near the remaining pines on the slope of al-Maliha, I still tell my kids with pride, and lump in my throat, that my classmates and I planted these pines.

I stand within the pipe for long moments, gazing at the olives in Beit Surik. Was I just a pawn here too, a "useful idiot" in the service of Palestinian nationalism? What will happen to these seedlings? Will the villagers indeed harvest the olives from them in the future, or were they just planted as a performance to the group of American Jews that came with the human rights organization? I hope they will thrive and that I will be able to show them to my children too.

Up in the village, a donkey brays and the children play. I recall how we—the Jewish and Israeli visitors—played soccer together with the village's kids before we planted the olives. Suddenly, the loud sound of a Border Police (known by its Hebrew acronym Magav) jeep's engine and the swish of wide tires are heard on the patrol road above me, coming down from the curves up on the slope. I quickly return my arm into the drainage pipe and wait for the jeep to pass. However, the jeep is coming to a stop, apparently just above me. I hear the jeep's radio rattling but cannot discern the words. Are they looking for me? Did they nonetheless see me on the water tower's camera? Can they see my bike outside? How will I explain my presence within the pipe; it's a bit suspicious, isn't it? But the jeep just lingers for a moment and continues its patrol. And I was not doing anything wrong or illegal, after all, I try to reassure myself. Israelis are allowed to enter the territories, and I only entered my forearm, I half joke with myself, noticing that while the whole situation—the pipe walk, the extension of the hand through the bars—is absurd and comic in certain respects, I am shaking, like I do every time I feel violence is imminent.

A few moments later I emerge from the pipe and hold on to my bike. Gradually, my shaking subsides and disappears. I am ready to continue my own patrol. I start climbing up a Jewish National Fund (JNF) "white trail" (that is, a relatively wide, not too technical trail) that parallels the fence and is on the edge of the "security planted" forest. The ascent is very hard, though, and the trail is very steep. I ride slowly, almost at a walking pace. The wheels' motion is not smooth and rolling, and the bike seems to advance like a caterpillar, rolling and stopping, from one pedaling stroke to another. In order to maintain balance, I zigzag along the wide trail. As I climb the wadi's wall, the sun starts to blaze on my back. I welcome the sun's warmth, but I shiver as I feel the security cameras peering at my back from the water tower.

Until that visit to Beit Surik, I did not think about the tower as anything other than a water pressure installation. Throughout the years, I was drawn to the tower's area because of the fence and the military memorial that I discovered at its feet, a memorial that commemorates a battle that took place there in the 1967 war. I felt a need to keep investigating—or is it keep agitating?—my fear of that "Land's End," to understand and feel the liminality of the place and to overcome—but also reproduce—the eeriness there. Was I enjoying the eeriness, the sensation of standing on the verge of the "territories," which I imagined as being full of hatred toward Israel, toward me? Yet the tower itself—I just thought about it as a symbol of Mevasseret's skyline, which I can see even from Mt. Scopus.

In that first visit to Beit Surik, I wanted to come to the part of the fence that stands in front of Mevasseret—the fence that parallels "our" fence—and to stand at the opposite gate. However, our Palestinian hosts became very anxious and said that the security cameras on the water tower would detect us approaching the fence and Magav would come soon and beat the hell out of us—their experience shows that they have to keep at least 150 meters away from the fence. Yet I could not resist the temptation (is this really the appropriate word?), and when everyone else was still busy with the olive seedlings, I snuck out and went to the fence. The feeling was so weird—to stand in front of Mevasseret's gate and not be able to cross. It took the rabbis' bus an hour and a half to get to Beit Surik from Jerusalem because of the military roadblocks, the traffic jams, and the long detour necessitated by the fence's winding course. I could have come with my bike from Mevasseret in less than ten minutes. Back at home, I dreamed that night of riding into Beit Surik through the gate in the fence (somehow, I had the fence's keys on my own key ring). I felt secure and welcome in the narrow streets of the village and wanted to continue my ride to the next village, which I could see lying behind Beit Surik. The villagers, however, became extremely anxious and implored me not to continue, because down the road it is actually "Iraq," and ferocious cannibals live there. Not a very sophisticated dream, I know. At any rate, I can't remember the rest of the dream—whether I turned back to safety or continued on to "Iraq."

When approaching the fence, during my "real" visit in Beit Surik, I knew I was endangering my Beit Surikian hosts. But I was confident that I could also get them out of trouble, should the soldiers come.[7] And after all, we were with a group of "respectable" American Jews (some of them even wore suits, a rare thing in this hot country, which signifies one's importance). Was I naive? Stupid? Orientalist? Probably all three. But I also felt I had to experience that—to stand so close to where I live, to the place I call home, and not be able to cross freely. Eventually, the Magav did not come that day, and the planting of the olives ended without any "problems."

Still inching my way up and trying to distract my mind from the peering cameras, I concentrate on the climb, focusing on my physical effort and the strain that is developing in my thighs. Now, however, the trail starts to meander among the trees, away from the fence. The slope becomes more moderate, and the trees hide the fence. Yet the trail turns more rugged, and thus I have to keep investing a considerable amount of pedaling power and mental concentration.

I am now about one hundred meters away from the fence, which is hidden

In front of the fence at Beit Surik, image taken from the Mevasseret side. (Photograph by Idit Wagner.)

behind the pines here. The feeling of suffocation eases a bit, and I work my way up in what may look like a typical JNF forest landscape. Now, as the path approaches a plateau, you can see wooden picnic tables among the pines, and, here and there, a stone plaque with the name of the person after whom this part of the wood is named. My patrol takes a left turn now, as the trail splits into a "fork." Descending sharply again, I fly over gravel and small rocks, jumping over roots that cross the trail and branches that have fallen from the trees. I notice that especially the younger trees are becoming brown, drying. Almost a decade of drought and low rainfall becomes evident on the trees. This is an expanding phenomenon in the whole region of the Judean hills. Even though I know that those pines were planted for various "security" reasons, I still feel very much attached to this landscape of pine forests. Ever since I was a child, the pine forests have represented "nature" and the "outdoors" for me. I love, yes, love, the dustiness of the pines during summer, and their freshness after the winter rains. I mourn the slow dying of the trees. If the trees die, and the desertification processes indeed continues, will I still love these hills?

I emerge at a part of the forest that is dedicated to the Jewish Polish doctor and educator Janusz Korczak. Korczak and his associate, the educator and administrator Stefania Wilczyńska, were murdered in Treblinka in 1942, with more than 190 children from the orphanage they headed in Warsaw. It is said that Korczak was offered by the Polish resistance a sanctuary, but he said he would go with the children nonetheless. Wilczyńska had returned in April 1939 to Warsaw from Palestine, having immigrated in 1938. I stop for a few minutes to watch the memorial stone plaque that was erected there in 2002, and contemplate the diabolical dilemma that Korczak and Wilczyńska must have faced. On the other side of the trail, just a few meters from the Korczak and Wilczyńska plaque, there is another memorial stone, commemorating the eleven Israeli athletes and members of the Olympic team that were murdered in Munich in 1972. Next to that plaque, another one commemorates dozens of Israeli teachers who, as reserve soldiers, "fell" during the wars of Israel. The forest's name here is the Teachers' Association Forest.

This is a remote area, not very accessible. Now and then, I meet here some walkers from the nearby settlement of Har Adar (located beyond the Green Line but "west" of the fence), other mountain bikers, or Khaled (pseudonym), a Palestinian Israeli (that is, a Palestinian with Israeli citizenship) and his herd of goats and sheep. Khaled comes from the village of Ain Nakuba. His village is one of the three remaining Palestinian communities in the "Corridor of Jerusa-lem."[8] (The two others are Abu Ghosh and Ain Rafa.) The rest were demolished and depopulated in 1948. Abu Gosh and Ain Rafa escaped this fate, mainly due to the friendly relations they maintained with the Zionist movement during the period of the British Mandate. Ain Nakuba was built in 1962 by refugees from the close and demolished village Beit Nakuba.[9]

Khaled does not speak a word of Hebrew—a very rare case for people from Ain Nakuba, Ain Rafa, and Abu Gosh, who work in Jewish Israeli towns or their own villages in the local tourism and hosting industry, namely, falafel and "oriental" restaurants that are open on Shabbat (Saturday, when all the kosher restaurants in Jerusalem must remain closed or risk losing the Chief Rabbinate's Kashrus certificate). It seems to me that Khaled's whole world is in these hills and his village. Today I don't see him here, but I can see by the droppings of the sheep and goats that he was here probably this morning. Perhaps I missed him when I was musing in the drainage pipe. When we meet, he often offers me a cup of boiling tea, and we drink, silently, while his dogs watch over the herd. I respect his decision(?) not to learn Hebrew. Or is it just comfortable for me that he does not speak Hebrew, for whatever reason (and I hardly speak Arabic) and we merely sip some tea together? Do I really want to hear what he has to say? On the other hand, am I just presuming that as an "Arab" he must have critical or "unpleasant" things on his mind? And if not, he probably *should* be critical, shouldn't he? Damn it, my mind is blowing...

Surprisingly, despite the relative inaccessibility of the area, this spot has a high concentration of memorials that work upon the Jewish Israeli national narrative of victimhood-heroism (the Holocaust, the wars of Israel, terrorism). Despite the open space around me, and the sensation of being in the outdoors, I feel the pressure of history, the weight of the nation-state's project of molding people into "loyal" nationals, so to speak. I envy Khaled, who, by being a Pales-tinian Israeli who doesn't even speak and read Hebrew, is free of the grappling, compunctions, and second thoughts that such a place produces in me. I feel that, on the one hand, I stand in an almost sacred place, and, on the other hand, I cannot avoid sneering at the too concentrated and obvious effort of nationalis-tic commemoration at this nowhere. But the country is strewn with such places, making it unavoidable to encounter such memorials in almost every space and place. Almost immediately, I become critical, distanced, and judgmental (aca-demic?), and at the same time, I feel that I shouldn't violate the sanctity of the site with my critical deconstruction. Then I'm angry that I'm not able to relieve myself of such dilemmas once and for all, and at the "state" that embedded the "nation" in such a deep manner in my soul. I doubt whether Khaled, as a "Noble Savage," a "native," an "aboriginal," you name it, knows or cares what historical story these plaques relay, and what string they pluck in my heart. On the other hand, by not being part of the narrative-community these plaques are aimed at constructing, Khaled is not only an outsider to Israeli society but also exposed to the risks of being seen by many Jewish Israelis as a threatening invader, his village's friendly "record" and Israeli official status notwithstanding.

With these thoughts in my mind, I speed off, wanting to get out of this "whirlpool," this sucking and pressuring site of "nation building." Yet, from bad to worse, I cannot avoid the fence. Eventually, all the trails here lead to it. Again on the patrol road that parallels the edge of the "securitized forest," I understand that the fence, too, is a national(istic) monument. It not only blocks suicide bombers, for which I am ever thankful, but it also constructs the Israeli citizen as a fearful subject, who is conditioned to be blind to what lies behind the fence, blind to who lives there and under what conditions. It is a fence for those who wish not to know and to maintain their fear. More broadly, the fence is part of the regime of organized ignorance and silencing, and the politics of fear that is so deep rooted in this land. It defines one's identity and belonging by the very act of separating. And these definitions are becoming ever more monolithic and dichotomous, and invested with so much emotional weight. The fence itself thus becomes an object and a structure invested with sacredness and emotional identification.

"I do not want to be constructed!" I cry out in my mind, I don't want to be *made* a part of the nation, of any nation. I want to confront my fears, not repress them. I again feel suffocated and entrapped: suffocated by my fears, the "real" ones and the "constructed" ones, and entrapped by them. I must break through the fence. I turn the bike back toward my home in Mevasseret. I have been enough in the "outdoors" today. Perhaps inside the four walls of my apartment, with my computer and books, I will find more free space. I think about Dr. Who (the BBC's science fiction series protagonist) and his spaceship—the *TARDIS*—the interior of which is much larger than its exterior. Perhaps the book I'm writing is my *TARDIS*.

As if reading my mind on its role as a technology of nation building and on its being a suffocating device, the fence "sends" a signal to me. Literally, a sign: one of those orange-colored signs of "MORTAL DANGER," just lying on one of the rocks on the side of the trail, upside down. I cannot ignore the sign. In an almost conditioned, Pavlovian reflex, I squeeze the brake levers and stop by the sign. How did the sign get here? Perhaps someone took it off the fence and threw it here? Perhaps it fell off a military jeep servicing the fence? Who knows. I turn the sign to the right side, reading it. I continue looking at it, and then, spontaneously, decide to take it with me. But the sign is big (perhaps 50 × 60 cm) and I cannot carry it in one hand—this will be too risky in the sharp descent that is ahead of me.

Contemplating what to do, I finally recall the plastic cable binders I have in my backpack for emergency repairs while away from home. I take out two binders and pull them through the sign's holes, in its corners, and then tighten the binders. The sign is elastic, and it folds. As I push the sign into my backpack, I am reminded, as I am almost every time I use these binders, how in Hebron the Palestinian "disturbers of the public order" were brought to the Tegart fort handcuffed with such binders, which were standard equipment of the soldiers. Often the binders were tightened so much that they cut deep into the skin of the prisoner and it was difficult to remove the plastic binder without seriously hurting or even harming the "detainee." (We soldiers had no police powers, but we nonetheless adopted the police jargon.)

Now the sign is in my backpack, but its top is protruding. Luckily, I folded it so that the printed side is hidden. Just in case, I cover the protruding part with a spare riding shirt I have in the backpack. I look a bit suspicious now, I think. But I feel a strong urge to take this sign, as if by taking it I really undermine the fence. Another quick look around, and I speed home.

And I *really* speed. Even though a strong east wind is blowing against me, swinging me from side to side on the bike and filling my lungs with dust from the desert, I ride this segment of the trail faster than ever. With the orange sign in my backpack, protruding, I feel that the whole Magav force is behind me. Did I "damage the fence," as the sign warns not to do? No, I just found the sign, at quite a distance from the fence. I did not touch the fence and did not sabotage it. But the piece of plastic in my backpack weighs much more than its actual weight. As I roll and skid down the curves of the path, I start thinking about the actual message of the sign: what is the source of the danger to the life of the person who damages or passes the fence? Aren't these actually two separate dangers? If the Palestinians on the other side of the fence are the source of mortal danger in the case of crossing the fence, who, then, is the source of the mortal danger in the case of damaging the fence? But the sign is written also in Arabic (and English). For the Arab-reading would-be fence crosser, are the Jews on the "other" side, just regular citizens like me, the "mortal danger"? Or is it the military/Magav forces patrolling the fence? The sign does not specify on these important questions (yes, these are important questions, and I'm not being ironic here), and leaves the issue ambiguous.

I reach the bottom of wadi Kissalon, pass the drainage pipe again, and climb back home. But suddenly a quick thought crosses my mind: what if I come here one day and see that someone has indeed broken the padlock and opened the gate within the pipe? Will I report this to the "authorities" or will I keep this information to myself? The question is simple, and the dilemma is clear but very painful. Can I have it on my conscience that a suicide bomber might cross through such a hole? On the other hand, I hate the fence exactly for its function of separating people, its imposition of predetermined identities on us. "This is just a hypothetical question," I respond to myself. "I will deal with it if indeed I see a 'hole in the fence' one day." As I push the nagging thought off my mind, I choose a trail that I usually do not ride on. This is a very steep trail, a single track that leads in a straight line up to Mevasseret from the wadi. It is hidden among the pines and thistles, and I feel safer here, with the thing staring out of my backpack. The trail ends in Mevasseret's Hermon Street. From here the separation fence is seen as just an ordinary road, winding among the hills, the barbed wire fence itself barely noticeable. There are only a few people in the street. No one is paying any special attention to me. Another two minutes, and I'm at home. I enter the door, smelly from sweat, partially because of the intense effort and partially because of the emotional stress, and my seven-year-old son, who is already back from school, immediately asks, "What is this, Dad?" "It's just a sign I found," I reply. "But what is written on it?" he keeps asking. It is in such moments that I'm happy that he goes to a Waldorf school, where they start really reading only in class three. The last thing I want now is to explain to him why the sign says "MORTAL DANGER," and why I brought this danger home.

I maneuver the bike through the apartment, "park" it in my "office" room, and then take off my backpack and take the sign out. I put it against the wall.

The strong orange is in sharp contrast to the wall's whiteness. Removed from its "natural environment," the sign looks now like just a piece of plastic, not a threatening warning. "It says," I tell my son, who follows me into the room, "that there is a border ahead of us." "What, you took it from the government?" he's asking, recounting the story I told him a few weeks ago about the "government" that built a "border" between "us" and the "Palestinians" on the opposing hill. "Not exactly," I answer. "Someone probably lost it." "So you should return it, Dad," he says, and goes out to the deck to continue playing.

A few weeks ago, he suddenly asked me where the "road" that winds through the wadi below Hermon Street is leading. "Who are the Palestinians," he asked, after I explained to him that the road is actually a "border." "They are our neighbors," I replied. "And there is war between us?" he pressed on, seeing my hesitation and sensing that I was hiding something from him. "Not between *you* and them," I tried to calm him. "But between you, Dad, and them? You said you were once a soldier, and Mom too," he insisted. "I hope not," I replied. "Dad, how was it to be a soldier? Do you sweat a lot in those boots they wear?" "Yes you do," I replied, "and it sucks to be a soldier." Seeking to "prove" my point about military "service," we then read (again) the part from *Tom Sawyer Abroad* where Tom is trying to enlist Jim and Huck in a military expedition "to recover the Holy Land from the paynim," not simply for the sake of religious duty but mainly to gain personal glory for Tom, who feels that his glory has diminished since he returned from their last adventure. But Huck and Jim remain unimpressed, and Huck surmises, "Now Tom he got all that notion out of Walter Scott's book, which he was always reading. And it WAS a wild notion, because in my opinion he never could've raised the men, and if he did, as like as not he would've got licked. I took the book and read all about it, *and as near as I could make it out, most of the folks that shook farming to go crusading had a mighty rocky time of it.*" The last sentence, I read in a funny intonation. We laughed.

Now Idit comes into the room and sees the sign. I quickly tell her the "story" of this sign, and suggest that she put the sign on various backgrounds and objects—an agriculture terrace, the gate to her parents' house, on our car, wherever—and shoot some photos. Idit, amused, looks at the sign and at me, and responds by saying that I should focus on my writing and leave photography to her ... She thinks my idea is "not that sophisticated" and that there are many images like that. I feel a bit offended by her sneer but realize that there is something in it. Yet I also feel that I have done something that is not to be taken for granted. I tell her about the sense of danger and adventure that I experienced when taking the sign and during my "visit" to the occupied territories through the drainage pipe. "I can see your point about the fence suffocating. I feel that suffocation too. But your patrols along the fence are just a game, an adventure," she responds. "You, at least, can 'patrol"; for them [the Palestinians] it's like living in a jail." "But I'm still suffocated," I retort.

Chapter Two

A FENCE BEHIND A FENCE
BEHIND A FENCE

Riding after the Unknown Soldiers and
Looking for a Breach in the Fence

June 25, 2010: Meeting a Former Enemy

I am standing with (retired) Colonel Munir Ibn Hassan (pseudonym) of the
Jordanian Armed Forces in front of the memorial plaque at the foot of Mev-
asseret's water tower, just a short distance from the gate in the separation fence.
It is noon, but not a very typical late June day. Usually, by this time of the year, it
is already around 30 degrees Celsius at this hour and the sky is painfully bright.
Today it is just 23 degrees, the sky is gray, and the wind is howling around us.

We look at the memorial plaque, which describes the battle that raged here
on June 5, 1967, between the IDF and the Jordanian military (it was called the
"Arab Legion" up until 1969, and then the name was changed to the Jordanian
Armed Forces). Back then, Ibn Hassan was a twenty-one-year-old lieutenant,
an officer in the Jordanian outpost of Sheikh Abdul Aziz, on the ruins of which
the water tower and the memorial plaque and plaza were built. While researching the Sheikh Abdul Aziz site, I read a newspaper article about a meeting between Israeli and Jordanian officers who fought in the battles in Jerusalem in the
1967 war. Ibn Hassan participated in that meeting and related his memories of
the battle here. He is now heading a Jordanian peace organization, and a friend

from the Hebrew University who's studying the Jordanian military connected us. I phoned him, presented myself to him, told him about my autoethnographic research of local history and landscape along my bike trails, and asked him if he would agree to visit the Sheikh Abdul Aziz site with me (I brought him here in my car . . .), as he is staying these days in Israel for a conference on agricultural cooperation among Israeli, Palestinian, and Jordanian farmers.

The aluminum plaque we examine now shows the "battle plan." "Is this how you remember the battle?" I ask the colonel. To my surprise, Ibn Hassan, who was, he told me, a senior officer in Jordanian military intelligence, replies that he does not read Hebrew. I am puzzled, but do not reveal my thoughts. I read to him from the plaque, and watch him while he listens. "The blue rectangles are Israeli tanks and armored personnel carriers," I explain, "and the red dashed lines are 'enemy forces.' That is," I add with an ironic smile, "you."

Ibn Hassan smiles back, and says, while looking at the battle plan, which shows the Israeli tanks storming in from the southeast, that the Jordanian force was caught by absolute surprise. He looks at me, thoughtfully, and adds that he could not imagine that tanks would be able to climb these rocky slopes. But the Jordanian soldiers, he says, fought well, nonetheless.

We fall silent for a few moments. Then I point out that the memorial plaque says that fifteen Israeli soldiers were killed there, and that the battle was fierce and included face-to-face combat in the bunkers and trenches of the outpost. Ibn Hassan nods, solemnly. It is an odd situation. I think about the battle that raged here, so close to where I live now. I don't ask if he himself killed one of these people. Instead, I ask, "How many men were killed on your side?" More than the Israelis, he responds, many more. He then notes that the place looks very different from what it used to be in 1967, even compared to his previous visit here in 1994, after the signing of the peace treaty between Israel and Jordan.[1] He wouldn't have recognized the place, he tells me, due to the new Israeli neighborhood built here. Hardly anything, indeed, remains of the old Jordanian outpost, except a few trenches and a sign reading "a double rifle position." Nothing remains of the small huts the Legion built here to house some of its veterans, in the form of a colony/settlement as in Roman times. Only a photograph in the Israeli Har'el Brigade's memorial book, the brigade that conquered this outpost and other places in this "sector" during the 1967 war, shows these houses.

We turn from the memorial plaque to survey the area from the observatory deck that was built here. The access to the deck is partially blocked by various thorns and small bushes that have grown due to lack of maintenance. The site is in fact beyond the Green Line and therefore not under the jurisdiction of the Local Council of Mevasseret Zion (even though access to it is only possible from Mevasseret, and Mevasseret's water tower and installations are part of the site). The Binyamin Regional Council, which is municipally responsible for the area, is beyond the separation fence in the Jewish settlement of Pssagot (which is not seen from here). Thus, the memorial site fell through the bureaucratic cracks, so to speak, and became a no man's land in terms of daily maintenance.

The observation deck is remindful of one side of a step pyramid, with five rows of fifty-centimeter-high concrete cubes that ascend to a small viewing surface at its top. Ibn Hassan hesitates before climbing—perhaps the cubes/steps are too high for him. I go first and extend my hand to him. He holds my hand and I pull him over the first row of concrete cubes. I am happy that his grip is not tight, but rather gentle, exactly enough to help me pull him. I don't like the custom of shaking or gripping someone's hand too tightly (in order to show strength or manliness?). How different this retired colonel is, I think, from Israeli high-ranking officers I have met over the years. There is not a bit of arrogance or dominance in him. Not that I have met so many Israeli high-ranking officers, and probably there are kind men among them too. But the ones I did happen to meet, as a soldier and a scholar, were almost invariably "tough"— bossy, omniscient (both personally and as commanders), and lacking almost any sense of self-humor. Ibn Hassan generates in me a much more humanistic impression. Is it because I want to find these qualities in him, or because they are really there? How would "his men" describe or think about him?

As we reach the top of this step pyramid, the separation barrier becomes the dominant object in the landscape. It cuts through the mountain and the valley. Arrows on a small aluminum direction sign in front of us point at "Har Adar," "Nebi Samuel," and "Jerusalem." There is no mention of "Beit Surik," even though the Palestinian village lies just in front of the viewer. I ask Ibn Hassan how the Palestinians saw the Jordanians, who ruled the West Bank in those days. Did they think of them as occupiers, as they see the Israelis? No, they considered each other as brothers, he replies. Many Palestinians served in Jordan's military (they, like their Israeli counterparts, had to sign up at age eighteen), and he had many Palestinian soldiers under his command. Then he adds that after the Israelis conquered the outpost, he fell captive to the IDF. He was held for two or three hours, but managed to escape when Jordanian artillery shelled the advancing IDF force. He fled through the mountains to join the retreating Jordanian forces. On his way through wadi Lauza, just below the hill we stand on now, he saw many Palestinian civilians seeking refuge and hiding in the caves of the wadi. He also met four soldiers from his battalion, running away in another direction. These were four Palestinian enlisted men from Nablus. In the midst of the withdrawal, their ways parted. In 1996, Ibn Hassan continues, an Israeli tractor working at al Jib (now the Israeli settlement of Giv'at Ze'ev) exposed human bones. The work stopped immediately (this was mainly due to Jewish religious considerations of not disturbing the [Jewish] dead in their graves).

It turned out that the bones found at Giv'at Ze'ev were those of the four Palestinian Jordanian soldiers that Ibn Hassan met on that night of escape from the Israelis (they were identified by their metal identification tags, which survived). They were probably killed that night, and their bodies remained in the field. Following the discovery of the bones, Ibn Hassan continues, the four were buried in Nabi Samwil (the supposed burial site of the prophet Shmuel/ Samwil/Samuel, choose your preferred name . . .) in a full Jordanian military service, attended by dozens of representatives of the Jordanian army and senior Israeli officers.

While Ibn Hassan describes the finding of the bones of the Palestinian Jordanian soldiers, recalling the march of the Jordanian military orchestra through the nearby Palestinian villages, we both look to Nabi Samwil, a distant landmark to the northeast. I suddenly remember the bones that I found as a twelve-year-old child while roaming in Malha, the former Palestinian village of al Maliha, which was close to my neighborhood in Jerusalem. My friend Amos, the "Huckleberry Finn" of my class, invited me one day to "explore" the place. While we walked among the bushes and the weeds on the hill, smoking dry hay "cigarettes" that Amos made, I suddenly saw, just in front of me, a skull. A human skull, the top part of which, including the eyeholes, peered out of the dirt. I jumped back, shocked and alarmed, and called Amos, half excited and half appalled by the sight, to "come and see." He came, and very calmly told me that these were the bones of Muslims who had "once" lived here and the rain had probably swept them from their graves at the top of the hill. We went up to the hill's top, and indeed, there, between the thistles and the undergrowth, Amos showed me many strange graves—they were like little rectangular "houses," with elaborate Arab inscriptions on them. They looked old, antique. Some of the graves were half ruined, the tombstones broken or cracked, and the inscriptions blurred. Bones—hipbones, arms, and palms—could be seen through the cracks and fractures in the tombstones. Night was falling, and we, suddenly not so brave anymore, started to run back to the safety of our street.

Ibn Hassan's story about the bones of his soldiers and my recollection of the bones from Malha somehow blend in my mind. When I take the colonel in my car back to his hotel in Jerusalem, we drive next to the grave of my father, in Har Hamenuchot (Resting Mountain), Jerusalem's biggest cemetery, which watches over Highway 1—the Jerusalem–Tel Aviv highway, Jerusalem's most important traffic artery. I recall my father's story about how in 1973, as a reserve soldier in the Sinai after the war, he found within an Egyptian-burned tank the scorched body of one of the tank's crew members. The body was black as coal, and when my father touched it with the tip of his finger, it crumbled into thin ashes, much like, as I had thought in the past, how a star collapses into itself and becomes a black hole. And isn't this the essence of war? To collapse into ourselves, to disappear into the black holes of history?

A week after this meeting with Munir Ibn Hassan, I decide that I will ride to see the graves of the four Palestinian-Jordanian soldiers. I do not doubt the colonel's story. But I want to see the place myself. It puzzles me much that these were soldiers of *Palestinian* origin, who were buried by the *Jordanian* military in a full military service, with the participation of high-ranking *Israeli* officers and with the approval of the Israeli occupation authorities (after all, the ceremony was held in a location under Israeli occupation in the West Bank). The meeting with Ibn Hassan and his story make me ponder about the fluidity, arbitrariness, and fragility of concepts of enmity. In some ways, I can understand that after the signing of the peace treaty between Israel and Jordan in 1994, there is not too much to wonder about in this military funeral, which perhaps represented goodwill and a way to come to terms with the past. Still, emotionally, I do feel that there was here something that revealed the capricious construction of enmity and postenmity. I sense that this story points at the unbearable absurdity of the politics of peace and war: I wonder whether among the Israeli officers that attended the ceremony there were some who fought against these Palestinian-Jordanian soldiers. And while the Israeli and Jordanian governments made peace and officially terminated the state of war between the two countries, the West Bank, where these four soldiers died and were buried, is still under Israeli occupation and is a limbo territory of conflict and violence. While

the burial of the soldiers themselves represented the formal peace and reconciliation between Israel and Jordan, the living family members of the soldiers
might continue suffering from the occupation. I think about the symbolism of
this funeral—that the West Bank Palestinian soldiers in the Jordanian army
continued to be so even twenty-nine years after their deaths (that is, in 1996),
even though Jordan had cut its administrative connections and denounced its
sovereignty claim over the West Bank as early as 1988. While I understand and
respect the respect the Jordanian military paid to these men after so many years,
the funeral also saddens me by revealing war's grip on people's identity even
many years after their deaths. For whereas Jordan "disengaged" from the West
Bank and canceled the Jordanian citizenship of the Palestinians who live there,
the Palestinian-Jordanian soldiers remained Jordanians nonetheless, thus sym-
bolizing, and maintaining, war's centrality in politics, its ontological precedence
over all other political institutions and practices.[2]

I also feel that these graves are an essential part of the story of the battle
that raged so near my home. Of course, there is ample evidence of that battle
in the place itself. There is the memorial plaque, and the story of the battle was
recorded by its Israeli veterans in a book.[3] Moreover, I guess I could have found
more Israeli evidence, stories, and testimonies had I wanted. But these would be
victors' history. Ibn Hassan's relation of the battle offered a different angle on the
story, the story of the *defeated* side. The graves of the four soldiers are material
evidence of the human cost borne by the enemy, a cost that we in Israel are often
only very superficially aware of. Even though they did not die in this specific
battle, and were probably killed a few kilometers north of Sheikh Abdul Aziz
outpost while running away, these graves are probably the single material Jordanian remains of this battle that *I* can locate. I feel I need to see these remains, to
try to experience and feel the plight of the defeated.

I know that often there are no real victors in war, and that the "victors" might
pay a terrible price for their "victory." For Israel, the 1967 victory turned out to
be a pyrrhic victory, leading to a never-ending occupation of another people and
the rise of messianic-religious nationalism. Despite this, however, the notion,
the myth, that Israel always won its wars with the "Arabs" is deeply rooted in me.
In the same manner, deep inside me there is the fear of suffering the same fate
that Israel inflicted on the Palestinians and the other Arabs throughout history:
to be expelled, defeated, humiliated. In the Sheikh Abdul Aziz site (called in
Hebrew Yad Assa—"Assa's Memorial"—after the Israeli captain Assa Yagori,

who was killed there during the battle), the memorial plaque tells that after the conquering of this and other Jordanian outposts in the region, "the remnants of the Jordanian forces fled in all directions." This was very brutal combat, very cruel. The four soldiers Munir Ibn Hassan told me about were among those "remnants" that "fled in all directions." So, I ride today to see, so to speak, those "remnants" that "fled in all directions," knowing that in the same situation I would have probably done the same.

Finally, I ride to Nabi Samwil perhaps because Ibn Hassan made such a good impression on me. In a sense, the "detour" to Nabi Samwil comes from my desire to continue the talk with the retired Jordanian colonel. Speaking very good English, manifesting self-confidence that nonetheless does not diminish his kindness and cordiality, the colonel fitted precisely into the image I, and many other Israelis, have of the Jordanian-Bedouin Hashemite "officer and a gentleman" character.[4] In this sense, Ibn Hassan is a reverse image of the Palestinian in my mind. As opposed to the Palestinian, he fights "honestly," according to the rules and laws of war (that is, directly facing the Israeli army in a "conventional" and "symmetrical" war, instead of using "terrorism"), and thus, loses; and after he loses, he is "mature" enough to "nobly" recognize his defeat and even be instrumental in concluding a peace treaty with Israel. So, in this respect, when I stand with Ibn Hassan on the observation deck in Sheikh Abdul Aziz, viewing the separation fence and Beit Surik, it is much easier to talk with him about war and peace than with the people behind the fence. For he is, on the one hand, a part of this landscape of conflict and emotionally involved with it (he fought here and lost men), but on the other hand, he is a foreigner who comes from a, literally, faraway kingdom.

Thus, on Sunday, July 4, 2010, I leave home at around 7:30 a.m. I set a course through wadi Lauza (in Arabic, "wadi of the Almond"), a dry riverbed that flows into the Soreq riverbed. The two riverbeds meet in the Arazim Valley, precisely on the trail that I ride to Mt. Scopus. I have ventured before into this wadi, but not too far—it is beyond the Green Line, in the occupied territories, and I was afraid to go up the wadi. This is the first time I will ride the entire wadi, ascending to Nabi Samwil on this trail. The night before, I thoroughly examined the route on Google Earth and Amud Anan—a popular Hebrew online geographic information system (GIS) and an interactive map that hikers and mountain bikers dot with countless pictures and notes on various sites. The Amud Anan map, like almost all Israeli maps, does not mark the Green Line. It only out-lines the route of the separation fence (which does not overlap this line) as a dashed stripe, tagged "security road." The Google Earth imagery, on the other hand, shows that the wadi Lauza trail crosses the Green Line and ascends to the north, eventually reaching Nabi Samwil. Both maps and GIS show that the separation fence extends west of the wadi, enclosing the villages Beit Surik and Bidu. On the eastern wall of the wadi, the Palestinian village of Beit Iksa resides on a high hill. This village was not enclosed by the separation fence, mainly due to its close proximity, 1.4 kilometers as the crow flies,[5] to Highway 1.[6]

I descend from Mevasseret through the Halilim wadi (Flutes wadi). The wadi is quiet and lonely this morning, and I quickly flow on the single track, clearing the familiar drops. At the bottom of the wadi, just at the entrance to the Arazim Valley, I turn left and head north. I ride on a wider dirt trail that leads to the remains of the Jewish settlement that was built here in the early 1920s and deserted after the 1929 Palestine riots. Now a national park called Einot Telem (Telem Springs), the place is being maintained by the Parks Authority. Work-ing there, I see Wasfi (pseudonym), a Palestinian man from East Jerusalem. (East Jerusalem was annexed by Israel after the 1967 war. Its Arab inhabitants are permanent residents of Israel but not full citizens. Although they can apply for Israeli citizenship, only a few thousands have applied over the years.) He cleans the trail of thistles and weeds. I stop and say good morning, asking how he is doing today. Wasfi once gave me water when I ran out on a hot summer day. The water he gave me was the tastiest and softest I ever drank—he opened a tap, which connects directly to a pump that draws from a groundwater reser-voir two hundred meters below us. Cool due to the darkness and depth of the underground well, and without chlorine added to it, the water smoothly poured through my throat and revived me before the long climb in the Halilim wadi back to Mevasseret that day. I filled my bottle and thought about the experi-ence of drinking springwater and water that is drawn directly from one's well. It was a bonding experience between the place and me. But while I remember the good taste of the water and feel attached to the place because of the water, I did not become friends with Wasfi. We just sometimes stand to chat a bit when we see each other. When he gave me the water, and I thanked him and praised the taste, he said, "Come whenever you want, and I'll give you more." His eyes glittered then, with joy. I felt then a good human connection between us, and was thankful for this. But later barriers of language and social-political status, I guess, prevented me from further developing that beginning.

"Not too well," he responds to my question of how he is doing today. "I don't feel so good." "So why didn't you stay at home today?" I ask. "How will staying home help me to earn bread for the children?" he snaps. "But can't you take a few sick days?" "No, I work by the hour." "I can help you cut these thistles," I offer. His eyes look at me somewhat amused, underneath the green Parks Authority cap he is wearing. The big, thick beard of a Muslim pious man covers almost all his face. I take off my sunglasses, and he can see my eyes now. But my full-face helmet remains on my head. I wonder what he thinks of my appearance. "No, thanks, you go on, I'm ok." "Are you sure? I can really help you." "No, no, thank you. I will get into trouble if the supervisor sees you working here." "Well," I say while opening my backpack and searching in it, "then give these to your children." I then hand him two chocolate-coated energy "power bars" that I keep to replenish myself during long rides. Again, I feel the almost inevitable sense of an encounter between a have and a have-not. I, who now toil on the bike out of choice (after getting tenure a few months ago I could have afforded to buy a second car had I wanted . . .), and the Palestinian day worker, who has no other choice but to toil. Was it insensitive to offer to work with him or to give him the forty shekels' worth of power bars (probably more than the value of two hours of working time for him)? Well, I really wanted to give him something, perhaps to return the favor of the water. He takes the chocolate bars, and simply says "thanks." He does not seem to be offended at all, but rather happy. But suddenly I also see fear in his look. As quickly as it comes, the fear in his eyes disappears. Why or what was he afraid of? I don't ask him. We then depart with the usual "peace be with you" wishes.

I now approach the Lauza riverbed. The trail continues on a relatively wide and comfortable gravel road. After two hundred meters, it ends with a thirty-meter-long, deep ditch and a dirt battery behind it. The ditch is, in fact, the Green Line. Well, not exactly: when the Green Line was demarcated on the maps in 1949, Moshe Dayan, the Israeli representative to the cease-fire negotiations, used a thick green pencil to mark it. At a varying width of one or 2 millimeters on the map, the line translates on the ground to a sixty-to-eighty-meters-wide strip. The "width of the line" is a strip of land the sovereignty of which was never decided. Therefore, I stand now on the "width of the line." This dead nonborderline now seems to me like a dried-up river.[7] On my left, I see on the hill the houses of Mevasseret's Reches Halilim neighborhood and above them the water tower at Yad Assa/Sheikh Abdul Aziz. On my right, another slope rises. This hillside is dotted with pine trees. Were they planted there deliberately to blur the Green Line, or did the "Israeli" pines on the hill of Mevasseret just naturally expand and migrate onto the opposing "Palestinian" hill? A beautiful grove of mature olives grows in the small valley between the two slopes; the soil is harrowed and plowed. I can see an old structure, a watchman's hut made of many stones that were cleared from the grove's soil (a *shomera* in Hebrew, *qasr* in Arabic). The hut, in previous eras, served the farmers as a place to sleep in and guard the yield during the olive harvest. I immediately think about *Palestinian Walks*, a book by Ramallah's (which is just ten kilometers away from here, "as the crow flies" . . .) lawyer and human rights activist, Raja Shehadeh. I just finished reading his book a few nights ago. In one of the chapters, Shehadeh goes out on a *sarha* (wandering) in the hills around his town and discovers a *qasr* that his grandfather and the brother of his grandfather built.[8] Shehadeh feels that in the *qasr* "time was petrified into an eternal present, making it possible for [him] to reconnect with [his] dead ancestor through this architectural wonder."[9] He finds within the *qasr* a stone-carved seat, and when he sits in it, he finds it to be exactly his size. He does not want to move from the seat. I envy Shehadeh's ability to connect with his ancestor in this way. I feel, compared to him, rootless. My father is dead now, and so are my grandparents. Their families are nothing but dust in Auschwitz. When my grandparents died, we sold their apartments. How I long now for those small, even shabby, apartments in Kiryat Yovel where so much of my childhood passed, with the love and grace of these Hungarian Jews who never became "real" Israelis. Indeed, from my father I did "inherit" the Hebrew University—when I walk in the corridors of Mt. Scopus, I feel that I, literally, walk in the footsteps of my father, who worked there too for so many years. Still, Shehadeh's connection with the *qasr* is much more intimate.

The landscape I see before me now looks so familiar and known to me. I admire the beauty of the grove, the dusty and chalky hills, and the *qasr*. I love seeing the contrast between the dry, yellow weeds and thistles on the slopes, which just a few weeks ago were green and flowering, and the dark, deep green of the olives. I lovingly examine the curved and grooved thick stems of the beautiful olives. Yet there is also something foreign in the grove. I know that it is not mine. I imagine Shehadeh sitting inside the *qasr*. Would he welcome me on my wanderings here, he who describes how his own ability to wander among the hills is restricted and circumscribed every year by the Israeli army and settlers? Could we become sojourners?

The grove, I know, belongs to farmers from Beit Iksa, just behind the hill to my east. On the top of the opposite hill—it cannot be seen from here—the separation fence encircles Beit Surik. Beit Iksa, on the other hand, is not "separated" by the fence (of course, it is separated from the rest of the West Bank, but it is not separated from Israel). I hesitate over whether to cross the ditch, to go beyond the Green Line, to trespass into the "real" territories (not like Sheikh Abdul Aziz, which, in effect, became connected to Mevasseret through a form of creeping annexation). Here I might encounter Palestinians in, I would dare say, their "home field" and not mine. It might not be like meeting Wasfi just a few hundred meters south of here, where he is considered a "minority" and I'm the "majority," and experiencing the resultant power hierarchies that constitute and accompany these definitions.[10] But I made a decision already to ride through this wadi, and I come with good intentions, I tell myself. I know that in some senses, *I* am now the "interloper," but I do not come to steal anything or harm anyone (immediately I think about the three old Palestinian men I met a few weeks ago in wadi Halilim). Am I just making excuses to soothe my conscience for trespassing on someone else's land? Or should I cross without hesitation because territorial and national boundaries are just politically constructed and "the question is not to whom the land belongs, but who belongs to the land?"[11]

I feel that I belong to this land, or rather, that I *want* to belong to it, and thus lift the bike on my shoulder and jump over the ditch. I then climb over the dirt battery (probably a barrier meant to prevent Palestinian vehicles from crossing into Israel, but not a real obstacle to my mountain bike . . .) and descend on the other side, within the olive grove. Now, even though just a few seconds ago I felt that I belong to this land, I nonetheless suddenly sense vulnerability—perhaps I don't belong *in* it?

I start riding again. The trail slowly ascends in the wadi. The olive grove becomes a narrow strip on both the sides of the dry riverbed. As I advance into the wadi, the trees become older, their stems thicker. They look impressive, majestic, with their wide and twisted stems, and the many concaves within them. Some of them are "Romans"—ancient trees. I know that they cannot really date back to the Roman period—I checked: it is too long ago for an olive tree. But I like the term the Palestinian farmers use to denote these trees. It shows to me that through centuries, if not millennia, people loved these trees and took care of them.

Stone terraces descend from the eastern slope, also strewn with olives. Occasionally, a pine emerges between the olives. The view of the old trees and the terraces relaxes me, as well as the familiar bodily experience of the riding, of the pedaling and sitting bent on the handlebar, which is "written" in my muscles and bones. On the saddle of the bike, among the olives and the terraced slopes, I finally feel that I do belong to and belong in.

Soon, I approach a body of water, as it were: a small spring, no more than a thin trickle of water from the dolomite rocks of the wadi's wall, drips its water into a shallow round pool, 1.5 meters in diameter. The pool is small, and the water in it is green. I stop by the pool and lean my bike on a Roman olive tree, which shades the spring. The day is already growing hot. Butterflies and dragonflies hover around the spring. In the muddy soil around the pool, I see the footsteps of jackals and deer, which come to drink the water at night. It is good to sit here in the shade, to rest a bit. I take off my helmet, sunglasses, and gloves, and dip the end of a stick I find there in the green water. Then I slowly move the stick in the water gently from side to side. I enjoy seeing the small ripples and waves in the pool. I cup my hand and draw some running, clear, water from the duct that channels the water from the spouting point in the rock wall behind into the round pool. The water is dripping into my cupped hand. The flow is very slow, as the last winters were quite dry. When my hand is full, I taste the water. The water is good, very light. "Stolen water tastes sweeter," I think, realizing that once I stop riding I again feel an interloper.

Then I recall the biblical story on how Gideon the Judge of the Hebrews chose his men to fight the Midianites by the way they drank water from the spring: those who lapped the water like dogs were chosen, while those who kneeled to cup the water in their hands were not. Judging by the way I just drank from the spring, I would not have been chosen by Gideon. As I think this, I understand once more how much my subjectivity was constituted by the military service and the "preparation" for it during history and Bible classes at school: in secular Israeli schools, the Hebrew Bible is studied often as a reliable historical source, the miracles and godly revelations notwithstanding. It saddens and angers me that even though it has been almost twenty years since I was released from the army, and almost thirty years since I studied this story in the Book of Judges, I still remember this tale in the context of the landscape, "Bibleizing" and militarizing this landscape. I look at my bicycle helmet, which I placed beside me on the rock, and at the knobby tires of the mountain bike. The bike suddenly looks like a very masculine machine, a vehicle that masters the terrain, that conquers it.

In the distance, I then see four or five human figures coming down the trail. They are too far away to tell whether they are Israelis or Palestinians. Should I mount the bike and hurry down toward the Green Line, toward the olive grove? No, I decide. I cause no harm to anyone just by being here. They will not harm me. But I feel a strong urge to ride away from there. As the seconds pass and I remain in my place near the water, the figures become more discernible. Now, a few dozen meters ahead of me, I see that these are five Israelis. They are dressed in jeans and bright t-shirts, and wear blue and green metallic sunglasses that glitter in the morning sun. As they come nearer I see that their t-shirts are actually "unit shirts"—shirts that IDF soldiers make at the end of a military course or training, with comical (or supposedly comical) prints of military "folklore" on them.[12] They are orthodox Jews, or "national religious," wearing "knitted skull-caps" and Tzizit (specially knotted ritual fringes), which fly along their hips as they walk. Two of them carry "shortened" M16 assault rifles.[13] They seem to me like soldiers on leave, probably settlers.[14]

I am relieved when I see that these are settlers. The five young men get closer, and I wave at them. They respond similarly, smiling at me, and talking among themselves. They do not seem to be bothered by my presence here. They look at my bicycle with some interest, and come to sit by the spring's pool too. One of them, while holding his M16 rifle in his right hand, bends toward the duct, and, while leaning on his left hand, I cannot believe this, actually laps water from the duct, just like one of Gideon's three hundred chosen men. His friends laugh at his prank/reconstruction of the biblical scene. I cannot suppress my smile. Despite my atheism, my "leftism," my scholarly critical education, and my antimilitarism, I still feel connected to these men. It amazes me how both of us—the "Gideonite" and me—thought about the same biblical scene here at the spring. However, while *I* am angry due to the re-creation of the Judges chapter in my mind, this man is obviously proud of reembodying, literally, this "history." It seems to me that by performing the biblical "drinking test" he is asserting not only that the Bible is "true" but also that this land is his. Yet, I understand his pride, even sympathize with it. I become confused, as two identities clash within me.[15]

We start talking, and it turns out that these soldiers-on-leave came here from the settlement of Har Shmuel, at the upper end of the wadi. "Where are you riding to?" the Gideonite asks me. "To Nebi Samuel," I reply, using the prevalent (at least among secular Israeli Jews) English name of the place (which, in fact, consists of a distortion of the Arab word *nabi*, a "prophet"). I prefer the English name and do not say the Hebrew name Kever Shmuel HaNavi (Tomb of the Prophet Samuel) not only because the English name is the one I have known for many years but also out of a conscious decision now not to let my body, my mouth, reproduce a biblical myth again today. Nabi Samwil, the Arab name, is also something I don't want to "give life" to now. Yet I remind myself that I ride there, to Nabi Samwil, to see the tombs of the Palestinian-Jordanian soldiers.

"It's a beautiful view from there," the Gideonite replies. "You can see about half of Eretz Yisrael [the Land of Israel] from there." I nod in agreement. I remember the place from a visit when I was very young, perhaps ten or eleven years old. My father used to take me then to tour various archaeological sites around the country, and he had a special liking for Crusader forts. Among the many forts we saw was also Nebi Samuel (the Crusaders built a fort there, on the "Mount of Joy," the place from which Jerusalem was first revealed to the eyes of the pilgrims). I remember a windswept mountain, with a huge stone fort on its top, three old and tall pines in front of the fort, and endless archaeological diggings around the place. Inside the fort, the dampness and coolness of a tomb cave. There were many orthodox Jews there, praying intently in a small and crowded vault, over a large domed tombstone covered with a blue velvet curtain—the tomb of the prophet. I felt claustrophobia there, and I feared the tomb. I kept thinking that these prayers might wake again the irate ghost of the prophet, who had already been startled from his eternal rest by the Witch of Endor on the orders of King Saul.

We went outside the crypt and climbed a steep stone staircase to the roof of the fort. From there the view was magnificent. We could see the whole Jerusalem hills at our feet, and for me it looked like endless open spaces of round-shaped hills, strewn with villages and pine forests. I have not returned to Nebi Samuel since then, but I sometimes notice it during my bike rides to Mt. Scopus. It is the highest mountain in the region, and the Crusader fort and the old pine trees dominate the whole area of my trail.

"Do you know anything about tombs of Jordanian soldiers there?" I ask the soldiers-settlers. They look at each other, at me, and say that they never heard of this before. "Why do you ask?" one of them inquires, with slight suspicion in his tone. "Well," I respond, "listen up . . ." and then I tell them the story of the four Palestinian-Jordanian soldiers. "But why do you want to go to the tombs of these four Arabs," one of them, who wears a t-shirt commemorating the exploits of his unit in the recent war in Gaza (2008–9), asks, disapprovingly, but also genuinely disappointed. "You should visit the tombs of the Palmach fighters [the Jewish "strike units" of the British Mandate period] who fell in the battle of Nebi Samuel in the War of Independence [1948]; they're buried in Kiryat Anavim's military cemetery, not too far from here," he adds. I weigh my reply, and say, "I will go to Kiryat Anavim one day too. But today, nonetheless, I'm riding to Nebi Samuel." I pause, and then I ask, "Do you think it's safe to ride in this wadi?" Talking about security issues relieves the tension, perhaps by reminding us that "we're on the same side." "Oh, it's perfectly safe," my interlocutor responds with a smile. "There are hardly any Arabs here now because of the separation fence."

I bid farewell to the five, don my helmet, sunglasses, and gloves, and mount the bike again. I continue to ride on the ascending path, and as the trail winds behind four huge oak trees, I lose sight of the settler-soldiers. Then, not too far from the spring, Ein Luz (in Hebrew, Spring of the Almond) is its name on the map, I see, on the side of the hill, the ruins of a Crusader farmhouse. I know that this is such a place thanks to the Amud Anan interactive map I studied thoroughly yesterday. Thinking about the Amud Anan map, I suddenly recall the origin of its name: it is, literally, the "Pillar of Cloud" by which god showed the way to the Israelites in the Sinai Desert, following their exodus from Egypt.

Some of the Crusader structure's walls are preserved. In particular, one high wall at the upper west corner of the compound looks like a single remaining tooth in the mouth of an old person. The place is eerie. But I decide to stray from the trail in the wadi and climb up to examine the ruins more closely. Why am I doing this? It is just an old ruin, nothing too spectacular or special, at least not on a first examination from the bottom of the wadi. Perhaps out of longing for my father.

I find a narrow "goat trail" that climbs sharply up to the ruins. As I crawl along it, many thumbtack-like seedpods of sainfoin ("cock's head," or, as they are also known among some Israeli mountain bikers, "Eichmanns"), dig into my tires. The knobby, wide, tubeless tires slowly crush the dry, hard seedpods as they roll over them. I am happy with the bike's durability and terrain-conquering abilities, even though just a few minutes ago I associated these properties with overt masculinity and militarism . . . And now I'm on my way to conquer these crusader ruins, crushing Eichmanns and led by the Pillar of Cloud. I grin when

The ruins of the Crusader farmhouse at wadi Luz. (Photograph by Idit Wagner.)

I think about my sequence of associations and images, and then recall *Eichmann in Jerusalem*, which I read not too long ago. I wonder what Hannah Arendt would think of my historical "welding" of the Pillar of Cloud, the thorny Eichmanns, and the Crusaders. Have I become too cynical or am I just tending toward clichés and symbols as a symptom of a midlife crisis I might be going through? I am looking for myself in these hills but cannot find myself. I want to be authentic and free, but cannot emancipate myself, even when I'm cynical, from the burden of the history and culture that produced me. For even when I find it ironic, and a bit funny, that the name Eichmann describes a thorny seedpod,[16] I still feel that just the thought of Eichmann as an annoying thorn is improper. On the other hand, perhaps the very use of this name to describe these thorns represents some popular resistance to the never-ending and all-encompassing efforts of the state to embed, to stick in, like the thorn, the Holocaust in every Israeli's soul?

Confused, I pause for a moment in the middle of the climb to gather my thoughts, and then I see the separation fence looming on the ridge ahead of me. The sight of the fence suddenly adds a melancholic element to the Crusader ruins. Ancient and current violence mingle in this small place. I can almost hear the earth crying "enough." Discouraged, I decide to see the ruins of the Crusader farmhouse perhaps at some other time. I turn back, down, to the wadi.[17]

I am returning to the main trail in the wadi and riding on it as it ascends to the north. The trail, after the Crusader ruins, becomes more rugged, full of melon-sized rocks and gravel. Perhaps this signifies the boundary beyond which Israeli hikers rarely continue—the trail up to here was relatively comfortable, and evidently it was partially smoothed by some machinery. My advance is slowed, and the bike flutters on the gravel in the uphill. Soon the trail turns so rugged and steep that I cannot ride anymore. I dismount the bicycle, and start walking it beside me on the steep rise. Every few minutes I stop to rest a bit, and when I look over my shoulder, I see the fence continuing its windings among the hills, going up and down the ridge on the western wall of the wadi. The fence just goes on and on, without any seeming end. My heart pounds quickly. The pine trees, which at the entrance to the wadi were growing in random patches, have now become a forest that covers the entire eastern slope. This forest must have been planted here—it is too dense and orderly to have grown naturally. Yet even though this is a typical JNF landscape, I still do not feel safe, now that I walk the bike. Knowing that the village of Beit Iksa, in the direction of which I advance, is not enclosed by the fence, I imagine hidden and unfriendly eyes watching me from within the pine forest. I become alert, feeling a tickling shiver in my spine. Then I think about the four fleeing Palestinian-Jordanian soldiers. How and when were they actually killed?

Added to the confusing character of this landscape—a Zionist-planted pine forest within the West Bank, and the separation fence that only partially separates it—is a small grove of fig, almond, and olive trees, which I see on the western slope as I stop to take a breath and look around me. High grass grows among the fruit trees. Here the fence line is quite low, just a few dozen meters above the bottom of the wadi. I recall the comment in the Amud Anan (Pillar of Cloud) map about this place. It is "an orchard that was planted by residents from Beit Surik before the time of the fence, and therefore, today, the fruits are unclaimed [Hebrew, *hefker*]." "How does the author of that comment know that the owners of the grove do not claim their fruits?" I wonder as I continue to walk the bike and consider the harsh connotations the word *hefker* brings to my mind (spoils of war and a no-man's-land [*shetach ha-hefker*]). The mixture of the beautiful orchard and the threatening and overbearing fence is hurtful. How many more orchards like this became "*hefker*" due to the winding fence, I wonder.

I am now approaching the end of the uphill climb. I sit on the saddle again, and start pedaling. The dirt trail soon becomes a paved road, which leads, in one direction, to Beit Iksa, and, in the other direction, to the Israeli settlement of Har Shmuel (named so after the proximate Nebi Samuel site). After some consideration, I take the road to Har Shmuel. I will ride to Beit Iksa some other day, perhaps. Thus, after a few hundred meters of easy pedaling, I arrive at the settlement of Har Shmuel, but, alas, it is surrounded by a high and seemingly strong metal mesh fence (this was not mentioned on the map!). I encircle the fence, but cannot find a breach or a gate. I curse my bad luck, but unwilling to turn back to Mevasseret before getting to Nebi Samuel, I continue to orbit the fenced settlement. It is a late morning hour, and there is no one in the street on the other side of the fence.

Suddenly I notice a small breach in the fence. I stop by the hole and consider whether I will be able to get in, with the bike. I could pass, but the opening is too small for the bike. Thinking what to do, and feeling an urgency to act, I decide after a few moments to release the bike's wheels and see if the frame will fit through the hole. I carefully pass the frame, it goes through easily, and then the wheels. Next, I go myself. Quickly I reassemble the bike. I rejoice at the success of my improvisation. "The Temple Mount is in our hands," I hear in my mind Menashe Noy, of the satirical "Chamber Quintet,"[18] parodying the now cultish words of Motta Gur, the brigadier of the IDF paratroopers during the occupation of East Jerusalem in the 1967 war.[19] Recalling Noy's parody of what seemed to be Gur's sincere emotionality, I start laughing. But as I enter this settlement through the breach in its own perimeter fence, I know that the joke is on me. The Quintet's humor, biting and sharp as it might be, is a satire that expresses the supposed liberal ideology of the "enlightened [Zionist] Left," a political species under the threat of disappearance (I don't want to think about a threat of "extinction"). Yes, "we" lefties can laugh as much as we want at the pathos of the Right, patronize many of the other sectors in Israeli society, feel sophisticated and open-minded toward the "other" (as long as he or she lives not too close to us), and be always, literally, politically correct. But would this move even a single stone in a single settlement?

I am just about to exit Har Shmuel, seeing the site of Nebi Samuel on the hill ahead of me. I make my way to the exit gate of the settlement, and then hear from behind me a roaring engine and a voice calling through a loudspeaker, "Bicycle rider, pull aside!" It takes me a few seconds to realize that the voice is calling to me. I continue riding, but look over my shoulder. I see a dark green Magav (Border Patrol) jeep closely following me. I pull aside, to the shoulder of the road. The jeep passes me, blocks my way, and stops too.

A soldier/policeman steps from the passenger's side. I can see another soldier/policeman in the driver's seat. The one who comes toward me carries a shortened M16 rifle, not in the "administrative" manner (across the shoulder, behind the back), but rather in the "ready-to-engage" manner (the weapon is hung with a long belt from the neck, horizontal to the soldier's body). He holds the weapon's pistol grip, his finger close to the firing trigger, but the barrel is turned low, to the ground. "Do you have an ID?" the Magav officer asks. I smile at him, but inside I start to shudder. I recall my childhood friend, Hayim (literally, "Life"), who was killed in Lebanon by "friendly fire." "Why do you need my ID?" I muster some courage, trying to sound casual. "Where are you from?" the officer responds, perhaps puzzled by my response. "I'm from Mevasseret Zion," I reply. The officer looks at me, and then examines my bicycle. He relaxes, now that he realizes that I'm an Israeli Jew. I relax too. My Ashkenazi, Central/Eastern European look, and my Israeli Tsabar Hebrew accent, as well as my expensive bicycle and "cool" riding clothes, were probably the ID the officer needed. "That's a nice piece of equipment you've got there!," he says, pointing with his M16 rifle's barrel toward my Scott bicycle. "Thanks," I say. I don't like the mastery gesture, the pointing with the rifle, even though I remember that I, too, as a soldier, used to do that. Machines that are extensions of our bodies: the rifle, the bike.

"Do you ride too?" I ask, trying not to become sulky. "Yeah, I live in the north, in the Galilee, I have a good mountain bike too." "Of what make?" I ask, feeling that the conversation is going in a better direction. We then talk a few minutes about mountain bikes and routes around this area. I tell him that I came through wadi Lauza and am going to Nebi Samuel. "You know, we thought you were a Palestinian coming from Beit Iksa, that's why we stopped you," he says.

"Why, can't they come here?" I ask. "No, they're not allowed; they cannot enter Israel." "But this is not Israel here," I answer back, almost automatically. "This is the West Bank." "The what?" he says. The soldier/policeman genuinely does not seem to understand my use of, now I realize, this archaic term. "The 'territories,'" I explain myself, finding it hard to actually say "the *occupied* Palestinian territories." "Aha," he smiles, probably still not understanding what I want from him.

"How did you see me?" I change the subject. "Oh, the security cameras at Nebi Samuel tracked you coming from the direction of Beit Iksa, and we were dispatched to detain you." He then points (with his hand, now) in the direction of Nebi Samuel, showing me a high, actually huge, antenna at the top of the hill. The antenna dwarfs the ancient fort there. Even though I see Nebi Samuel from various points along my ride to Mt. Scopus campus every day, I realize now that I never "saw" this antenna before. The "security landscape" is so natural and merged in this country, says my friend the geographer Amiram Oren, that people hardly notice it.

The officer's voice penetrates my contemplations: "The operations room can see the entire sector (*gizra*) with the cameras from Nebi Samuel, Mevasseret's water tower, and Har Adar." Is he bragging or just friendly and carelessly sharing this information with me, I wonder. I suddenly have an idea: "Do you think I could ride back on the fence's patrol road to Mevasseret, and you'll open the gate for me there?" He laughs, friendly: no, that road is strictly a security road and only security vehicles can use it . . . Obviously, I am not a "security vehicle."[20]

Nabi Samwil turns out to be not only an archaeological and religious worship site, as I remembered from my childhood, but also a small Palestinian village of a few dozen little houses at the edge of the "National Park Nebi Samuel." The first thing I see at the end of the sharp incline leading to the place is yet another separation wall. Just in front of a few Palestinian houses, the huge antenna I was shown a few minutes ago is rising to a height of at least forty meters. The antenna is walled by massive concrete plates, identical to the eight-meter-high concrete plates that make the separation wall in parts of East Jerusalem. The sight magnetizes the gaze: the high, naked concrete plates dwarf everything that is near them. Many devices of communication and surveillance are attached to the high mast. One of them probably detected me along the trail from wadi Lauza to Beit Iksa. It is so ironic that the ancillary equipment of the separation fence has to be fenced and walled too, I think. Of course, this is expensive and sophisticated electronic machinery and, naturally, the army would like to protect it from sabotage. Yet, this special guarding, in this case, the *fortification* of this equipment, indicates, I sense, how much the fence itself is actually a vulnerable structure too. The fence, which is often referred to in Israel, especially by Israeli officials, as the "security fence" (*geder ha-bitachon*), is insecure itself. A fence behind a fence behind a fence, vulnerability behind vulnerability . . .

I continue to gaze at the giant antenna, disbelieving—Israeli citizens would rarely tolerate such a structure in such immediate proximity to their houses, mainly due to fears of intense electromagnetic radiation. The antennas and equipment at the top of the water tower of Mevasseret, at Sheikh Abdul Aziz, are little toys in comparison with this giant structure. Here, in the occupied territories, the "backyard" of this country, it is a different story. I recall the book of Ariella Azoulay and Adi Ophir, *This Regime Which Is Not One*,[21] which I read recently. Azoulay and Ophir talk about the "occupation" not as a temporary military situation but as an inherent component of the Israeli regime itself. In this system, they argue, there is a democracy mainly for Jewish citizens, and a large "backyard" of authoritarian and arbitrary military rule over the noncitizens, the Palestinians of the occupied territories. I knew all this before reading the book, by reading *Haaretz* (literally, "The Land/Country") daily and from my own experience at Hebron. But their book forced me to think about these issues in more explicit and conceptual terms. I remember that on reading the book I once went to vomit. And this was not because of the quality of their analysis . . . Recalling this and seeing the huge walled antenna, I suddenly feel that I'm going to vomit again. I feel (or imagine I feel, but the sense is still very real) the intense radiation that the antenna emits. I sense the insecurity and vulnerability that it symbolizes and further produces. I breathe in the odor of the sewage that runs openly on the road beside me, next to the Palestinian houses. The radiation, the fear, the odor, the wall. These are the materials of subjugation.

As I continue to stand in front of the antenna, fighting the urge not to vomit while thinking about Azoulay and Ophir's book, concepts from the works of Giorgio Agamben, Hannah Arendt, and Michel Foucault buzz in my mind. I think about the "state of exception," "discipline and punish," "the right to have rights," and "bare life." Am I imposing these categories on what I see here, or do the concepts just naturally emerge from this site? What does it give me to think about these concepts besides getting more frustrated and angry? I feel the heavy weight of belonging to a place, to a polity, to a system of control that obliges me to confront, literally, these concepts. While in many Western countries (and the "the West" is what I not too long ago believed Israel is a part of), the camp, the state of exception, bare life, and the surveillance society exist too, they are usually at the margins of the polity or sophisticatedly camouflaged. In my country, they manifest themselves openly, without any shame: right in the middle of a "national park" so close to Jerusalem.

It depresses me so much to acknowledge this. I know that I belong to the privileged elite of this regime. I don't have to be here today—like many of my colleagues, I could withdraw to my office on campus and deal there with other peoples' troubles. This would surely earn me academic prestige and acknowledgment. That is a lot of what IR is about, after all. But the knowledge that I stand here now and experience a reality that insists on staying in an unresolved condition, full of internal contradictions and paradoxes that continue to produce daily violence and oppression, creates in me such distress and resistance that I feel I nonetheless have to keep investigating it. Investigate in order to become bitter and sad? Yes, this could happen too. But investigate also to retain some self-respect in front of this system, which seeks to impose its deep abnormality as normal—and normative—in my own subjectivity.

I headed back home about an hour after arriving in Nebi Samuel. I came back through Jerusalem's neighborhood of Ramot, which is very close to Nebi Samuel,[22] instead of returning through wadi Lauza. From Ramot, I went down into the Arazim Valley, and from there returned home. It was a long detour, but I felt that I had had enough of this "geography of fear" and the occupation for a single day. My choice of return route was the decision of a person who has the privilege of freedom of mobility. Considering the place I was returning from, this freedom was not an obvious thing. For while I could ride through Ramot, the residents of the small village of Nabi Samwil are not permitted to use that road. If they want to go to Jerusalem, they have to drive north (instead of south), and cross a checkpoint in the separation fence, the fence that actually turned their village into a small Palestinian enclave between Jewish Jerusalem and its northwestern surrounding Jewish settlements. From the checkpoint, they would have to take a long detour to Palestinian Jerusalem (and that, too, only with special permits issued by the Israeli authorities). And while I, in my home, am able to decide, for example, who to invite to visit, or who to sell the apartment to, if I like, in Nabi Samwil both these things, among many other things, are impossible for the Palestinian noncitizens. Every day hundreds of uninvited visitors—Jewish worshipers who come to the tomb of the prophet Samuel, and some of them also ritually bathe (to religiously purify themselves) in the spring of the village—come to the place. Occasional "viewers" like me pass in their community too. The villagers, on the other hand, cannot plant trees, even in their own courtyards, because their village is considered a part of the "national park," and they cannot invite Palestinians from other localities to visit them in their village because of the fence. And, of course, they cannot do anything regarding the giant walled antenna.[23]

Before returning home, though, I did find the grave of the four Palestinian-Jordanian soldiers, the actual reason for my ride to this place. A Palestinian resident of the village, about my age, who was walking up the hill into the village while I was watching the walled antenna, showed me the way to it after I asked him if he knew anything about the grave. We spoke in Hebrew, and he inquired how I knew about the tomb. I told him about my meeting with Colonel Ibn Hassan. He seemed very happy to hear this, and said that he had attended the funeral and saw the colonel and the Jordanian army orchestra. "It was very honorable," he added. I wanted to continue talking with him, but he seemed reluctant. "Why not?" I asked. "It is unbecoming," he replied, avoiding my look. Then he added, "I don't know, someone might think you're from the Shabak [Israeli security service, Shin Bet], you know, asking all these questions, looking around . . ." "But I'm just a cyclist," I wanted to reply, yet I didn't.

I realized that perhaps the man indeed thought I was from the Shabak—I did snoop around and ask strange questions. Twenty, even fifteen years ago, I thought, I would have been quite flattered if someone had thought I was from the Shabak. I remembered how important and honored I felt when I was summoned, on finishing my BA, to be examined at the Mossad, the Israeli foreign intelligence and espionage service—the twin brother, but more prestigious among the two, of the Shabak. A "connected" professor gave my name to someone there. Yet I failed the Mossad tests, and continued on to graduate studies and an academic career. Perhaps it was something I said to the psychologist who examined me at the end of a long day of psychometric tests. I remember that she asked me what is common to water and air, and I replied that both are just mediums (*tavech*—not a very common word in Hebrew). She looked at me strangely. Then she showed me a series of Rorschach images, and I involuntarily burst out laughing (that was because I could not stop thinking about a relevant skit from *The Chamber Quintet* in which a young man is examined by a female psychologist who shows him various Rorschach inkblots. Each time he says, initially hesitatingly but then very seriously and resolutely, that he sees there is a "pussy," in Hebrew a *kous,* a woman's genitals [even though in some cases the picture, he argues, is upside down]. The psychologist remains very professional and businesslike).[24]

Perhaps an unconscious, or semiunconscious, element within me deliberately caused me to fail those tests. Perhaps I was too afraid to serve in the Mossad (even as a desk analyst, the job I was tested for—definitely not an "agent" job), and I did so like the freedom of university life. But I felt, nonetheless, that I had missed an opportunity. Not only had I lost the chance to get a job with a steady income and various other benefits, a job that was in line with my education in IR, but I had also missed an opportunity to belong to what I perceived then as an esteemed elite class that was shrouded in secrecy and daring. I felt I had missed an opportunity to be a part of the real core, the pure essence, of the State of Israel—its security apparatus (*maarechet habitachon*).

Moreover, I wanted to join the Mossad also in order to atone, so to speak, for my meaningless military service, to reverse my fears of being a combat soldier, those fears that led me, eventually, to what was perceived then as a humiliating position (for it involved no "real" fighting, as in Lebanon against the Hizb'allah militia) in Hebron at the headquarters of the Judean Regional Brigade. The feeling gnawed at me that there was something hidden, sublime in the realm of "real" security and "service," something I would never be allowed to reveal and experience. Now, when the Palestinian man told me he thought I might be a Shabaknik, something old awakened in me: I still felt that sense of a missed opportunity and, stupidly enough, I was flattered, even if just fleetingly, for being identified as belonging to this apparatus, to this status.

I parted with the man and went to the village graveyard, where he said the tomb was: inside the fenced and gated national park compound of Nebi Samuel (where the tomb of the prophet and other archaeological remains are). The cemetery lies at the foot of the northern side of the fortress. I could not enter the cemetery itself, though, for it too (how not) was encircled by a concrete wall the height of my shoulders, and a higher mesh-wire fence as a second separating layer in front of the wall. A fence behind a fence behind a fence . . .

But I managed to peer beyond the wall and fence and see the grave that the man described to me. The soldiers' grave was a rectangular concrete platform, wide enough to cover four human skeletons lying just next to each other. The platform was made of concrete that was once painted white, with no special decorations or marks. A small limestone plate was placed at the end of the concrete platform. The inscription on it faced the inner side of the graveyard, and therefore I could not read or photograph it. Thus, eventually, the soldiers remained unknown to me.[25]

The grave lies amid the other graves in the cemetery, among the weeds. I was a bit disappointed. I expected to see something more *respectful*, I assume the word would be. Somehow, I had in mind something like the tombs of the Israeli soldiers at the Mt. Herzl military cemetery in Jerusalem, where my cousin, who committed suicide when he was a soldier, is buried—well-groomed (with flowers) cut-stone uniform graves with a relatively large stone "cushion" as a headstone. Here the naked concrete plate, the undecorated grave, the relatively small headstone—it all puzzled me. I began to doubt the colonel's story. The image I had of the colorful Jordanian military orchestra marching through the site and the various dignitaries who participated in the ceremony was not in line with this simple, common, concrete grave.[26] But perhaps, I thought when I recalled the work of George L. Mosse on military graveyards and their sanctification of war, it is better this way.[27]

At home, I realized that something important had happened to me in Nebi Samuel/Nabi Samwil: I went on this ride in order to continue my pleasant, comfortable meeting with the retired Jordanian colonel. I wanted to sense the fear of the defeated, and congratulate myself for being on the victorious, powerful side. Yet, I was exposed, to a small degree, true, to the suffocation and misery caused by the occupation. Yet while in this case, too, I was on the more powerful side, I felt great insecurity—my own inner insecurity in my identity and my role in the insecurity and dispossession of the Palestinians. The fleeting sense of satisfaction that I felt for being identified or suspected as a Shabaknik was replaced with a sense of fear, namely, fear of myself—why, after all these years, was I still allured by this image of the agent of the spearhead of the occupation?

I also began to think about the fence as a structure, technology, and mechanism that perpetuates the occupation. This is not only because the fence sends long "fingers" into the West Bank or encircles villages like Nabi Samwil or Beit

Surik, thus making enclaves and usurping, in effect, large Palestinian territories that remain on its Israeli side. It is also because the fence *hides* the occupation and its wrongs behind it. Israelis become indifferent to these wrongs because the fence—along with other measures and policies—reduced almost to zero the price they have to pay for the occupation in terms of Palestinian violence targeted at them.[28] Knowing that, on the one hand, the fence, with its complex system of monitoring devices and patrols, prevents suicide bombers from reaching Israeli towns and cities, and recognizing, on the other hand, that the fence enables the Israeli public to become indifferent to the continuance and deepening of the occupation, I felt that I had reached an emotional impasse regarding this structure and the regime that is protected and maintained by it. I became frustrated when I realized that I could not be at peace with myself, let alone with the other.

During the next months of my research, I increasingly rode along segments of the fence in my area, and continued to think about this winding barrier in the hills. Following a "lead" I received from a friend with whom I had shared my thoughts about the fence, I eventually met with several residents of Mevasseret who in 2004 played a key role in a public and legal campaign that resulted in a precedent-setting ruling of the Israeli High Court of Justice (HCJ) in the case of Beit Surik.[29]

The government of Israel decided to erect the fence/barrier in the summer of 2002, mainly due to public pressure to do something about the suicide-bombing attacks. Initially opposed to the idea of a physical separation between Israel and the West Bank, a separation that might have endangered the settlement project, Prime Minister Ariel Sharon may have realized that the fence could actually provide an opportunity to confiscate more Palestinian lands by further dismembering the West Bank into an "archipelago" of noncontiguous Palestinian "islands."[30] In early 2004, the construction and infrastructure of the fence drew near the wadis and hills between Mevasseret and the close Palestinian village of Beit Surik, and construction there was about to start. According to the initial plans of the military and the Ministry of Defense, the fence was supposed to be positioned in extreme proximity to the last houses of Beit Surik (perhaps fifty meters away), thus obliging the villagers to obtain—and renew periodically—special permits from the military in order to access their agricultural lands. But following the appeal of the local council of Beit Surik and seven other neighboring Palestinian villages to the HCJ, the court ruled that the Ministry of Defense and the IDF not only must weigh strict security considerations regarding the route of the fence (for example, military topographic issues) but also must give high priority to the interests and needs of the "local population" (that is, the Palestinians) so that the injury to its interests would be proportional to the degree of added Israeli security.

The appeal of the Palestinians was supported by the group of Mevasseret residents, who, in what turned to be a crucial element in the appeal, managed to enlist the Council for Peace and Security—an organization of retired generals and senior officers from the IDF and other security agencies—to the cause of the Palestinians. The council was, in fact, one of the bodies that suggested and lobbied from the outset to build the separation fence between Israel and the Palestinians, playing a major role in the Sharon's government's decision to adopt the initiative. Therefore, it had considerable epistemic authority in this matter.

During the Beit Surik appeal, the Council for Peace and Security was acknowledged as an *amicus curiae* (friend of the court), and the court considered its arguments to be "very serious."[31] The court concluded, "Only a separation fence which is built on the foundations of law [in Hebrew, *mispaht*] will provide security for the state [of Israel] and its citizens. Only a separation route which is based on the way of the law will lead the state to the desired security."[32] Perhaps not incidentally, most of the Israeli Mevasseret activists also adhered to the motto "A just fence is a secure one."

The group of Mevasseret activists consisted of a few dozen persons who were highly committed and involved. Together with officials and members of the community of Beit Surik, they organized several joint communal markets at the halfway point on the "interlopers' path" between Mevasseret and Beit Surik—exactly the place where the gate in the fence is presently located, where I once stood with my bike and recalled my soldier time in Hebron (see chapter 1). Spending long hours in the town's mall, the activists also collected hundreds of signatures from Mevasseret residents on a petition that called for redirecting the fence along the Green Line. The petition was handed to the court. There was also a joint kite-flying event, with children from both localities. In addition, the Mevasseret activists visited Beit Surik four or five times (the opposite was not allowed by the army), and promised that they would harvest the olives of Beit Surik for the villagers should the fence not be redirected eventually. These events were designed to convince the court that there is no fear of Beit Surik in Mevasseret and that the fence should be erected along the path of the Green Line and not along the proposed route of the military.[33] These joint activities carried a message of peace and optimism, and created a sense of comradeship between the activists from Mevasseret and Beit Surik. "But these were just fantasies of peace," one of the Mevasseret activists told me. "We woke up too late— why haven't we done anything like this in the last forty years [of occupation]? Now, nothing will remove the fence."

The most prominent activist from Mevasseret was Shay Dror. His story tells something about these supposed "fantasies" of peace. Whenever I ride along the fence, I think about him.

Shay Dror is sixty-six years old, a landscape architect and gardener from Mevasseret. All the activists with whom I talked corroborated my sense that this man was the "engine" behind the campaign. A former sergeant in the IDF's paratroopers brigade (this is how he chose to present himself to me in our first conversation, on August 2, 2010), he was the employer of several workers from Beit Surik. One day in early 2004, the Beit Surikian employees showed him a map the military had distributed to the villagers. The map informed them of the planned route of the fence in their village. Dror was shocked at the extremely close proximity of the fence to the Palestinian residents' homes. He was enraged by what he considered to be the immorality of the act, which would deprive the villagers of most of their lands and encircle them from three directions. He also feared that the fence in this suffocating route would alienate the people of Beit Surik, who would respond with violence. He then initiated what was a one-man campaign against the fence's route, "one sergeant against the whole General Staff of the IDF," as he saw his struggle. He played a key role in many of the activities and initiatives described above, and, most important probably, he was the one who harnessed the Council for Security and Peace for this cause. "As a simple soldier in the IDF, I followed your lead through 'rivers of blood.' Please do not disappoint me now," he implored the retired generals of the council. His determination and resolution worked.

Dror saw his Palestinian employees and other people of Beit Surik as friends. He told me how he stood in Mevasseret's mall and convinced people that they could not turn a cold shoulder to their neighbors from Beit Surik, whose faces and names many of them had known for years. Indeed, people from Beit Surik used to come daily to Mevasseret to work in many of the homes as electricians and plumbers, and they even built many of the houses in the town. Considering the timing—early 2004, just after the height of the suicide-bombing campaign—Dror's actions were extremely courageous. He could easily have been beaten, or worse.

Then Dror told me that while he is very satisfied that he and the group of the Mevasseret activists managed to influence the redirection of the fence, he remains very sad and hurt by the affair. His hard feelings stemmed from the fact that most of his Palestinian friends and colleagues from Beit Surik simply broke off contact after the court's decision. He said that he had heard from foreign peace activists that his friends from Beit Surik told them that for them the conflict dated back to 1948 and not to 1967. They were bitter. They told the foreign activists that their land was taken from them twice: in 1948 and currently, with the fence. (This is true: even the corrected route effectively cut several thousand dunams from Beit Surik.) But for Dror the detachment of the Palestinians was hard and offending. He now tells himself that what he did was primarily for his own sake. He believes he acted morally and that the results of his activities, mainly the redirection of the fence's route, carried material benefits for Mevasseret in the sense that the corrected route prevented the Beit Surikians from turning to terrorism by not becoming too bitter.

I found his relation very moving. Dror and his friends' success in rerouting the fence made me optimistic about the ability of the ordinary person to have an effect on political decisions and processes. But I also became very sad when I realized that the separation fence is not merely a security-oriented structure or a political tool in the struggle over land and space, but also a construction that separates Israeli Jews and Palestinian Arabs in emotional and personal terms. The segment of the fence that I see everyday when I ride my bicycle in and around Mevasseret cut off personal ties between people like Shay Dror and people who worked with him from Beit Surik, whom he deemed friends for many years.

Dror was probably offended that his Beit Surikian friends could not make the distinction between "Israel" as an occupying state and regime and "Israel" as represented by people like him, ordinary, good-willing citizens. At first, I identified with Dror's hurt. The affair, as he told it, seemed to contain some elements of exploitation by the Beit Surikians of Dror's and the other Mevasseret residents' goodwill and help. It also seemed to me that the Palestinians insisted on maintaining their identity as victims—why did they abruptly break off contact with Dror and bring the issue of 1948 into the affair, I thought. It bothered me a lot to discover on the website of the Local Council of Beit Surik that there is no "Mevasseret" on the map there, and instead there is Qalunya—the Palestinian village on whose ruins and agricultural lands Mevasseret was built.[34]

But on a second consideration, I understood that there might be good reasons for the Beit Surikians' bitterness: the fence indeed cut their access to livelihood sources in Mevasseret and other Jewish towns and villages in the region (apart from actually working in the Jewish localities, many Beit Surikians used to rent homes and rooms for other Palestinians who wanted to work in Israel and benefit from Beit Surik's proximity to Mevasseret). The fence also cut them off from places and spaces that they continue to see as Palestinian, even if populated "currently" by Israelis. Why should they not call Mevasseret Qalunya when even one of the prominent activists from Mevasseret told me that what he laments most is the fact that the fence cut off his previous easy access to regions and areas that he sees as having been "his" since biblical times? I cannot be angry with people for their dreams, I realized. While before the fence the Beit Surikians could at least come and work in the place that earlier generations in their village knew as Qalunya, as well as other regions and localities in what they dream of as "Palestine," the fence completely blocked this access.[35] Finally, the fence did take significant parts of their agricultural lands, even after its route was redrawn, and it clearly carries an unwelcoming message of suspicion toward people who were not violent against Israel.

The people of Beit Surik were in shock when the fence was eventually erected I was told by Mustafa Joubran (pseudonym), a forty-year-old construction contractor from the Palestinian-Israeli village Ain Nakuba. He is a former resident of Beit Surik who became an Israeli citizen in the mid-1990s by marrying a Palestinian-Israeli woman from Ain Nakuba. He, too, was involved in the 2004 campaign. From Beit Surik's point of view, said Mustafa, they were peaceful all these years, and the construction of the fence tagged them as enemies of the Israelis. But they still remember very kindly the work of Shay Dror, Hagay Agmon-Snir and the other people from Mevasseret, he added.[36] "Do you still visit Beit Surik?" I asked. Mustafa offered me coffee and cakes, while we sat in the living room of his house in Ain Nakuba. This was the first time I had entered an Arab house as an invited visitor (as opposed to an uninvited soldier). His little daughter was sitting in his lap, listening to our conversation, which was in Hebrew, trying to understand what we were talking about. I recalled how in Hebron the army used to expropriate—for limited times—a whole store or the roofs of Palestinian houses just like this one, usually to post there a lookout to secure a road for Jewish settlers. I remembered the little children crying when they saw the soldiers settle in their house. We didn't cry then in the children's rooms that were converted into mini–military bases, with boxes of ammunition, military mattresses, rations, and binoculars and night vision goggles all around us. Now tears came to my eyes. Moreover, I could not stop wondering at my feeling of confusion about this man's political-legal status: just a few years ago, he was a Palestinian from the West Bank, and now he had "immigrated" to Israel and become an Israeli citizen. And I sit as a welcome guest in his house—how arbitrary are the categories that make us into enemies.

Mustafa probably did not see my tears. He told me that even after the erection of the fence he continues to visit his twelve brothers and sisters in Beit Surik. It takes more than an hour to get there, with the long detour through the Kalandiya checkpoint (at the northern edge of Jerusalem). When his little daughter complains about the long detour, he tells her that the fence is against thieves. Indeed, thefts and burglaries have considerably decreased in Mevasseret, the local newspaper reported once, thanks to the fence.

"But what is some theft of a car or stereo system compared to the theft of land and dignity?" Rotem Mor, another activist from the 2004 campaign, asked me.[37] Mor, a thirty-year-old social activist, as he defines himself, operates a project called Jerusalem Reality Tours. He takes people, mainly international visitors, but also Israelis who are interested and willing, to tour Jewish and Palestinian rundown neighborhoods in various parts of Jerusalem. There they meet the residents person to person, and stay at their houses for a meal or a sleepover. As opposed to the activist who told me that the campaign was a fantasy, Rotem did feel a sense of "we-ness" and strong comradeship with the Beit Surikians during the campaign. He even considered changing his permanent address with the Ministry of Interior to Beit Surik (this was also in order to dodge the occasional "closed military zone" orders that the Israeli military used to issue in order to prevent Israelis from Mevasseret from entering Beit Surik—as a permanent resident of the village the order would not have applied to him). Like Shay Dror, Rotem also felt that a considerable part of the struggle was that "we [the residents of Mevasseret] needed to feel that we were doing the right, moral thing." However, unlike Dror, who could identify with the motto "a just fence is a secure one," Rotem could not accept the concept of a "just fence" from the outset: the fence divides a land that he believes belongs to the two peoples equally, and it prevents communication between Israelis and Palestinians. Even violent communication is better than noncommunication, he said. But in the Beit-Surik–Mevasseret region, the fence actually transformed a *nonviolent* reality into a conflicted and military one, changing the consciousness of the residents on both sides. The destruction of the land by the massive infrastructure works of the barrier was an extremely difficult sight for him, he told me. Tension was brought to a small and quiet place. Madness was created by mad actions. "The land is too small for the fence, [and] one day the citizens—Israelis and Palestinians—will knock it down," he continued. "So why did you take part in the campaign to *redirect* the fence, instead of objecting to its very existence?" I asked him. "In 2004, the fence was a fait accompli, [and] joining the rerouting campaign was the lesser evil," he sighed.

Rotem upset me quite a bit with his remark that even violent communication is better than noncommunication. I also could not have disregarded the apparent paradox in his words: if suicide bombings are a violent communicative act on the part of the Palestinians, what makes this act more acceptable than the coercive communication that is embodied in the fence? Being the weak, oppressed part of the conflict did not seem to me a justification for this supposed means of communication.

Nevertheless, he prompted me to think about this disturbing point. Of course, he did not support or advocate suicide bombings or any other form of Palestinian violence that Israelis call terrorism. But he saw such violence as a call—a shout, actually—for attention on the part of the Palestinians. In a sense, I had to admit, he was right. The fence not only prolonged and perpetuated the occupation but it created a reality in which Israelis perceive the Palestinians as a nuisance, at best. Most of us consider them as wild preying beasts that *deserve* to be caged and silenced behind the fence due to their barbarous conduct during the second intifada and because of the chance for peace they supposedly declined—according to the prevalent Israeli "why the Oslo process failed" narrative.[38] The fence helps us to forget or even not be aware of the fact that the intensive suicide-bombing campaign of the second intifada started only after the IDF's initial harsh oppression of what began as a popular Palestinian uprising. Moreover, this harsh oppression was planned by the military for many months prior to the actual eruption of the intifada, turning the intifada, in fact, into a self-fulfilling prophecy.[39]

The fence thus serves as a conclusive material proof of the "blame" the Palestinians carry, and it reduces their plight to a problem that is *manageable* by means of the hi-tech tracking, alarm, and surveillance systems of the fence. I recalled a senior professor in my department talking about the need to move from a paradigm of conflict resolution to a paradigm of conflict management. Furthermore, I realized after talking with Rotem that the fence is not only a security/conflict management structure; it also harks on the Israeli desire for the collective *punishment* of the Palestinians. It has literally cemented this desire, and every day that passes shows that it is possible to realize it with a relatively low (international) political price.

My anger at Rotem's comment that violence is also a form of communication—whether we like it or not—was somewhat dissolved by his pragmatism, which was manifested in his understanding that joining the 2004 rerouting campaign was the lesser evil, or even just due to the fact that the campaign itself created a momentary feeling of comradeship and a joint cause between the Mevasseretites and the Beit Surikians. I recalled Mustafa Joubran's remark—which he made without me raising the issue first—that people in Beit Surik still remember kindly the work of Shay, Hagay, and the other activists from Mevasseret. I understood that everything we do and say eventually matters in the "broad picture." This realization shed a new light for me on Rotem's work with weakened and oppressed Palestinians and Israelis in Jerusalem, on his knowledge of Arabic and Palestinian music and culture, and on his genuine and deep pain over the fact that the fence tears the beautiful hills and brought militarization and madness to the two quiet communities. And above all, on the fact that he was personally involved in a campaign that ended up fixing a gigantic barrier in the middle of the landscape that was so dear to him.

He was the first among many people—colleagues, activists, friends—with whom I talked about the fence that let his pain over these realities be expressed to me in a way that was not trying to cover his vulnerability with a discourse of security and/or legal/historical rights/nostalgia. I envied Rotem for being able to be so honest and true to himself. I realized that the various mantles I wrapped myself with—the Shabak/Mossad analyst that I did not become but that still resides in me, the leftist Zionist peacenik, the IR scholar—were just meant to prevent me from looking into myself. I went out to ride along the fence following four dead Palestinian-Jordanian soldiers and a retired colonel. The ride eventually led me to understand that in a sense there is a separation fence or wall inside me too, that I will not be truly a part of this land until I am able to identify with and contain the pain of *both* its peoples. When Rotem invited me to ride with him (he has this funny-looking folding bicycle . . .) to the ruins of Qalunya, the 1948 depopulated and demolished Palestinian village, I felt that this trip would be a good way to start looking for a breach in my inner separation fence.

Chapter Three

RIDING TO QALUNYA, PART I
Truing the Wheel of Time?

September 21, 2010: The Jerusalem Syndrome

Kfar Shaul Mental Health Center in Jerusalem specializes in treating persons who are stricken with "the Jerusalem Syndrome"—a psychiatric condition whereupon a visitor to the holy city believes he or she has divine powers, has been assigned a messianic duty, or is the embodiment of a character from the scriptures. Hundreds of such tourists have been treated in this mental health facility.[1] It is 9:00 a.m. now, and I am waiting for David (pseudonym) from the nearby bicycle shop to open. Until he does, I sit at a picnic table among some pine trees, in a small grove on the western side of the hospital. My bicycle is leaning against the table, and I rest after the long climb to here on a trail called the "Romans' Acclivity" (Ma'aleh Roma'im)—a steep old Roman road, still partially paved with Roman cobblestones, which cuts directly through the mountain from Mevasseret to Giv'at Shaul. From Qalunya to Deir Yassin.

The hospital is a patchwork of many old domed stone houses, newer concrete structures, and additional construction. Sometimes, an old house "has grown" a more modern concrete part on its side. Also covered with limestone, according to the Jerusalem municipal bylaw, which requires that all buildings in the city be covered with such stone, the modern houses' coat of stone is nonetheless more polished and white. The older houses' cover is rugged and gray. The arched windows of the stone houses stand in contrast to the rectangular windows of the modern structures. The entire scene is peering through a belt of pines, figs, and eucalyptuses that encircles the hospital's courtyard, behind a fence of high and thick metal bars.

The old stone houses were once the Palestinian village of Deir Yassin, which was depopulated in April 1948, during what the Israelis call the War of Independence and the Palestinians call the Nakba (catastrophe). I think about the battle and consequent massacre that took place here on April 9–10, 1948. Between 100 and 120 persons, among them many women, elders, and children, were shot dead by the Jewish "dissident" militias Irgun and Lehi, which stormed the village in order to "cleanse" it of its residents and Arab forces. It is argued that the event—and the many exaggerated reports and news stories about it (by both Jews and Arabs)—was pivotal in the flight and/or expulsion of the Palestinians from other localities in the Jerusalem region and elsewhere in the country.[2]

I vaguely knew about the Deir Yassin massacre many years before, but never read anything about it. When recently looking for materials about Qalunya, the depopulated Palestinian village below "present-day" Mevasseret, I searched Benny Morris's book *The Birth of the Palestinian Refugee Problem Revisited* for the name Qalunya (otherwise transcribed as Qaluniya) and found this description that the Jewish "dissident" militia, the Irgun Zvaii Leumi (IZL, National Military Organization), circulated to justify the events of Deir Yassin: "terror and dread among the Arabs in all the villages around; in al Maliha, Qaluniya and Beit Iksa, a panic flight began that facilitates the renewal of road communications [to besieged Jewish Jerusalem] . . ."[3] This led me to read more on Deir Yassin, as well as on the events that preceded and followed the occupation of this village.

I wanted to enter the hospital/village, but the guard at the gate said that entrance is allowed only to "authorized personnel." Well, I thought, this is, after all, a closed institution. But what an insane idea to place a mental health institution in such a location of bloodshed and massacre, I continued thinking while circling the compound to locate a breach in its fence, to no avail this time, though. "Madness is created by mad actions," I recalled Rotem Mor saying about the separation fence.

Now, sitting at the picnic table in the grove outside the hospital and looking at the houses from behind the fence, I try to imagine the pillars of smoke rising above the village in 1948, and the sounds of the explosions and shootings, of crying, which were probably heard and seen in Qalunya too, on the range opposite here. If the IZL's message about the "panic flight" that ensued after its action in Deir Yassin is correct, then I live today in Mevasseret at least partially thanks to what happened here—the massacre.

It's 9:10. The bike store will be open only in twenty minutes. I take out my notebook and look for the phone number of Gadi Kadman (pseudonym). Kadman, as he describes himself on his website, is a retired software engineer who decided to establish a volunteer enterprise of free guided tours and hikes across the country that seeks to deepen the connections between the "people and their land." Kadman espouses a nostalgic Zionistic perspective that stresses the links between "knowing the land," *tiyul* (hike), romantic relationships among the hikers, and "Israeli" music (namely, Ashkenazi/Central-Eastern-European-informed tunes and style). I found out about him after searching the Internet for the "the legend of the flute," and finding a version of it on his website. The legend, which tells about the poor herder with the magic flute who married the daughter of the evil *mukhtar* of Qalunya (see the prologue to this book), appears on many websites, including on the Scouts website and the Ministry of Education's.[4] I called Kadman yesterday to ask him if he remembers where he found the legend that he posted on his website. He told me to call him this morning, and we will have time to talk.

I take out my cell phone and dial the number. Kadman answers almost immediately and I present myself again—a researcher from the Hebrew University's IR department, who's interested in the history of the region where he lives. I tell him about the legend, which I heard being told in the wadi itself and also read about on several websites, including his, and ask him if he remembers where he heard it first. His answer surprises me quite a bit: "Of course: I made it up," he says, without any hesitation. I ask him to elaborate, and he says that he thinks that ten or fifteen years ago, when he had just started guiding tours, on a trip to this wadi, someone asked him about the origin of the name Halilim. In order to satisfy the curiosity of the hikers, Kadman simply invented the story on the spot, and since then has repeated it many times and published it on the Web.

I pause for a few seconds, and then, perhaps because of the unwavering confidence in his tone, I cannot but think about the episode from Jerome K. Jerome's *Three Men in a Boat*, in which two of the three boaters, George and Jerome, see a "monstrous trout" showcased in a little riverside inn, and each person who comes into the inn tells them self-assuredly that it was he who, in fact, caught the fish. Eventually, George wants to take a closer look at this "most astonishing trout" and climbs on a chair to get a better view, but then the chair, naturally, slips. "George clutched wildly at the trout-case to save himself, and down it came with a crash, George and the chair on top of it." Jerome scolds him, "'You haven't injured the fish, have you?' But he had. That trout lay shattered into a thousand fragments." They then discover that the supposedly stuffed fish "was plaster-of-Paris."

Unlike George and Jerome, who find out that the legendary fish at the inn was in fact a faked one, I cannot tell for sure if indeed Kadman himself authored the flute legend or heard it from someone else. Then I ask, "But why an Arab story?" "Because it sounds more legendary and romantic," he replies. "It sounds more *authentic* and engaging," he adds. I smile with sympathy and some amusement, partially due to the recollection of the *Three Men in a Boat* episode, and partially because by now I know better. "Would you like to hear the real origin of the name wadi Halilim (the wadi of the flutes)?" I ask. He replies positively, and then I tell him that I had discovered that before 1948, the wadi was named in Arabic wadi a-Zananir, literally the "valley of the sashes or belts," probably because of the holes in the elongated caves (Merahair a-Zananir, الزنانير "the caves of the belts").[5] According to Zeev Vilnay, one of the founders of and the highest authorities on Zionist cultural geography (*yediat haaretz*, "knowledge and *lore* of the country"), the translation of the place's name to Halilim (flutes) in Hebrew is probably the result of confusion between *zananir* (sashes, belts) and *zamamir* (Arabic, "flutes").[6] The Governmental Names Committee of Israel, of which Vilnay was a member, officially changed the name of the wadi from Zananir to Halilim during a meeting on January 4, 1955 (Vilnay was absent from that meeting).[7]

Kadman thanks me for my elaborate explanation, but says that as a guide of experiential tours he is not so much interested in historical facts and accuracy. We talk a bit more, and then the conversation ends. I close the phone, and think about what I just learned. The minutes pass, it is already after 9:30, and the bicycle shop has not opened yet. Perhaps because of this delay, which forces me to confront my thoughts, I increasingly feel gloomy. Here, in Deir Yassin, which was a central place and event in the escape of the Palestinians and their expulsion to exile, I hear that someone supposedly made up a story about an

"Arab" herder and his sweetheart because it sounded authentic, romantic, and legendary enough to explain the name of the wadi near my home. Qalunya, on the lands of which was located the Halilim/Zananir wadi, was occupied on April 11 by the Palmach (a Jewish pre-state militia and a subunit of the largest militia, the Haganah), a day after the Deir Yassin massacre. I realize that the placement of the mental health hospital in the village of Deir Yassin and the renaming of the Zananir wadi are examples of different ways of deleting or repressing the history of the land: Deir Yassin was turned into a restricted mental health institution, while fabricated legends about the wadi have dehistoricized (even if unconsciously or unintentionally) the village of Qalunya, which, in its own turn, was almost completely destroyed. Must it be this way? Must we be so disrespectful toward the history of this land, toward the history of the Palestinians, whom we defeated in 1948, even if they were/are our enemies? I think about all the youths, soldiers, and hikers who hear the "legend of the flute," and how the story integrates into a broader dehistoricization of the Palestinians in this land. True, I personally became aware of the very existence of Qalunya only after hearing the story told to the soldiers in the wadi one morning not too long ago. And I don't know enough about the 1948 war. But at least I am becoming aware of this gap in my knowledge. On the other hand, how many people who hear the legend in the wadi bother to check the historical, not legendary, past of Qalunya and the 1948 war?

I think about Zeev Vilnay, who invented many legends about the land, often "spicing" his stories with Palestinian lore and fables, or "converting to Judaism" Palestinian stories, in order to reconnect the Jewish immigrants to the Land of Israel. Vilnay lamented that due to the long Jewish exile from the land, the Zionists don't have enough legends about the country. He saw legends as strengthening the emotional links between the people and the country.[8] I love legends. Now I recognize, though, that in a contested territory like Israel-Palestine, legends also help to ease the burden of the "real" history.[9] In their turn, those legends become themselves a new burden.

Eventually, David of the bike shop arrives, and apologizes for the delay. We enter the shop, and while he starts truing the front wheel of my bicycle—a few days ago I crashed, again, on that curve in wadi Halilim, and the wheel came somewhat "out of joint."[10] I suddenly feel the strong grip of the "Jerusalem Syndrome."

October 10, 2010, Lost in Translation

Today, too, there is no whistling of a flute, or anything like it, here at the foot of the cave of the flutes. A headwind is blowing from the northwest, and from behind me, to the south, I can hear the rustle of the Jerusalem–Tel Aviv highway. It is the late afternoon rush hour on the highway, but in the wadi, there is no rush. The wadi is still. I hear a bird's whistle, carried by the wind from the upper part of the wadi. The cave is still quiet.

I have been standing below the Halilim cave for long minutes now. Returning from Mt. Scopus to Mevasseret, I am proud of my success in crossing with the bike today one of the most rugged parts of the Halilim trail, on the ascent. It is one thing to "clear" that "drop" on the downhill, and another to overcome it on the uphill. A different kind of concentration, a quieter and more intensive one, is required. All the muscles of the body—legs and arms, back, neck, and abdomen muscles—work as the wheels steadily override rocks and gravel in the winding ascent. It is not every day that I manage to cross this section so smoothly. I felt that the bicycle was under my total control today. It responded directly to my body, without disputing me or submitting any complaints about my conduct. It was a true extension of my body. What a wonderful machine it is, simple and reliable, controllable and responsive. It is my instrument for generating a "temporary autonomous zone" every day.[11]

After waiting for a while to hear the flute, I eventually decide to continue riding. I'm getting cold in the wind without pedaling, and the elongated cave will not play any tune for me. I continue on the trail, and suddenly, behind a curve in the path, materializes Zuheir (pseudonym), one of the three aged Palestinian day workers I meet in this wadi from time to time. The outdoor landscape always has this element of "suddenness." Even though I often meet people along the trail, it is always a surprise to see someone else on the trail: "suddenly" I see a deer, "suddenly" I see a Magav jeep, "suddenly" I see a man. Zuheir is returning to his home in Beit Surik. "So what do you call this wadi in Arabic?" I ask him after we greet each other.

I'm not sure why I ask this, for I know the answer: wadi a-Zananir. Perhaps I ask because I just want to "verify" my theories on the transformations of this place. But the element of suddenness strikes again. "We call this wadi— wadi al Khalil," Zuheir replies, with a smile. "No, I meant in Arabic," I respond, perplexed for a moment. "Yes, I know," he answers, "wadi al Khalil. It means 'the friend of god'—the name of Ibrahim, like the city of al Khalil, you know [Hebron]." Al Khalil/Hebron, the city where according to Jewish and Muslim tradition Abraham/Ibrahim the patriarch is buried. I recall now that Abraham is mentioned in the Quran too, as the "friend of god." "Don't you call this place wadi a-Zananir?" I ask.

Zuheir contemplates my question for a minute and then answers, "No, I don't know what that word means."

I don't know how to respond to this. This sounds so ironic—the process of dehistorization has taken a complete circle: the wadi, which in pre-1948 Qalunya was the "wadi of the belt" turned in post-1948 Hebrew into the "wadi of the flutes," and then a legend was invented to explain this new name. Now I learn that Palestinians from the region know the place as wadi al-Khalil—due to the resemblance to the Hebrew Halilim. And not only that: Hebron, the city of "my" Tegart fort, follows me here too.

It is growing chilly and dim as the afternoon begins to fade into a cold evening. By now, I know how long and arduous is the way Zuheir has yet to walk. He will continue down through this rugged wadi, and later will climb via wadi Luz. Then he'll cross a checkpoint in the separation fence to the north of Har Shmuel, and will enter the Palestinian village of Bidu. From there he will get a ride for three shekels (less than one dollar), in a Palestinian van that collects returning workers, to Beit Surik. I know that Magav might detain him or harass him—he will be seen by the security cameras of Nebi Samuel. It is not the time to start a historical discussion about my research now. We say farewell. I will be home soon. There, I decide as I continue the climb on the trail, I will edit the (Hebrew) Wikipedia entry for "Nahal Halilim" and tell the story of the translation mistake.

A few days later, after editing the Wikipedia entry, I noticed that someone reedited some of my additions. My addition stating that the wadi's name comes from a mistake between Zananir (sashes, belts) and Zamamir (flutes) remained untouched. Yet, my other comments were deleted by another user: the comments that the case of the Halilim legend exemplifies the way the Palestinian residents of the land have become a subject of folklorization, and that, in this context, it is interesting to note that Zeev Vilnay regularly invented similar "Arab" legends in order to (re?)establish the connection between the Jews and their land. I reedited the entry in order to keep all my comments. A duel of deletion/addition ensued for several days. Eventually, a "Wikipedia administrator" sent me a message, saying that the style of this last comment was not "encyclopedic" and any further attempt to insert this passage again would cause her to block my access. I did not insist and thus found out that there are certain hurdles in the wadi that I cannot pass. But mountain biking taught me that there's always another trail: at least, in my own book, I am sovereign to write whatever I want . . .

May 3, 2011, in the Morning: A Blood Debt at the House of the "Last Nazi"

"During the night of the 10th–11th of April [1948], Qalunya, with whom[12] there has been a blood debt since the riots of 1929, was occupied and the village was destroyed."[13]

Blood debt. The words keep floating in my mind whenever I come here, to the ruined summerhouse of Mufti Amin al Husayni in Qalunya. The mufti (an Islamic high cleric and scholar) was the head of the Supreme Muslim Council and the Arab Higher Committee during much of the British Mandate period in Palestine. He is seen by many Israelis as the instigator of the 1929 Palestine riots as well as the embodiment of the connection between Palestinian nationalism and nazism. Amin al Husayni is also perceived in Israeli Zionist historiography as one of the chief Arab leaders responsible for the Palestinian defeat of 1948, due to his refusal to accept the UN 1947 partition plan for Palestine between the Jews and the Arabs, and his major role in the initiation of the Palestine war in late 1947. I come here today to ponder this concept of "blood debt," and to inquire whether I, too, consider myself a debtor of this supposed debt of Qalunya, and if so, can/should I put it aside.

Hidden in the lush vegetation (tall thistles, cacti, weeds, and many trees: pines, almonds, olives, and ailanthus), stands what is left of Husayni's house. In fact, this house is almost all that is left, materially, from the village of Qalunya on this slope. The other houses of the thousand-inhabitant village that once stood here were destroyed in the 1948 war by a Palmach force that occupied the place during the battles on the road to besieged Jerusalem. There was a detachment of the Arab Deliverance Army here (volunteers from the various Arab countries that came to aid the Palestinians in the 1948 war), which harassed Jewish transportation to Jerusalem on the highway. The villagers themselves fled a few days before the occupation, after hearing the news from Deir Yassin.[14]

On the main trail of the depopulated village of Qalunya. *At the distant fore,* the Israeli village of Motza Illit and Highway 1 to Jerusalem. (Photograph by Idit Wagner.)

What remained of Qalunya after this war was demolished when Mevasseret Zion was built and populated mainly by Jewish immigrants from North Africa (1956). The agricultural terraces of the village were covered with a Jewish National Fund planted pine forest. The trees were planted in the late 1950s, to "improve the landscape" and save travelers to Jerusalem from being bothered by the "unpleasant" sight of the ruined Palestinian village, so that "various questions" would not be asked.[15] The village's main spring turned, in recent years, into a nonregulated, "piratical" *mikveh*—a pond in which religious Jews come to wash and ceremonially purify themselves (even though the water is not very clean, to say the least). A café that once stood at the edge of the village is now a school for Jewish children with special needs. Sporadic cacti and old, narrow trails on the southwestern slope of Mevasseret are also material remnants of the village.

Like the mufti's house, the trail that leads to it is hidden among the weeds and thistles of late spring. This is a forsaken place, even though it lies just a few dozen meters down from the Soreq Road, which leads to Mevasseret's southern entrance. *At the Side of the Road and at the Edge of Consciousness*, is how Noga Kadman's book on the depopulated Palestinian villages characterizes these places. She couldn't have chosen a better title.[16] I navigate carefully along the narrow trail, for I know from previous visits here that somewhere close to the house there is a deep, open pit: an archaeological excavation. The digging is surrounded only by white marking tape and a small sign with the symbol of the Antiquities Authority. It is easy to miss it with all the thistles around. The trench is said to be a granary from the period of the Kingdom of Judah during the second half of Iron Age II in Canaan.[17]

Successfully passing the granary pit, I dismount the bike and watch Amin al Husayni's house. The ruined old house is, at least in its external appearance, reminiscent of an archaeological site. Of course, this is not a "natural" archaeological remnant, if such a thing exists at all—it was *made* into one only about sixty years ago. The Israeli law of antiques stipulates that a site or an object can be considered "antique," and consequently enjoy the resulting legal protections and special status, only if it originated prior to the year 1700 (CE) or as otherwise determined by the minister of culture. The mufti's house was probably built in the nineteenth century, on land that was usurped by one of his ancestors from a poor fallah (Arabic, "farmer") in Qalunya.[18] But there must have been other houses and sites in Qalunya that predated the year 1700, the boundary that separates archaeology, which is rigorously protected by law, and "history," which can be deleted and demolished more easily.[19] I wonder whether the archaeologists who excavated in this area (and there were several archaeological excavations here, in the valley of Motsa) found, while searching for prehistoric, biblical, Roman, Byzantine, and Crusader remains, evidence of the "Palestinian period" of this region, and if so, what they have done with these findings. But there is no Palestinian period in the archaeology of this land not only because the concept "Palestinian," as a nationalist signifier for the Arabs of Palestine, originated in the mid- to late nineteenth century (and, thus, again, does not fall under the realm of "antiquities" according to Israeli law) but also because the "periods" in the country's archaeology are named according to the foreign rulers who occupied and ruled it: the Roman period, Byzantine period, Early Muslim period, Crusader period, Mameluke period, Ottoman period, and so on. Thus, imperial history makes it harder, from the outset, to grant recognition to the local history of the land's inhabitants, including in this place, Qalunya, or to perceive it as something worthy or "important." According to this imperial logic of periodization, how should the current era be termed—the Israeli/American period?

Archaeological identification of sites is often tenuous. But the identification of the mufti's house is easier and more certain. In a YouTube video that I saw, two elderly Palestinian refugees from Qalunya returned to visit the area in 2009. When shown this house, one of them clearly identified it as the *qasr* (Arabic, "palace, villa") of Haj Amin al Husayni, "the leader of Palestine," as he says. Meir Broza, a native of Motsa, a Jewish village that was established in the 1890s in immediate proximity to Qalunya, also identified this house as the mufti's.[20]

The mufti is perceived by the Israelis as a bitter enemy of Zionism who incited the Muslims to attack the Jews prior to the 1929 Palestine riots, in which 133 Jews were murdered by Palestinians, mainly in Jerusalem, Hebron, Safed, Haifa, and Tel Aviv.[21] One hundred and sixteen Palestinians were killed in the riots too, the great majority of them by British armed forces that tried to suppress the outburst. Hundreds of Jews, though, were protected and saved by their Palestinian neighbors during these "events."[22] This is a fact that Israelis tend to forget. "It is easy to forget this," told me Hillel Cohen, a colleague from the Hebrew University's Middle Eastern studies department, who studied the period. "This forgetfulness makes it easier to deal with the expulsion of the Palestinians in 1948." I asked Hillel about 1929 last summer, when I discovered 1929 along my trail in the Arazim Valley. Not too far away from here, from Qalunya, there is another depopulated Palestinian hamlet—Beit Thulma. The national park Einot Telem, where the Palestinian worker Wasfi once drew cool groundwater for me, marks the place today. In that place, a sign of the Parks Authority tells, there was a small Jewish settlement during the 1920s (Emek Ha'arazim, the Cedars Valley), which was deserted in the 1929 riots. The sign doesn't tell, though, that Jews and Arabs lived together, in very good relations, in that small place by the springs that today are almost dry and give only a trickle of water.[23] *Thulma*, in Arabic, means, by the way, "plentiful." Water was plentiful then, in the springs. Today, plentiful water can only be found deep in the ground. On August 24, 1929, when a mob from Qalunya came to lynch the Jews of Emek Ha'arazim, their neighbor and friend, a Palestinian person called only by his first name in the reports I found—Ismail—stood up against the mob and talked them away. That night he hid his eighteen Jewish neighbors in his house and gave them

The ruins of the Jewish village of Beit Talma. The village was deserted during the 1929 riots, its occupants saved by a Palestinian neighbor and smuggled into Jerusalem. (Photograph by Idit Wagner.)

Arab clothes with which to disguise themselves. The next morning they managed to flee to Jerusalem.[24]

What happened to Ismail after this? Did he live to see 1948? Did his family? Did he or his family regret the help he offered his Jewish neighbors in 1929? Beit Thulma does not exist anymore; only Emek Ha'arazim's story is told on the sign at the park. I told this story one day, when I rested at Einot Telem, to the Jewish wardens of the Arazim Valley and Jerusalem Park—within the jurisdiction of which the site is situated. Perhaps, they said, they would be able to edit the sign one day. One day . . .

Closer to here, in Motsa, the neighboring Jewish village of Qalunya and "present-day" (what a cliché, but a necessary one in this context . . .) Mevasseret, the story of 1929 is harsher, and involves a strong sense of *betrayal*. Perhaps this is why it is better known and more often told than the Emek Ha'arazim/Beit Thulma story. Perhaps this is why I, too, come here, to the mufti's house.

In Motsa, seven unarmed Jews, in the Maklef family house, the most out-lying Jewish house of Motsa, were brutally massacred by their Palestinian neighbors, with whom they believed they had friendly relations until then. The mukhtar (headman) of Qalunya promised the Jews of Motsa the day before the massacre that they would be protected and had no reason to be afraid. But this was to no avail. The Palestinian attackers were, according to a refugee from Qalunya, responding to the news/rumors from Jerusalem about a supposed Jewish attack and massacre of hundreds of Muslim worshipers at the Temple Mount, and about an alleged Jewish assault on the nearby Palestinian village of Lifta.[25] "In this manner, our village [Qalunya] was the first that practically expressed its belief that there is no other way but to strike iron with iron, and that armed action is the only way to reclaim our rights. And I will not exaggerate if I say that the residents of our village Qalunya are the first among the Arabs who have taken *military* initiative."[26]

Standing in front of the mufti's house in Qalunya and staring down at the Maklef house in Motsa (that house still remains there, although a different family has lived in it since 1930), I think about the complexity of the "situation" of Palestinians and Jews in this land. Here, a massacre. In Emek Ha'arazim/Beit Thulma, just a kilometer and a half to the northeast, friendship and rescue. I wonder what brought these men from Qalunya to fall upon their Motsa neighbors in such a manner, to murder Batya Maklef, a midwife that helped bring into this world many of the village's children, and mutilate the body of her daughter? I know that civil wars and intracommunal conflicts are terribly bloody and brutal. Israelis, too, have massacred Palestinians throughout the decades, either on their own private initiative or as soldiers who "just" followed their orders. I also assume that the Qalunya villagers must have been resentful toward the Motsa settlers for purchasing village lands not always in the fairest and most honest ways.[27] And I can imagine that the Jewish colonists' attitude toward the Palestinians was, at a minimum, touched by condescension. In the broader context, I know that the years prior to these events were characterized by increasing stress—economic, religious, political—between Jews and Arabs, and that Palestinian society felt the growing pressure of Jewish immigration and colonization of the land.[28] I can understand—but, of course, not condone—the background behind this brutal massacre. But once more I feel the inherent tension that exists between scholarly understanding of events and the emotional response that such events elicit in me, especially when I am out in the field, literally, so close to the place of actual bloodshed. I cannot *not* feel the sense of betrayal and anger, even though I rationally know that 1929 is long gone, in many senses.

I examine the exterior of the mufti's house. It has two levels, built of thick walls covered with hewn limestone. Two old olive trees grow at the entrance to the upper level, on each side of the doorstep (there is no door in the opening). Cypresses and pines, some of them quite old, almonds, cacti, and ailanthuses surround the house. Several large arched windows open in the walls. The windows have wide ledges and rusting steel shutters; some are open, as if someone just woke up, and some are closed, as if the occupants left and locked the house. None of the windows is glassed or has any remains of glass.

I enter the house, walking the bike beside me. I am alone here, no one is watching me, the house is semi-demolished. Where am I entering? The sense that this was someone's *home* is very strong. But this is not a home *anymore*; it is just a ruin that belongs to the state's Authority for Development, the organ of the Israeli government that is responsible for the lands and estates of the Palestinian "absentees." What, then, am I entering—a home or a ruin? Should I consider myself an interloper or an uninvited guest? Or is the question irrelevant now?

I cross the doorstep and, first, examine the ceiling. This is, after all, a half-demolished structure. The ceiling, where it still holds up, is supported by a cross vault. As far as I can tell, it will not collapse today . . . Little round holes in the walls, above the windows, probably let light and air in when the shutters were closed. The floor is covered with rubble from the partially destroyed ceiling and roof. A thick layer of plaster painted in azure-cyan crumbles from the walls. Blue was traditionally used in Palestinian houses to ward off the "evil eye," I recall from a line in a seminar paper on the politics of Islamic demonology written in my course Science Fiction, Fantasy, and Politics. The student wrote an analysis of Salman Rushdie's *The Satanic Verses* as part of the "real" and "imagined" worlds of demonology in Islamic culture and their political meanings. Well, in this house, the coloring did not help much, I think. Then again, the house still stands.

Underneath the azure plaster, on the walls, stones and dirt are tightly knitted together. No concrete or other industrial materials hold up the walls, just

Jerusalem limestone and dirt. Where the plaster has fallen, the exposed walls of dirt and stone seem, on the one hand, an elaborate work of masonry artisanship, and, on the other hand, the result of haphazard piling. There are no remains of furniture or other household stuff. They were probably looted many years ago. The sight of the empty house reminds me that Idit and I should soon start boxing our apartment's contents, as we soon depart with the kids for a sabbatical leave on Vancouver Island. It'll take much time to box all my books and take them down to our storage room, so the apartment will be ready for renting. I feel uneasy, sensing the fine line that separates a momentary refugee, who has time to pack hardly anything before leaving his house, and a secure and *fortunate* person like me, who can plan his leaving several months ahead, and also be able to return.

I look at the thick walls of the house, and the dirt/stone inner filling. Even though it is partially destroyed, it is still beautiful and gives a strong sense of belonging in the landscape. I try to picture the house's furnishing and think about the long summer afternoons in the dusty courtyard, under the old pines and cypresses. I imagine the mufti sitting here, receiving his guests, and then I recall the narration of Baruch Katinka, a Jewish construction engineer whose Jewish-Arab contracting company built the Palace Hotel in Jerusalem for the High Muslim Council of Palestine, which the mufti headed. Katinka and his partners also built a private house for the mufti (in which the mufti never actually dwelled, for he had to escape Palestine before the building was completed) in the Sheikh Jarrah neighborhood in Arab Jerusalem, very close to the Mt. Scopus campus. Katinka, who was at the time also a member of the Haganah, the main Jewish militia in Mandatory Palestine, tells in detail about the deep-seated hatred the Mufti felt toward the Jews, on the one hand, and, on the other hand, about his courteous and friendly relations with him, personally. "I was invited every year, as his private guest, to the [Muslim] Nebi Musa pilgrimage parades, and, on the last day of [the Jewish holiday of] Passover, the mufti even used to send to me a *hamutza*: a big plate of hot Arab pita breads, cheese, butter, olives, and honey, so that I would be able to dine on fresh leavened bread [upon the end of the holiday]."[29]

Passover this year ended just a few days ago. Although we don't keep Passover Kashrus in our home (we do eat *chametz*, "leavened food"), and I don't experience anymore my childhood anticipation for the end of Passover so that I'll be able to eat bread again, the thought of the *hamutza* at the end of the holiday

Inside Mufti Amin al Husayni's house. (Photograph by Idit Wagner.)

On the trail, outside the house of Mufti Amin al Husayni. (Photograph by Idit Wagner.)

stimulates my taste buds. I take a sandwich from my backpack and sit on the southern windowsill. While I eat my sandwich, I see just underneath the house a small dry creek in which, during one of my previous visits here, with Rotem Mor, at the end of this winter, rainwater ran. I recall Rotem's deep and sincere sorrow, no, it was agony and distress, about the destruction and depopulating of "beautiful Qalunya" when we explored this small creek and drank water from it. It is indeed a beautiful place, and the old black and white pictures of the village show a serene and homey rural community. But when Rotem yearningly said "beautiful Qalunya," and was so profoundly sad about the destruction of the village, sad in a heartbreaking and almost existential manner, as if he himself or his own family had lived there and were banned from returning, I felt estranged from him. "How could he be so, well . . . , so 'Palestinian,'" I thought. I remembered Meron Benvenisti's discussion of the post-1948 nationalization of the Palestinian landscape by Palestinian writers and their sympathizers, the glorification and idolization of the demolished and occupied landscape. This idolization is directed at a struggling Israeli-Zionist national identity using the same tools created by the latter: the worshiping of images and mythic physical features and "natural" landscapes.[30]

For many Palestinians, whether they are dispossessed refugees in the diaspora, occupied noncitizens in the "territories," or second-class citizens within Israel, the memories, myths, and images of the pre-1948 Palestinian landscape are indeed, as the title of Whalid Khalidi's book reads, All That Remains or almost all that remains.[31] But hearing Rotem embracing this discourse, I felt that he was trying to avoid, even run away from, his Israeliness by absolutely "buying-into" the no less idolizing narrative of Palestinian nationalism. At the same time, I envied him for his ability to connect wholeheartedly with something sublime and authentic—imagined as it was—as "beautiful Qalunya." For when he said "beautiful Qalunya," I imagined the "real" Qalunya of the 1930s and 1940s, based on my fleeting passages during army patrols in Palestinian villages in the south Hebron hills in the late 1980s and early 1990s. I thought about houses in which humans and livestock shared living spaces, sewage running open in the streets; no electricity; windows covered by leather sheets, not glass; meat hanging in front of butcher shops, in the open air with clouds of flies hovering around it; burning smoke from woodstoves used for cooking . . . But then I also thought about the stone-built thick-walled houses; the almond, fig, olive, and pine trees among the houses; the terraces; the clean and cool springs; the running creeks; and the narrow village trails trod by people for hundreds of years. Yes, I too could see "beautiful Qalunya."

But what about the *people* of the village, I think now. This is a *human* geography I love and feel connected to, even if the village has been demolished for more than six decades now. The trails on which I ride on these slopes, the figs I pick at the end of summer on my way back from campus, the terraces I admire, even this house of the mufti—all these are the inheritance of the people of Qalunya to me, an inheritance that was indeed forcefully imposed on them by Israel, my state (booty?! Is there such a thing as just conquest?). I cannot be hostile or even indifferent to these people—to love a place means also to feel for its people, for their history and present.

I finish my sandwich, come down from the windowsill, and look again at the house from the outside. The variable-sized, matte brown limestone that makes up its walls, the lichen that is attached to the outer stone walls, the trees that surround it, the scent of the field that enters through the openings, the view of the valley below. I can absorb almost the whole house and its details in a few looks. This ability to absorb the house in one glance is unlike the imperceptibility of modern buildings, including my own apartment building a few kilometers up the hill, this "residential machine," which is so big that you can never encompass it in one or two looks, only when you stand far away. I recall one of the few times I did encompass my residential machine in one look: this was a few months ago, when I visited Beit Surik, beyond the separation fence. From there, on the opposing ridge of Mevasseret, I was amazed by the view of the huge residential complex of Meron and Hermon Streets, where I live: seven-story-high buildings, with cascading levels built one on top the other, like big ziggurats or step pyramids (quite a common architectural feature in Jewish Jerusalem and its satellite towns). Dwarfing the hill on which they are built, the buildings protrude to the eye also because of the glaring white-polished limestone that covers them. The whole view reminded me of a fortress on the hill. I knew that there are various constraints and limitations when planning and building such "saturated housing projects" for hundreds of families. But I felt that the architects could have at least aspired to plan something that would continue the landscape and integrate with it, not rupture it and challenge the eye. Here, in the last house of Qalunya, the ability to behold the house in a few looks from so close, the house blending into the landscape, gives me a strong sense of intimacy with this place, even though I still feel like an uninvited guest and even though I am aware that I simplify this place into a symbol of authenticity.

While the pines, cypresses, and olives around the house are quite old and seem pre-1948, the ailanthuses are much younger. Ailanthus, an invasive species in this country (what to call it? Palestine? Eretz Yisrael?), arrived from Taiwan in the 1920s. The species also invaded the inner parts of the house, and several young ailanthuses grow within the rooms in which the roof is shattered. When I see these trees, I recall a conversation I had a few months ago with a Magav patrol team in the Arazim Valley. I asked them what or who they were looking for in their patrol, and they responded, "Shabachim" (Palestinian interlopers). We were resting in the shade of an ailanthus tree, and I mentioned that this tree, too, is an interloper, a *shabach*. "We should deport these trees too, then," one of the soldiers joked. But it is not that easy to "deport" the ailanthuses, which are an extremely invasive, hardy, and adaptive species. The whole valley below the mufti's house is occupied by ailanthuses. Occupation upon occupation, the ailanthuses are the agents of desolation that finish the work of demolition and marginalization. When I think about the images of this hill before 1948,[32] the ever expanding ailanthuses (they send out suckers that quickly develop into separate trees) become in my mind the strangling baobab trees in Antoine de Saint-Exupéry's *The Little Prince.*

But beyond being invaders and agents of desolation, here, and along other places on my trail to campus, ailanthuses provide thick and broad patches of shade. This is unlike the olives' small and the cypresses' narrow perimeters of shade, or the pines' wide and large circles of shade, which are nonetheless thin and porous, letting in the scorching rays of the sun during the flaming days of summer. On such days, I am happy when I pass with my bike under an ailanthus tree. I "collect" the shade and the momentary relief and coolness, and "store" them in my body for the continuation of the ride.

I don't know why this specific house was not completely ruined. Perhaps the Palmach force that occupied the village did not have enough explosives in 1948, or perhaps it was indeed the azure paint. Or, as a colleague told me not long ago, when we walked together along my trail, perhaps the bulldozer operator who leveled the ruins of the other houses here after that war had to go to relieve himself and forgot this house, and thus it remained standing. It may be that there was a more serious or rational reason for not completely demolishing the house. But I liked the ironic tone I thought I heard in my colleague's words. I liked it because, despite my aversion to the owner of the house, the house's supposed incidental survival challenged both the Palestinian idolization of the landscape *and* the one-dimensional and sometimes hypocritical mode of historical memory in Israel, this historical memory that aims to mold Israelis as a homogeneous and obedient self-righteous people who will gladly "serve" (read: sacrifice themselves, often in vain, for) their state. Here, just because of some trivial coincidence, a supposed abomination was left.[33]

The mufti was indeed an ally/client of the Nazis.[34] In 1937, he fled from Mandatory Palestine, realizing that the British held him accountable for the Arab revolt/uprising that erupted in 1936 (and lasted until 1939). Eventually settling in Berlin, he advanced Nazi propaganda and anti-Jewish incitement in the Arab world; was actively involved in recruiting thousands of Muslims from the Balkans to a division of the Waffen SS; personally met Hitler for an interview, in which the Nazi leader promised him that should Germany occupy the Middle East the first task would be to kill the Jews in Palestine; and tried to prevent the emigration of several thousands of Jewish children from Hungary, Bulgaria, and Romania to Palestine. He wrote to the foreign minister of Hungary in June 1943 that it would be better to send the Jewish children to a place where they would be "under active supervision, for example in Poland."[35]

After reading this about the mufti, after *absorbing* all this evil history in recent months,[36] I became ill for several days. Yet, I also noticed that in Israel his Nazi past is usually noted when mentioning him as a Palestinian leader, as certain Zionist historians and Israeli officials try to connect, sometimes equate, nazism and Palestinian nationalism. On the other hand, many other Nazis and Nazi sympathizers, often seniors, were, in effect, ignored by Israel when its interests favored this.[37] Thus, Amin al Husayni became Israel's "Last Nazi." This instrumentalization of the Holocaust attests to the "poverty of spirit and imagination that afflicts us all."[38]

Standing there, in the slowly decaying house of the mufti, which the "baobab" ailanthuses are slowly wearing down from within and without, and watching the slope of Qalunya through the open window, seeing the Maklef house down the hill, I sadly realize that perhaps the real irony is that it is *this* house, the house of the Last Nazi, that is the last remaining house of Qalunya. I understand that my coming to this house and my thoughts about it are actually a manifestation of my desire not to fear the memory of this village. My default instinct, as a product of the Israeli culture of conflict, is to assume that the house and the village it was a part of are a supposed "proof" of Palestinian brutality and deep-seated hatred and anti-Semitism, even before the occupation of 1967, the original sin, according to the Zionist political Left. For the Maklefs were not armed settler-occupiers as the Israeli settlers of the West Bank are today, and the Palestinian national movement hardly ever denounced the mufti's Nazi past.[39] If ever, the mufti was marginalized in Palestinian historiography mainly because of his poor leadership in the 1948 war, which eventually led to the Palestinian defeat, the Nakba. But then I think, perhaps it is this poor leadership, and, more generally, the low level of political organization of Palestinian society during the 1948 war, that "endears" the mufti so much to the Israelis. Having had national leaders, inept as they were, the Palestinians are created in the Israeli popular and political (though not always the academic) discourse as a coherent and unified society that willfully obeyed the orders of its Nazi-inclined leaders to wage war on the supposedly pragmatic Jewish Yishuv. Yet, unlike Zionism,

Palestinian nationalism was not highly developed in 1948. Various local Palestinian communities had different interests, not always corresponding to the hypothetical clear and unambiguous dictates of nationalism. Some were bent on fighting the Jews; others, like the villagers of Deir Yassin in western Jerusalem, concluded local peace or nonaggression pacts with the Zionist leadership or their immediate Jewish neighbors. Most of the Palestinians were very reluctant to live under Jewish sovereignty, but most of them also did not want to fight and were tragically dragged into the conflict.[40] Here, in Qalunya, there was in April 1948 a dispatch of the Arab Deliverance Army that harassed the transportation route to Jerusalem, and some of the villagers attacked Motsa's school. But in early January 1948 the villagers also "chased away an [Arab] armed band and prevented it from 'doing anything.'"[41]

Indeed, the Mufti and his aides often pressured and even used terrorist methods in their efforts to make Palestinian communities adopt or accede to active belligerence toward their Jewish neighbors. But this, again, shows the messy and complex nature of the 1948 war's intracommunal dimension. For the Israelis, it is convenient, nonetheless, to ascribe many acts of aggression and ethnic cleansing that were performed by them in 1948 to the fact that the Palestinians unanimously and enthusiastically "chose" to follow the lead of fundamentalist and evil leaders such as the mufti or heed their leaders' supposed call to escape their villages.

But I know that just as it is easy for Israelis—me included—to cling on to the memory of the Last Nazi or the memory of the raging 1929 mob, it is no less important to think about Qalunya as a living village that existed here for hundreds of years, if not more (the origins of the village are apparently in Roman times, when the Tenth Legion's veterans were given land here to establish a colony, and hence the name Qalunya, which preserves the Roman Colonia).[42] There were in it people who loved, raised families, worked the land, and marveled at the landscape of these hills for many generations. The story of the village does not pertain solely to the Israeli or Jewish "period." Suddenly it strikes me: the mufti ran into exile in 1937 (and died in Beirut in 1974). Who lived in the house in the eleven years between his escape and the 1948 war? And why do I call this place "the mufti's house" when it is logical to assume that other people, too, shared the house with him? At least one of them, I hope, was not a "Nazi." . . .
I realize that precisely by coming to this house, and viewing the Maklef house from its window, I declare my wish to remember Qalunya, to keep its presence

in this landscape, so that such an all-out war as the 1948 war, a war that resulted in the smashing of a whole society, will never recur.

The demolished and depopulated Palestinian villages scare me. Perhaps I am thinking as usual from the privileged place of the victorious side, from a standpoint of hegemony and relative security, or just from historical misreading. Yes, I know that had the Palestinians and their Arab state allies won the 1948 war, it might have been the other way around—that the Jewish Yishuv might have been depopulated and demolished. The mufti had shown his willingness to join the worst enemies of the Jews, and there were open discussions among Arab states about a jihad and slaughtering the Jews of Palestine. The Holocaust, which ended only three years before these events, made it very clear that the Jewish people needed a safe haven. But why at the expense of the Palestinians? Why not in Sitka, Alaska,[43] or somewhere in British Columbia, I half joke with myself, and half not, recalling a science fiction novel I teach in my class and a conversation I had a few years ago with a University of British Columbia political scientist who told me very earnestly that he is sure that should there be a real threat of the extermination of Israel, the Canadian government would "make room" for us in BC.

The complex politics of the mufti, the Arab countries' leaders, the Zionist Yishuv establishment, the British, and the other Great Powers; the endless debates between historians on individual and collective liability and responsibility up to 1948; the Alaska/BC "options," all this suddenly seems so close and immediate, so heavily felt, on the one hand, and so remote and unrelated, on the other hand, when I stand here on this familiar and beautiful slope, in this house that I feel is so alien and yet so natural to me. I suddenly feel worn out, in my body. Where will I muster the strength to continue the ride to campus today, as I am just at the beginning of the trail, close to Mevasseret? I think about the book I will write, the many ways in which it might anger or hurt so many people who know what "really" happened, who was/is right, and who was/is wrong. I imagine the solemn and angry faces of experts and historians and their adherents, "on both sides," a cliché I so often repeat during my classes on campus, to keep my students at bay, to keep myself at bay. War is always a tragedy and a cliché/ farce at the same time, and often only in retrospect and after seeing the "broad context" can one appreciate more fully what happened. But what scares me right now is simply the ease with which these old and deep-rooted Palestinian villages were destroyed. "When I left, sappers were blowing up the houses. One after another, the solid stone buildings ... exploded and crashed," says Harry Levin, a Jewish American journalist who accompanied the Palmach force on the night of the battle here in Qalunya. "One after another, *the solid stone buildings... exploded and crashed,*" Levin's words echo in my mind.[44]

As I stand in front the mufti's crumbling stone house, my bicycle beside me, and as I watch the slope where once there was a village, I feel how such village houses failed to provide the protection that their thick and organic walls seemed to have promised. Then I think, perhaps the Israelis demolished all these houses in Qalunya and in hundreds of other Palestinian deserted/depopulated villages during and after the 1948 war, not only due to the usual military reasons that are often cited (that is, to prevent the Palestinian and Arab forces from recapturing these villages and using them once more as bases for attacks on Jewish transportation and localities) or due to "development" needs after the war. Of course, there was also a desire to prevent the refugees from returning or even harboring a hope of return: the places they knew as their homes were destroyed. But these village houses—they were so native and so historical in the sense that the knowledge needed to build them went far back in time. The masonry artisanship was a natural part of the land, creating a human landscape that was continuous and blended into the hills. Once their owners were driven away or prevented from returning after their escape, perhaps the houses themselves were a reminder of the fact that much of the land on which the Jewish state was established was conquered and that even such an organic, native landscape is no guarantee of communal survival. Territories that only a few years ago were the home, with all the deep meanings of this word, of an other society, which had lived here for centuries, were taken—indeed, not without a heavy human toll for the Jewish Yishuv—in a relatively short time. Perhaps destroying these villages stemmed also from awe and fear of conquerors, of a generation of settlers.

Tears come to my eyes when I think about that "generation of settlement" of 1948, with which I so much identify yet also feel estranged from. I take my class notes from my backpack—in today's afternoon class I want to talk with the students about the subject of revenge. I sit on the ground in the shade of an ailanthus, and read the famous words of Moshe Dayan, the chief of the IDF general staff, in his April 1956 eulogy for Roee Rothberg, a young man killed by Palestinians at the Gaza border.

Why should we complain about their fierce hatred of us? Eight years they have been sitting in refugee camps in Gaza, and before their eyes we turn into our possession the land and villages in which they and their ancestors dwelt. Not from the Arabs of Gaza, but from ourselves we should claim the blood of Roee. How did we shut our eyes from looking squarely at our fate and from seeing the destiny of our generation in its full cruelty? ... Beyond the borderline surges a sea of hatred and desire for revenge, which is looking forward to the day when serenity will dull our vigilance, to the day when we will listen to the ambassadors of harassing hypocrisy, who call upon us to lay down our weapons. To us, and only to us, cries out the blood of Roee from his torn body. For we have sworn a thousand times that our blood will not be spilled in vain, and yesterday we were fooled again, we listened and believed. Our reckoning today is with ourselves, we are a generation of settlement, and without the steel helmet and the muzzle, we will not be able to plant a tree and to build a house. We should not be deterred from seeing the animosity that foments and fills the lives of hundreds of thousands of Arabs who sit around us. Let us not turn away our eyes, lest our hand will weaken. This is the predestination of our generation. This is the choice of our lives—to be ready and armed, strong and determined, or that the sword will be dropped from our fist and our lives will be cut off.

Dayan was right in identifying the causes of Palestinian ("Arab") hatred and resentment in his time. His militaristic worldview about the never-relenting need to be ready and armed, is shared—even enshrined—by many Israelis today too. I know that on a certain level and in a certain kind of political reality, he was correct. *Si vis pacem, para bellum* (if you wish for peace, prepare for war). But the problem is that we have prepared too much for war, and almost given up on peace. Ignoring—and worse still, actively making people forget the disaster the Palestinians suffered in 1948—will prevent Israelis from a recognition that is the first step toward peace with them in whatever kind of solution to the conflict. No Israeli official will dare to say today that "we turn[ed] into our possession the land and villages in which they and their ancestors dwelt," because the land was always ours by historical and/or divine right, and it was empty or invaded by Arab occupiers/illegal immigrants from other countries in the Middle East, wasn't it?[45] Today Dayan would be immediately categorized as an "anti-Zionist" and marginalized politically. Yet such dullness and deliberate ignorance, which come from Israeli realism that is mixed with pain and fear, and perhaps shame too, continue to contribute their share to Palestinian frustration and prevent healing or at least a closing of the wound of 1948 simply by pretending that such a wound does not—should not—exist. Forgetting and erasing the memory of the Nakba as a moment of founding violence, a la Walter Benjamin, also means not recognizing the disaster that made *us*, Israelis, into a people of conquerors that still live on their swords and who came to cherish this way of living.[46] Forgetting the Nakba, as a human tragedy, before even thinking about its concrete political causes and implications, means that we perpetuate our identity as conquerors. "We are born to be conquerors," I mutter to myself.

I hope I am not an "ambassador of harassing hypocrisy" now, I think as I mount the bike and pedal away from the ruined estate. I turn my head for a last look, for this visit, at the house. Then I feel the unresolved tension between my desire for authenticity and nativelike connection and knowledge of the land, on the one hand, and my being a product of the politics of occupation, exclusion, and dispossession, on the other hand. I feel the tension between my wish for an apolitical human and personal mutual contact, recognition, and understanding and the all-encompassing conflictual political context, in time and space, from which this wish stems from the outset. I feel my fear of the "sea of hatred and revenge," as well as my fear of living in a society that fetishizes the "steel helmet and the muzzle." Is there a way to break this vicious circle?

Chapter Four

RIDING TO QALUNYA, PART II
L'Hôte

May 10, 2011: We Are Both from the Same Village . . .

It is Israel's Independence Day today. Independence Day always invokes in me
a sense of stress. It comes a week after Holocaust Memorial Day and only a day
after the War Dead Remembrance Day. It is the culmination of a week of nationalistic and militaristic commemoration, in which I always feel that there is
hardly any escape from the heavy pressure of all the sanctified commemoration
rituals. It is as if a blanket of orchestrated—but at the same time, sincere and
deeply internalized by so many citizens—agony and ceremonial pathos covers
the country. Anyone who refuses to or simply feels they cannot participate in
the public demonstrations and exhibitions of uniform and sacred grief (like, for
example, ultra-orthodox Jews or Palestinian Israelis, who, for different reasons,
don't always stop everything they do and stand still during the commemoration
siren—an act that is one of the central litmus tests of being a "true" and "loyal"
Israeli) is shunned and denounced for being a "dissident," "defiant," or merely a
social "parasite." These are not days for doubts and serious questions about the
causes of war and the lack of peace or about any other meaning of the Holocaust for current times except the need to be strong in the face of the constant
(and partially Orwellian 1984-like) "existential threat" that Israel still faces (in
recent years, read: Iran).

The same applies to nonparticipation in the almost mandatory rituals of jubilation during Independence Day. As evening falls and the War Dead Remem-

brance day ends, Independence Day starts with an extravaganza of fireworks and street carnivals, and with almost everybody barbequing on their decks or in parks, and, in fact, in any other available corner (including roundabouts and side-walks). The feeling that you have to be sad and grieving and then, in a matter of a few hours, change your skin and be joyful and celebratory—in public—always creates in me a strong opposition. Moreover, the inability to escape all this, as the private and public spaces are invaded and colonized by the state and its "loyal" citizens/believers, generates in me also deep frustration and estrangement.

But today, nonetheless, we are going to have an Independence Day picnic. Idit's friend Ma'ayan (pseudonym) called yesterday evening, just as they finished the fireworks on Mt. Herzl, where the central Independence Day ceremony takes place, and asked if we were "doing something tomorrow." She suggested that we join their family for a picnic. We said ok; it's better to be outside than to be crammed with the kids in our apartment, without being able to open any window due to the heavy barbeque smoke that will engulf the entire tenement. Perhaps we can find some quiet spot near Mevasseret, "far from the madding crowd." I suggested we go to Ain Lauza, the spring in wadi Lauza that I discovered after riding to Nabi Samwil last year. That spring is now a place I often wander off to with the bike to reflect quietly. I thought that it would be nice and quiet there, beyond the Green Line indeed, in a place hardly known to anyone. Ma'ayan was a bit reluctant—is it safe there? She and her husband Nissim (pseudonym) are on the extreme political Right. Nonetheless, they rarely venture into the "territories," mainly due to personal security fears. I explained to her that I often rode to this spring during recent months, that the spring is on the "Israeli side" of the separation fence, and that the region is constantly monitored by security cameras and patrolled by Magav. There would not be any trouble, I promised. This satisfied her, and we agreed to meet there at 10:00 a.m.

I went ahead with my bicycle. I wanted to be there early—perhaps someone else would "occupy" the (already occupied) place before us, despite its relative anonymity (those "Gideonite" settlers, perhaps . . .). When I arrived, there were three Magav soldiers patrolling the wadi, to make sure that no Palestinian "interlopers" entered Israel on Independence Day. As they were about to continue their patrol, Ma'ayan and her family arrived, in their car. "You see, I told you it's safe here," I said, pointing to the soldiers, who smiled contentedly. I felt ironic, but I don't think that Ma'ayan or the soldiers perceived my irony.[1]

The dirt road in the wadi, which until a few months ago was relatively narrow and partially rugged, is now hard packed and wide, and cars, too, can drive on it easily. The reason for this change is that the wadi was turned into a work site of the Israel Railway Company, which is now constructing a new railway line between Tel Aviv and Jerusalem. The new line will replace the old Ottoman-laid track that winds its way up to Jerusalem along the Soreq riverbed. Instead of almost two hours on the old track (hardly anyone uses it), travel on the new track should take only twenty-eight minutes, the railway company boasts. Six kilometers out of the fifty-seven-kilometer-long new track will pass through the Occupied Territories. Of those six kilometers, several hundred meters will be in tunnels and a bridge under and over the lands of the villages of Beit Surik and Beit Iksa, the villages located just above this wadi—to the west and east, respectively.[2] Here, in wadi Lauza, the tunnel that comes from Beit Surik's direction will emerge from the slope and the track will cross the wadi on a bridge that will then enter another tunnel, underneath Beit Iksa's land. This small infringement in the Occupied Territories here was a result of pressure laid on the Israel Railway Company by the residents of the Reches Halilim neighborhood in Mevasseret, who demanded that the tunnels' portals be moved north of the wadi below their houses (houses that are tangent to the Green Line), due to the expected noise and air pollution during the construction work and after the activation of the railway line. On the other hand, an appeal to the High Court of Justice by residents from Beit Iksa to stop the work was rejected, mainly, the court said, due to a delay in filing it.[3]

The digging and infrastructure works turned the peaceful and secluded wadi, with its beautiful olive groves and ancient terraces and *qasrs* (watchman's huts), into a site where the sovereign shows its might, "just for the sake of it," says Rotem Mor. The works reflect a mode of thinking that considers the land as the total possession of the sovereign, of the occupier, who not only may transform and mold it at will but also has the perceived right to, physically, trample it. The fast track to Jerusalem was exposed to countless critiques regarding its economic necessity and its physical planning. The railway company, a government owned company, admitted that it could have tunneled the whole segment in the Jerusalem Corridor area, thus avoiding the harm to this wadi and another one—the Black Canyon in Nahal Yitla, a pristine wadi at the foot of the Jerusalem hills (within Israel of the Green Line). But because the work has already begun, any change of plan will cause unpredictable setbacks, and therefore they should stick to the original plans of long and massive bridges across the wadis between the several tunnels. Logical and not impossible to understand, one may surmise, especially when taking into account the huge financial investment and the complex set of contractors and subcontractors that the railway company hired for this project. However, at the same time, this is a mode of thinking that reveals a very violent concept of custodianship of space. If one has the capability to mold and transform the landscape by means of massive digging and construction, and if nonetheless one does not realize this potential, then this becomes a wasted opportunity.

As Ma'ayan and Nissim, and their two children (they are the same ages as our children [four and eight years old], and have known them since infancy), unpack their picnic baskets, I tell Nissim how sad I am about the destruction of this wadi. The spring and its close surroundings remain an island of green and beauty within the rocky, exposed slope that the bulldozers' teeth created here as preparation for the opening of the tunnel's portal just above our heads on the hill. More digging will come soon, for the massive concrete legs of the bridge. Yet, the railway company dug out and moved several old olive trees from the slope into the bed of the wadi, and thus enabled the High Court of Justice to reject the appeal of the villagers of Beit Iksa not only by arguing that they delayed in filing it but also by proving that no damage was being done to the appellants' trees. The company promised to return the trees to their original place once the construction work is finished, or to compensate the owners should the trees die. The trees are watered now around the clock with pipes that were laid especially for this purpose from the groundwater pump at Ainot Telem, five hundred meters southward within Israel of the Green Line. "The Occupation at Your Service," they should have put such a sign here . . .

Nissim becomes uneasy when I tell him about the many planning errors that could have been avoided had the railway company and the government been more attentive to the various appeals and reservations of different "green" and civil society groups that objected to the route. I also mention the absurdity of the railway company's claim that the track will "one day" fork to Ramallah, and that therefore the track is not to be considered a violation of the occupied population's rights, for it will serve it too. "Why do you find this absurd?" Nissim asks. I hesitate for a moment. After all, if indeed the track will be connected to Ramallah, this might be very good thing. "Well," I respond, "because for this to happen, they will first have to dismantle the separation fence. Do you see that happening any time soon?"

Nissim says that he doesn't, and in fact, that he hopes they will never dismantle the fence. His mother was badly injured a few years ago, when a suicide bomber exploded himself in the Ma'hne Yehuda marketplace in Jerusalem. She suffers terrible pains to this very day. At any rate, he says, he's definitely in favor of the railway line, and thinks that "every modern state" should have such a fast track. "And the harm to the landscape will be minimal, eventually, when they do the restoration work here. You tell yourself that they even carefully moved the trees," he says. I want to tell him that I didn't say they transplanted the trees so *carefully*—a few days ago I was here and saw that they used heavy bulldozers to dig the trees out, not a designated crane and soil-sawing tools that exist for this purpose. But before I say this, Idit and our kids arrive in our car, and this puts an end to the conversation about the train.

The children are happy to see each other and begin playing and running among the trees and the terraces that the bulldozers spared. Idit and Ma'ayan set out the picnic and Nissim seizes the opportunity to quit the uncomfortable talk. He begins to make a small bonfire in which to roast potatoes. I rest in the shade of the olive tree that grows near the spring. Everything looks calm, and I recall my promise to Idit not to bring up politics during the meeting. Ok, I tell myself, I should let go a bit, at least for the sake of the children—and not to ruin the nice day for them.

This is the first time we have met with Ma'ayan and Nissim for two months. The previous time, an angry debate erupted regarding the 1948 war. Ma'ayan repeated the well-established, popular Zionist narrative that in 1948, Israel was defending itself and barely managed to gain independence after thwarting the armies of seven Arab countries. She was very upset when I told her that this is what I was brought up on too (we're about the same age), but that I had discovered, after reading more "serious history," that following the initial stage of the war, which was indeed a defensive one, Israel fought a war of occupation and committed many acts of ethnic cleansing, and that the invading Arab armies were inferior in military method, lacked motivation, and, eventually, were low in numbers and the quality and quantity of their armaments. It was not exactly the heroic story of "the few against the many" that is taught in Israeli schools and repeated in the media. "I know you know more than me, historically," she replied, "but I know that I'm right, nonetheless." That ended the debate.

Idit was not angry with me after this talk, but she asked that I not bring up politics with Ma'ayan and Nissim again. "But *I am* a political scientist; how can I avoid talking about what I am?" I protested. She knows that, but she and Ma'ayan have managed to preserve their friendship over the years *only* by avoiding politics. As I recall this, we suddenly hear the roar of jet planes and the rumble of helicopters in the sky. Four El Al (Israel's national airline) Boeing passenger jets and four IDF air force gunships slowly pass over our heads in a structured formation, heading west toward the Tel Aviv metropolitan area: the "Independence Day Flyover." I am amazed—not by the flyover itself, which I don't find that impressive. Rather, this is the first time I have seen this kind of overt cooperation. While the joint flyover of the air force and the commercial airline is a thing that can make sense, as many of the airline's pilots and chief executives are former fighter pilots ("our finest lads") and as anyone who has flown El Al and experienced the security interrogations before boarding the plane can tell, the joint flyover still symbolizes in a very crude manner the mix between the civilian and military spheres in this country. The children stop their game and run to us. Ma'ayan is looking up at the sky and, excitingly, tells the kids, hers and mine, "Look, it's the air force flyover!" Her eight-year-old exclaims, "Wow, those are Cobra helicopters!" "No," his father corrects him, solemnly, "Apaches." As the jets and helicopters pass on, Idit and I remain silent. "So what," I hear my four-year-old daughter saying, "we too will fly in an airplane to Tanaga [she meant Canada] soon." "What corps will you be in the army?" Ma'ayan's son asks my son. "I want to go to the paratroopers, like my dad," he continues. "I don't want to go to the army; my father says it sucks," my son replies, sincerely, and they happily return to their bug search among the stones.

A few minutes pass, and we adults keep ourselves busy with the bonfire and the potatoes. Suddenly we see a group of about twelve people coming up the trail. As they approach, we can tell they are Palestinians. Ma'ayan looks at me reproachfully—I said it was safe here ... Nissim stands up and holds the wooden stick with which he was handling the fire and the potatoes. I keep sitting on a stone in the shade of the olive. "They know it's Independence Day; they came here on purpose today, to tease and defy, to declare ownership," Nissim says. The Palestinians near, and we see that they are a group with several adults and children. They greet us with "Shalom," in Hebrew, and go to the opposite side of the spring. There is no fear in their conduct, they speak loudly in Arabic,[4] and I can see why Nissim thinks they came to "tease and defy." Obviously, these people came to make a point here, I concur with Nissim's view. Then I recall that Rotem told me recently that on Independence Day, many Palestinians tour the country too, visiting their demolished villages and forfeited and occupied lands, because for them it is the unofficial Nakba Day. The official Nakba Day is May 15, the day when the British Mandate in Palestine ended and Israel declared its independence (in 1948). But many Palestinians get a day off on Israel's Independence Day, which is celebrated not according to the Gregorian calendar but according to the Hebrew moon calendar—on the fifth of the month of Iyar—because they work for Jewish employers, who close their businesses during this day. The Hebrew and Gregorian calendars rarely match, and so the Palestinians get to mark, in effect, two Nakba Days. *Two* Nakba Days, I think. At least "we" mark only one Holocaust Memorial Day and one War Dead Remembrance Day.

I go to them, smiling, and welcome them, offering some of our food. "You know," the older among them, he looks to be in his early seventies, tells me after taking a pita with hummus from me and as we sit under a tree, "this place is in our village's land." I hear pride and self-confidence in his voice, and I know that some time ago I, too, would have considered his tone "defiant." "Oh, so you're from Beit Iksa," I say, with some guilt, thinking about the rejected HCJ appellants. After all, *we* are the interlopers today. "No, no, we're from Motza," he answers. "What do you mean from Motza? There are no Arabs in Motza," I am quick to respond. Then I realize, "Oh, you're from Qalunya, right?" And immediately I add, "We're from Mevasseret." The man's eyes shine with excitement. He extends his hand to shake mine. "Come, come," he calls, in Arabic, and the others to join us, "he's from our village!" Four or five men come nearer, including one who films the scene with a video camera. The elder man, who still holds and shakes my hand, tells me, "My name is Taher (pseudonym), I was born in Qalunya and was four years old when we turned refugees. My grandfather was the mukhtar [headman] of the village. After 1967, I worked for many years in Mevasseret, as a truck driver, at the quarry. Our family, we live now in East Jerusalem, in Jabel Mukabber." I am impressed by his openness and feel his need to talk. He treats me as if indeed we are both from the same village. I tell him my name, and turn to find my four-year-old daughter. Taher is asking me now how long we have lived in Mevasseret. "Only five and a half years," I reply. "And before that?" he asks, somewhat disappointed. "Oh, I was born and raised in Jerusalem." And then I add, smiling, in Arabic, "In al Quds" (القدس, literally, "the Holy," Jerusalem's name in Arabic. The Israeli state Hebraized the name to Urshalim [al Quds]). He smiles too. My Arabic is rudimentary, and he notices this immediately.

We continue talking, in Hebrew. "Why did you think we're from Beit Iksa," another elderly man joins the conversation. "This is my brother," Taher steps in. "Because you said it's your village land here, and this is, in fact, Beit Iksa's land." "No, no, this land belongs to our village. I clearly remember coming here as a child," Taher says, decisively, but I insist, "No, believe me, I know, I am writing a book on this area." Why do I insist on this territorial accurateness, when I see that he is so excited? Perhaps this is my way of dealing with *my* excitement— this is the first time I have met a refugee from Qalunya. Knowing how much village identity and property are important in Palestinian society, I don't want him to think that I have "invaded" *his* land. Then I tell them that I actually know quite a lot about their village. "Can we film you?" a younger man, perhaps twenty-five years old, who holds the video camera, inquires. "What for?" I ask, with some apprehension. "We're just making a documentary about our village," he replies. "It's ok, he's my nephew," Taher steps in again. "I study economics at Mt. Scopus," the young man says. "I am Murad" (pseudonym). He smiles at me, and then adds, "Professor, don't you recognize me? I took your intro to IR course three years ago." Unfortunately, I don't recognize him; there were more than two hundred students in that class . . . But this helps to dissipate the apprehension I felt. Now I too feel that we're from the same village . . .

Nissim approaches us. He was standing a few meters away until now. He looks me directly in the eyes, and says, "Please tell them not to film my family." "Of course," Murad says, but Nissim does not respond to him. I feel his contempt for what I'm doing now, and I regret it. Yet I really want to talk with these people. My son, seeing a video camera, comes, excited, and sits in my lap. He's seen me several times before being photographed during interviews, and he wants to be a part of the happening too.

"Can you tell us anything about how our village was demolished?" asks Taher's brother (who still has not introduced himself). "What village, Dad?" my son interposes. "I'll tell you about it once," I say to him, and to Taher's brother, "Do you remember the event?" "No, I was born after that war," he replies. "And do you?" I ask Taher. "Yes, of course, I remember how my mother and me and my brothers ran away . . ." "Oded," Idit suddenly calls me, "please come for a moment." "Could you excuse me for a minute?" I say and go to Idit with my son. Idit is standing with Ma'ayan at the opposite side of the spring's pool. "Oded, this is really inappropriate now, with the children and Ma'ayan and Nissim here," she says. Ma'ayan and Nissim move away to the bonfire. "I see you're excited," she continues, "but tell them that you will talk with them some other time." "But they are refugees from Qalunya," I reply. "Take their phone number," she says.

I return to the group. "I'm sorry, but it seems that this is not the best time to talk. Could I take your phone number, and we'll continue this later?" Murad takes out his cell phone, and says, "Give me your number. I'll call you." "Ok," I say and give him the number. My home number.

I return to the families and sit close to the bonfire, looking at the embers that roast the potatoes. Nissim is standing next to me, silent. I see the Palestinians talking among themselves, quietly now, and then they start leaving the spring, returning toward the Green Line and Arazim Valley. We wave good-bye to each other. As "East Jerusalemites" (another Israeli-invented/imposed category), and unlike Palestinians from the West Bank itself, they are permanent residents of Israel (but, in contrast to "Israeli Arabs," they don't have full citizenship). Thus, they enjoy the same mobility rights that Israeli citizens enjoy within Israel. They, too, can pass back and forth across the Green Line, at will. I wonder whether the patrolling Magav team, which will surely stop and check them down the trail, is aware of this—that they are allowed to *enjoy* mobility, not just be entitled to it.

Ten minutes later, when they are no longer seen, I decide to ride after them and continue the talk not in front of the children and Ma'ayn and Nissim. I feel an urgent need to continue the conversation with them. I tell Idit, quickly mount the bike, and start pedaling toward the wadi's mouth. But it seems that the earth has swallowed them. There is no sign of them along the trail, nor in the Arazim Valley. I desperately look in all directions, on the slopes of the hills, on the trail, in (the crowded with picnickers) trickling Ainot Telem springs, but in vain. I feel a big missed opportunity. They disappeared like Qalunya itself, I think. Who knows if they'll really call me. I turn my bike back, and return to Ain Lauza. When I return, Ma'ayan and Nissim say they have to leave soon. The ambience is grim.

I rode back through the Halilim wadi. Idit and the kids returned with the car. The heat was intense, but I did not care. I was deep in my thoughts, trying to process the events in Ain Lauza. I arrived about half an hour after them. "You groveled before those Palestinians," Idit told me after I took a shower. "And you also alienated Ma'ayan and Nissim, again." Her voice was sad, and at the same time matter-of-factly dry, as if she was just mentioning a fact. She understands my excitement—she has come to Qalunya with me several times, and she knows all my dilemmas and burdens. But for her, the conflict in this land is much heavier, literally, than for me. While I unload this burden in my notebooks, talk about it with my students (even though most of them are not too happy about this . . .), or vent my fear and sorrow on the bike trails, she has not found yet the means that will enable her to ease the weight that this culture of violence puts on her heart. The only way she sees for us to live at peace with ourselves is to emigrate.

Was I groveling before the Palestinians, I kept thinking that night. I was surely very agitated before they came—the usual stress I feel on Independence Day, the tension that arises during every meeting with Ma'ayan and Nissim, the El Al and air force flyover, the children's conversation . . . Yet, I don't think I was humbling myself when Taher's group arrived. At least, I did not *want* to humble myself. I sensed a challenging posture on their side, the supposed audacious and teasing "defiance" that Nissim talked about. But I did not interpret this posture as infuriating or unbecoming. First, I was sorry that we went to Ain Lauza today. We could have gone instead to the Giv'at Ram campus of the Hebrew University—a gated compound with wide green lawns and flowering, colorful gardens among the laboratories and other natural science buildings. (This is the home campus of the faculty of mathematics and sciences. Mt. Scopus is the home of the social sciences, law, and the humanities.) Only university employees and students are regularly allowed into the university's campuses. (Others require a special permit from the security department—this has been the policy since the 2002 terrorist bombing of the Frank Sinatra cafeteria at Mt. Scopus.) We had picnicked in Giv'at Ram many times before, with Ma'ayn and Nissim too, but somehow I wanted to be today in the "real" outdoors but also to remain close to home, to Mevasseret, without getting stuck in the never-ending traffic jams of Independence Day. And in a sense, I also wanted to be abroad, out of Israel, so to speak. Ain Lauza, the separation fence that looms above it notwithstanding, seemed, at the same time, more open and secluded, literally beyond the Green Line—not in "Israel proper" and more authentic than the carefully gardened Giv'at Ram campus. The trickling spring, the dark green olive trees, the beautiful agricultural terraces, the ruined Crusader farmhouse in the background (I thought this would interest Nissim—he is an amateur archaeologist), and the yellowing thistles and weeds of early summer–late spring, they all allured me much more than Giv'at Ram's evergreen and generously watered gardens.

But when Taher's group arrived, I knew that because we were now in the occupied territories, at least in the "official" occupied territories (that is, unlike Israel "proper," where an unofficial military regime applies), it was we who were actually defying or challenging him and his family, they who for that matter became in my eyes, at least for a moment, the representatives of the noncitizens of this country. Their "defiance," then, struck me as a response to *our* uninvited presence there, especially when Taher said that the land there belongs to his village and I thought that he was talking about the neighboring Beit Iksa. I felt I needed to stress that we were just peaceful visitors on a picnic, that we had not come to take possession of the place in any forceful manner. True, I managed to convince Ma'ayan to come to this spring, from the outset, only thanks to the machinery of the occupation that controls this environment (Magav, the separation fence, and the surveillance cameras). Yet it was just because I wanted a quiet sanctuary from Independence Day and all that accompanies it. This is also why I chose a place I could ride to with the bike through the mountain trails, to evade Independence Day's commotion. I felt that even though Ain Lauza does not belong to me legally and politically, I belong in it, emotionally. When the Palestinians came today, I sensed the intense tension between me and my family and friends' presence here, a presence made possible, on the one hand, mainly thanks to the occupation regime that grants us protection and privileged rights and, on the other hand, by my sense of connectedness to this place.

I wanted to do the seemingly impossible: to distance, differentiate, myself from the symbols of Israeli coercion and militarism that were all around there: the Magav patrol on the ground, the colonial railway tunnel and bridge works that destroyed the landscape and consumed the hills from within, and the air force and El Al flyover that dominated the sky only a few minutes before Taher's group arrived. When I learned that Taher was in fact from Qalunya, I experienced a further mix of emotions and feelings: surprise to discover a real human being from Qalunya even if he was only four years old when he left the village (did he really remember his escape from there?); a wish to learn what happened to him and his family after the war; sympathy and care toward the small child, whose family and he had fled from the village; fear of this "living heritage" of the village and his almost explicit claim to the "right of return"; and, at the same time, a hope to somewhat rectify things by salvaging Qalunya's erased memory and in this way (and only in this way?) give it some life. I wasn't groveling. I was struggling to normalize an inherently abnormal situation and reality, to normalize a torn political self, and to reconcile fear and hope.

May 18, 2011

Rotem Mor and I are sitting in the living room of Raja and Nabeela Ibn-Daud
(pseudonyms) in the Sheikh Jarrah neighborhood in East Jerusalem. They are
refugees from Qalunya, in their mid- and early seventies, respectively. Rotem
came to know them through his involvement with the "Sheikh Jarrah Solidarity" group—a joint Jewish-Palestinian movement that conducts weekly antiset-
tler demonstrations and vigils in this neighborhood, an area in which a Jewish
religious settler society is claiming to have pre-1948 property rights. The settlers are basing their legal claim on an Israeli law of 1970, which allows Jewish
Israelis to reclaim previously owned lands and properties in what was between
1948 and 1967 Jordanian-ruled Jerusalem. No parallel law exists with respect
to Palestinian-owned properties in post-1948 Israeli-ruled Jerusalem. Three
Palestinian families have been evicted so far from their houses. The settler society plans to evict more residents and build a compound of two hundred apartments. The house of Raja and Nabeela is one of the houses that the settlers
have their eyes on, says Raja. They fear that some time in the future, eviction
procedures will be opened against them too.

It is a one-floor house, a not too big rectangular structure, covered with pro-
cessed limestone plates, with wide straps of cement in between. This neighborhood was built by the Jordanian government in the 1950s to settle the refugees
from various villages around Jerusalem who fled to Arab Jerusalem in 1948. A
grapevine grows over a parking space, in which an old Subaru car is parked.[5]
Our bicycles are leaned against the poles that support the vine. I love the sim-
plicity and modesty of the house—its exterior and interior remind me so much
of my grandparents' home on Nissan Street in Jewish Jerusalem, also a house
built for refugees in the 1950s. The living room is small, and we sit on old so-
fas (Rotem and Raja) and wooden ornamented chairs (Nabeela and me). Raja
is coughing every few minutes, and Rotem responds by saying, "Sacha, Sacha"
(Arabic, "bless you, bless you").

Nabeela puts small tea glasses on the table and a plate with biscuits and
cookies. I eat the cookies happily. We arrived here from Mt. Scopus, not too
far away at all, after Rotem gave a talk in my seminar Journey to the International. Rotem talked about his visit to Cairo a few weeks ago. He said he heard
it calling him to come and see the events in Tahrir Square with his own eyes.

He returned energized and thrilled—he felt that a whole generation of young people there wants to know, to learn and explore, to change their world. There is something enchanting and captivating in Rotem—people feel that he talks from his heart, and that this is a big heart. The students listened intently. It was the first time, one of them told me after the talk, that he had thought about the "Arabs" as anything other than (potential) enemies. This student, by the way, wrote a brilliant paper on a meeting between *The Little Prince* and Machiavelli's *Prince*. To Rotem he said he was happy that he had come to hear him, even though he had had serious qualms about attending class that day. Prior to the talk, he had Googled Rotem, and seen that he had "evaded" military service. (In fact, Rotem did serve a year and a half, as a soldier-teacher, and then decided to "quit." He was in a military jail for several months and then released.)

I think about all this as I bite into the cinnamon cookies and sip the hot tea, accustoming myself to the room. Raja and Nabeela don't ask me if and where *I had* served in the Israeli military. We speak in English. They know Hebrew, but prefer English. Rotem jokes with them in Arabic from time to time, and I ask for a translation. In Cairo people in the streets were confused by his perfect Palestinian Arabic accent and his European external appearance. Some thought he was a spy and "reported" him to the police. To the police he showed his European Union (EU) passport (in recent years more than one hundred thousand Israelis have applied, and received, German, Polish, Romanian, Hungarian, and other European countries' passports) and told them that he was a student in Damascus, hence the good Arabic. It would not have been wise, he said, to identify himself as an Israeli citizen. I try to focus back to the conversation in this room, but perhaps because of the encounters of the recent month, perhaps because I sit in the living room of refugees now (and they might become refugees once more), or perhaps under the impression of the crumbling of the old order in the Middle East and the eyewitness report of Rotem from Cairo, the question keeps looming in my mind: should I apply for a Hungarian passport (it entitles one to an EU passport too), just as a precaution? No, I push the thought away. I would not be able to live in Europe, let alone Hungary with the sharp rise of anti-Semitism in that country's politics.

I return my attention to the conversation between Rotem and our hosts. Raja and Nabeela are both retired now. Raja was a hydrologist, and Nabeela a nurse. They worked for the Jordanian, Israeli, Palestinian, and UN authorities. Veterans of the conflict, if you will. Raja and Nabeela are second cousins, and they both grew up in Qalunya. They show us the ownership documents of their family houses and a rental agreement of another house between Nabeela's father (owner) and a Jewish family from Motza (tenant). The agreement is in three languages: English, Hebrew, and Arabic. All these houses, though, were long ago demolished.

We continue talking. They treat us with great respect and kindness. I tell them about my book and my bike rides in Qalunya. They are moved and surprised. They did not think any Israeli would even know about their village, let alone want to write about it. (But do I really write about the village? Or, do I write about *me* through the village? And, is there a difference for that matter?) "No," I say, "I'm not the first one." Then I tell them about Meir Broza's book on Motza, which has a chapter on Qalunya, and about Meron Benvenisti's book *Sacred Landscape*. Actually, I have the book here in my backpack. I take it out, and quickly leaf through it. There it is, on page 113: "The largest and most prosperous village along that section of the road to Jerusalem was Qalunya, which was situated in an area with plentiful water and abundant greenery," I read aloud. "True, true," Raja confirms, enthusiastically. "I miss so much the taste of the fresh water from the village's spring," he says. "Even if the water was not pure and clear by modern standards, we were immunized ..." "And you say this as a hydrologist," I say, and we all laugh.

I continue reading: "In the village, whose population was about 1,500 ... were the summerhouses of a number of well connected Jerusalem families, both Muslim and Christian: Husseini,[6] Nusseibeh, Maroum, and Niqula." Raja nods in agreement. He seems thoughtful, absorbed in his memories. "Mufti Haj Amin al-Husseini maintained a large house and a vineyard there," I continue. "The villagers raised olives and fruit trees, as well as vegetables." I flip the page to page 114. As I do this, their two-year-old grandchild—they babysit this evening—runs into the room, with his toy truck, laughing. We all laugh at the cheerful commotion. Nabeela holds him, and hands him to me. Surprised, I lay down Benvenisti's book, and lift the toddler. We look each other in the eyes. He is a beautiful child. I go into the parent mode, and make "funny faces" and stroke his gentle hair. The boy smiles. I softly talk to him in Hebrew. He giggles. Then he wants to go back to his grandmother. I feel elevated, and joke with Nabeela and Raja about the pleasures of being grandparents (you have a baby again, without having to wake up at night ...).

"Shall I continue reading?" I ask. "Please do, professor," Raja replies. From the moment we arrived, I noticed how respectful he is to me as a Hebrew University professor. I feel genuinely honored by his respect. Not too many Israelis treat me with similar respect. "A roadside restaurant, coffeehouses, and shops made this a pleasant stopping place for travelers on the main road to Jerusalem."

The rest of Benvenisti's relation discusses the 1929 riots, and the clashes between Motza and Qalunya in the 1930s and up to the 1948 war. I recall Idit's request when we met Taher and his family at the Ain Lauza spring on Independence Day not to discuss war and violence in front of the kids. Even though the text is in English, and the toddler surely would not understand a word, I decide to stop here. "God has pity on kindergarten children. He has less pity on schoolchildren. And on grownups, he has no pity at all . . .,"[7] the words of Yehuda Amichai's poem flash in my mind. Thinking about the poem, I decide to spare not only this child but also his grandparents that bloody history lesson. They already "took" this class in 1948, when they were young schoolchildren. I close Benvenisti's book and let Nabeela take the lead. She tells about growing up in the village, about the games the children used to play, the sense of open spaces, and the beauty of nature around them. The taste of the fruits that grew in her parents orchards. Raja speaks about riding horses in the summer along wadi Qalunya ("what you call today Nahal Soreq").

"Have you been to the village recently?" I ask. "No," Nabeela replies. It is too painful for them. Often they see the valley and the slope when they drive on the Tel Aviv highway, but they don't stop. I want to tell them that the valley itself, where they had the orchards and rode horses, is soon going to disappear too. Indeed, it had already disappeared under the planted pines and the "baobab" ailanthuses. But now it's literally going to disappear: in the next year, the Israeli ministry of transportation will start constructing a bridged bypass and a two-way tunnel for Highway 1 right over the valley of Qalunya (Nahal Arza, in Hebrew). The quarrying and mining materials that will be produced by the works will be spilled in the valley, to "flatten" it—probably due to the same unconscious motivation that stands behind the digging of the train tunnels in wadi Lauza. These are the last days of the wadi they once called home. But I see that perhaps this is not the right time to talk about this. It is getting late, and Raja's coughing becomes more frequent and intense.

We part from the couple after about two hours of conversation. It is dark now. I start riding back to Mevasseret. Rotem stays in Jerusalem at a friend's. On my way home, in the dark Arazim Valley, my flashlight's beam is reflected in the eyes of jackals and deer that have come out to graze or prey in the dark, at the end of a hot day. I think about the conversation with Nabeela and Raja and my recollection of "God Has Pity on Kindergarten Children" and wonder why Amichai's poetry has been ingrained in me for so many years now. Amichai, who fought in the 1948 war, wrote from an antiwar and anti-ideological point of view, rejecting the heroism and glory of war, and refusing to hate his enemies. He hollowed out many of Zionism's symbols and notions, such as the (supposed) yearning for peace, the (avoidable) inevitable wars, the (false) unity between the private self and the national collective, the (made-up) Israeli only government/ regime, and, perhaps above all, (the myth of) Jerusalem. I think about Amichai's warm acceptance in the Israeli public—how surprising it is in light of all this. I recall the literature classes in high school in which we learned many of his poems; his various poems that were incorporated into popular songs, played to overflowing on the radio; and the many prizes and honors he received from the Israeli establishment. In many senses, he is Israel's iconic poet. Was it only his evoking and heart-penetrating texts that enabled this? Or was this embracing of him exactly *because* of the not-too-difficult-to-discern challenge he posed to Zionism and Israel? Amichai, who saw himself as a prophet trying to run away from his destiny, the one who "out of three or four in a room stands by the window, forced to see the injustice among the thistles, and the fires on the hill," yet whose love for this land and its people is so evident. His distancing that creates intimacy, his rebuke that comes from deep love and care. But most important, I realize, as I slowly glide down the moderately descending path, perhaps it is the fact that his poetry is so powerful and people sense the humane and universal *truth* in it, his precision and authenticity—this is what makes it too painful to really accept and identify with his perspective and prophecies. Thus, tragically, the wonderful poetic means, the mastery of the Hebrew language, and the sophisticated and yet simple to understand images and metaphors become the essence that endears him so.

Then I suddenly understand that like Amichai, who allegedly thought about every experience he had in the "real" world as a basis for a poem,[8] I, too—despite my being in the world, on the trail with the bike, and with the people I meet— am starting to think about these experiences as "material" for my stories. Worse still, I am starting to live a storied life, in which I become a "figure" in the story I write about myself. As the landscape I expose is revealed to me in all its sadness and pain, I revert to the imagined world of the story in order to cope with the burden, to give it meaning. But these are real people and places, not stories or images! I am a real person too. I must never let the story come ahead of the "real," but is this possible at all? I am not sure anymore. Frustration strikes me strongly. I am filled with rage at myself for sitting with Nabeela and Raja and "Amichaizing" the situation. I should have listened to them more carefully, not to myself and the aesthetics of a dead poet. And why can I talk with Nissim, whose mother was terribly injured in a terrorist bombing, about war, while with these refugees not? They could have heard the more "problematic" part of Benvenisti's history of their village had I continued reading it. I stop the bike in the middle of the dark trail. I let my anger and frustration out in a shout of agony. A pair of jackals is startled by my shout and run out of the bushes on my side, crossing the trail and disappearing among the thistles on the other side of the path.

A few days after this meeting, I call Raja and Nabeela. Nabeela picks up the phone. She is happy to hear from me. I ask if perhaps they have second thoughts about having a joint tour in Qalunya. I tell her, cautiously, about the coming construction ("There is a plan to start building bridges and tunnels in the wadi of Qalunya soon—"). "Yes," she stops me, "we saw the signs on the road to Tel Aviv recently." Indeed, the ministry of transportation put along the road some big advertising signs—"beginning of work signs"—that publicize/threaten/ boast of the approaching construction project. The grandiose images on the signs leave no doubt as to the future look of the valley.

No, unfortunately, they will not be able to come. Raja is not well. And, to tell the truth, he is troubled enough by the threat of the settlers in their neighborhood, Sheikh Jarrah. What about her, I wonder. "I loved Qalunya, but it died long, long ago," she responds. "Perhaps it's better that they bury what's left of it now." Her voice trembles. There is a long silence. I let her words permeate my mind. "Loved ... died ... bury." Suddenly I think about my grandmother, my father's mother, who never wanted to join my father on his trips to Budapest, to see their old home there. My father flew there quite a few times after the fall of communism. But she never wanted to go there, even though she would often talk about their home and life in Hungary.

"I understand," I finally tell Nabeela. Then I say that I soon leave for a long sabbatical in Canada. Perhaps we can meet again when I return? Yes, I can call them when I'm back. "Have a safe journey and return in peace," she adds, warmly. "Thank you," I respond. My eyes are filled with tears due to this simple, but so meaningful, blessing: *return* in peace.

May 31, 2011

The telephone is ringing. It is morning; I am just about to leave home for campus. An unrecognized number appears on the phone's display. "Hello?" I answer. "Shalom, is this Oded?" An unrecognized voice, calling my unlisted home number. The old paranoia of being summoned to military reserve service floats in me in each time I receive such a call. Alternatively, it might be some telemarketing agent. Neoliberal economics and militarism, two of my main phobias in a split second. No, it is neither one: in both cases, the caller's number would be hidden. "Yes . . ." I answer, hesitantly. "This is Taher speaking." I linger for a second or two. "Taher, from Qalunya," he continues, "you remember, we met at Ain Lauza." "Taher!" I'm very surprised but happy: "Ahlen, ahlen!" (Arabic, "hello, hello"). I did not believe he would call. It's been three weeks since we met on Independence Day/Nakba Day, and I have not heard from him since. "Listen, I would very much like to meet you, in Qalunya, and talk about the village," he says. "Yeah, this sounds good," I respond. "Would you like to tour the village together?" I'm very excited. I'm eager to know what he can tell me about the village, to where he can lead me there, and I also want to share with him my knowledge and feelings. "Sure," he says. "I'll bring two of my nephews with me, if this is ok with you." We set a tour for June 11.

June 11, 2011, 2:00 A.M.

I scream, but my voice is mute. I am terrified. I know this is just a nightmare, yet I cannot wake up. Again, I shout with all my power. Finally, I can hear my voice—dry and weak, it hardly manages to utter some words in my choked throat, but it is still discernible. I wake up. Idit is sitting on the bed next to me, her hands on my head and body, relaxing me. "It was just a bad dream," I say after a few moments, and rise from the bed to go to the washroom. She returns to sleep.

After the washroom, I go to my desk and find my notebook. I write down the dream, so I won't forget it. Perhaps it would have been better to forget it, but it's too late: I have let this research project become me and vice versa.

I'm invited to watch a movie on Qalunya's village life. The movie will be screened on a wall of one of the village houses. Actually, there is only one house left, the Husayni house, of course. So the movie will be screened there.

I ride down to Qalunya from Mevasseret. When I arrive at the place, I realize that this is a special movie, one that you can enter into. Something like Woody Allen's *The Purple Rose of Cairo*. No, actually in that movie the character in the film comes *out* of the movie into the real world. Here it's the opposite, or is it? At any rate, I enter the movie's world. It's a trap! Inside I discover many people who turned into devils and demons, and they lash and flog every newcomer. The cruelty is terrible. People crawl on the ground without their limbs, which were amputated by the terrible whips. Everything is flooded with blood, which reaches up to my knees. My shins, knees, elbows, and arms are nonetheless protected thanks to the guards I wear every time I go riding. The demons try to whip me too, but I'm guarded. Meanwhile, new people enter the village, from the porous wall of the house. They are now beaten, indiscriminately, by those who entered just before them, who after a certain time grow limbs again and join the tormentors.

June 11, 2011, 5:00 P.M.

We meet next to Qalunya's former café, which is now a school for (Jewish) children with special needs. This was one of the "pleasant stopping places for travelers on the main road to Jerusalem" that Benvenisti writes about in his description of Qalunya, when travelers—not "commuters"—still stopped before ascending to Jerusalem from this low point in the valley. I think nostalgically about a past I did not experience myself. Taher has brought two of his nephews with him: Nasser and Isa (pseudonyms). Nasser is a lawyer, in his early thirties, registered with the Israeli bar; Isa is an accounting student at the Hebrew University, around twenty-five years old. We shake hands, and sit for a few minutes on a low stone wall near the café/school. It's Saturday—Shabbat—but I came with my bicycle even though I could have taken the car today. Still under the impression of the nightmare, I thought that if there is a need to escape during our tour in the desolate trails of Qalunya, the bike will be a perfect means.

But apparently there will be no such need. They look welcoming, happy that I came. After we exchange greetings and the small talk trails off, I take off my backpack, and draw out of it a plastic cylinder. Inside, there are several maps of Qalunya. I found these maps in the Hebrew University's Maps Library and brought them for Taher today, somewhat as a welcoming gift, somewhat as an authentic "artifact" from the village itself. I take the maps out, and spread them on the stone wall, between us. These are (1) a British Survey of Palestine map at a scale of 1:10,000 from 1934, showing the village and its surrounding lands and plots. Each plot of land is marked by its owner, and the map indicates what crops are grown there. I scanned the map in four large parts in high resolution, and taped the printed parts together. (2) A 1:20,000 Survey of Palestine physical map of Jerusalem and its environs from 1945. I scanned and enlarged the part in which Qalunya is shown. The map clearly indicates where the cemetery, mosque, different springs, and school of the village were. The school and mosque are demolished now, and Mevasseret's southeastern neighborhood is built on the location of most of the village houses. But the cemetery, according to the map, is somewhere on the southern side of the Tel Aviv–Jerusalem highway, where there are no houses. I've ridden in that estimated site a few times before, searching for the cemetery, but could not see any remnants. "Do you know where the cemetery is?" I ask Taher, and show him the location on the map. "Of course," he replies, and points in Motza Illit's direction (Upper Motza), on the hill in front of us, not on the map. "You want to go there?" "Yes," I answer. "But before we go, these maps are for you." I also give him a CD with the scanned files.

Isa takes the materials I brought and carefully, very carefully, scrolls the map into the cylinder, and puts everything in his shoulder bag. His eyes are wet. "Thank you," he says, and puts his hand on my arm. "This is the first piece of paper we have from our village." Nasser and Taher also thank me quietly. I'm moved by their thankfulness.

After a few moments of silence, I say, "Shall we go to the cemetery?" Taher leads the way, and we set foot on a dirt trail that leads up to Upper Motza. After the cemetery, we will go to a hidden spring they didn't know about from their previous visits here, and then Taher wants to show me the plot of land on which his house stood. This "going to see" the remaining sites of the village grants the tour the nature of a study trip, but I know that this is only the outer layer of this journey. I cannot tell exactly the purpose of this tour. Perhaps it is to examine whether we are indeed from the "same village," as Taher said in the Independence Day/Nakba Day encounter at Ain Lauza, or, maybe, whether we can and want to be from the same village.

As we walk on the trail to the cemetery, we talk about Qalunya and Motza. Taher brings up the subject. He asks if I know where the Maklef house is. I say I do (a different family lives there now, but in the same house where the massacre took place). Taher then tells me that in 1967, right after the war and the Israeli annexation of East Jerusalem (to which his family escaped in 1948), when his father and he started to visit the site of demolished Qalunya, Mordechai Maklef, who had known his father since childhood, met them once in Motza and invited his father to return to Qalunya. Mordechai Maklef, a survivor of the massacre who was nine years old in 1929, became in 1952 the chief of the general staff of the IDF. I always wondered how his early childhood experience influenced his military career, but could find no historical evidence for such a connection, only vague indications. Vagueness—the frustration of the historian. When I hear Taher's story, I'm not sure if Taher and his father properly understood Maklef's words (namely, not their literal meaning), and from where Maklef got the moral (not the mention legal) authority to make such an offer. "Supposing that there was such an offer indeed," the cautious scholar and, even more so, the frightened Zionist/Israeli in me jumps off . . . But then again, perhaps it is *I* who cannot accept that Maklef would have made such an offer and that Taher and his father understood it right. Could it be that it is indeed so simple, the "solution" to this conflict? People-to-people reconciliation?

"You know, it wasn't the inhabitants of Qalunya who killed his family," Taher's thick and vigorous voice cuts through my thoughts. "These were Bedouins [Arab nomads] who did not belong to our village." This is exactly what the defendants from Qalunya told the British court in Jerusalem in 1930 during the trial of the Maklef family murderers. "No, no, you're wrong," I respond, somewhat agitated. "These were villagers from Qalunya who committed the murders; there is evidence of that." No, he states, these were Bedouins. His grandfather, who was the mukhtar of Qalunya, told his father so, and he told Taher. As Taher keeps talking about the supposed Bedouin killers, I recall that he indeed said when we met a month ago that his grandfather was the mukhtar of Qalunya. During the trial in 1930, Qalunya's mukhtar argued that he did not know about the massacre until a day after it happened. To that and the mukhtar's efforts to provide alibis for the suspects, the British presiding judge responded, "I will compliment you. You are the biggest liar I ever heard in my life. I have already heard many liars in Palestine, but you are the greatest among them. Go

The Maklef house in Motsa, the location of the 1929 massacre of seven Jews by their Palestinian neighbors from Qalunya. Here began the "blood debt" between Motsa and Qalunya, which culminated in the depopulation of the village in 1948. (Photograph by Idit Wagner.)

back to your village and let everyone there know that you are a liar. Be ashamed in your white hair [read: old age]. Go."[9]

A British imperial judge, especially one who uses such a derogatory style, is not necessarily the right authority to cling to in matters of morality. Moreover, I know that if indeed the mukhtar lied to the British court, the judge should not have wondered or been angry about this so much, because "what system of justice can determine that it is allowed to occupy a land but not to lie at the conquerors' court?"[10] And perhaps the mukhtar lied not so much due to his desire to protect the murderers but more out of fear of possible vengeance on the part of their families should he incriminate them or out of shame for failing the Jews of Motza, whom he had guaranteed would be safe. It is probably impossible to know. Nonetheless, I find Taher's words about the Bedouins disturbing.

Why does he not recognize, no, admit, that the murderers were from Qalunya? On the other hand, I think as we walk up the trail to Motza Illit that if occupied people are not obliged to speak the truth to the occupier, then I should remember that for Taher *I am* the occupier. No matter how many maps and "papers" from his village I might give him. It is probably difficult enough for him to take this tour with me and to converse about these events in *Hebrew*, even though he was the one who contacted me. When I, and my people, am willing to speak the truth to him, and to his people, about the occupation, not only that of 1967 but also that of 1948 and before, and the post-1967 occupation (for the occupation—not only in the "territories," but also in Israel of the Green Line—is not a single historical moment but a daily developing practice), perhaps he will be willing to speak the truth about the riots of 1929 to me.[11]

"And what guarantee do you have that once the truth is told, they [the Palestinians] will not demand—with international legitimacy, that is—that we leave this country or that the Jewish state be replaced with a 'state of all its citizens'? Finding out the truth about the occupations of the land will simply endanger the justness of Zionism," I hear in my mind the voice of one of my most clear-eyed students, a zealous Zionist herself. "The only guarantee I can give you is that violence will continue as long as we keep lying to each other. A necessary condition for peace is that people tell each other the truth," I replied to her. But I kept silent as to the *sufficient* conditions. I know they must include a deep reform of the "Zionist regime," the Israeli ethnocracy,[12] in terms of control of space and the structure of power relations in the society, even—or perhaps at first—within the pre-1967 borders.

"I wish I could be a Zionist, but I can no longer be," I then recall the words of one of the Mevasseret "separation fence activists." I remember the extreme pain caused to this man when he said these words, to reach this realization that he cannot identify anymore with the ideology he was raised on, an ideology that is nonetheless still a part of his identity in very intimate meanings that he cannot always resist. I understand that in certain respects I am like him too: I also feel that I cannot identify anymore with Zionism as an ideology that in practice took the form of dispossession and exclusion of the Palestinians, and by doing this, sentenced the Israeli Jews to continue to be a generation of settlers, who live here behind separation fences and only thanks to the muzzle and the steel helmet, as Dayan aptly said. Yet, perhaps like that student of mine and many other Israelis too, I am also afraid of Palestinian nationalism and *its* culture of

denial and violence, and too afraid of the "day after Zionism" to be able to explicitly challenge this structure of power/knowledge. But I do, after all, challenge
it, at least here, in Qalunya, on the microlevel. Is this pathetic, hypocritical, or
admirable and, more important, positively helpful? I've heard the whole range of
responses, and to be honest, cannot decide . . . Perhaps it's all of these together.

While I conduct this minihistorical trial and reckoning in my mind, we pass
the location where I believe the cemetery should be, according to the British
map. It's a plot full of impenetrable ailanthuses and high thistles. "No, the cemetery was not here," Taher says. "It's just a bit further up." A few dozen meters
up the trail, and there we see several old sheds and a house. "It's in the backyard
here, behind the sheds and the junk. My grandfather is buried there." "Are you
sure, in this backyard?!" I ask, disbelievingly, and, perhaps still under the influence of the words of the British judge and the whole controversy between Taher
and me about the Bedouin killers, I add, skeptically, "How do you know?" "My
father showed me the grave many years ago, and I often came here afterward;
the man sometimes lets us in," he replies. I don't know if this can really be true.
How could anyone live with a cemetery in his backyard? On the other hand, in
Mal'ha/al-Maliha, near my childhood neighborhood in Jerusalem, they built
a middle school close to the cemetery of that village, and some graves are still
visible just behind the school. In many other ruined and depopulated villages
and towns (including what became in 1948 West Jerusalem), Muslim graveyards
were defiled or covered with construction (however, Jewish cemeteries in East
Jerusalem and Hebron suffered a similar fate before 1967).

I look at the backyard with dismay, and think about the cemetery where
my four grandparents and my father are buried, Jerusalem's Har Hamenuchot
(Hebrew, Resting Mountain) cemetery. It is so close to here, just on the opposing hill to the southeast. Dense rows of tens of thousands of rectangular
boxlike gravestones and narrow, all too narrow, lanes separating the graves. In
recent decades, due to lack of burial space, they started building massive concrete terraces there to add more space, and also to bury people in catacomblike
designated concrete walls (in Israel, for religious and historical reasons [that is,
the Holocaust], there is hardly any cremation of deceased people's bodies). A
very gloomy and crowded place. But at least we can visit the graves of our family
members without asking the consent of anyone. I turn my gaze to Taher and see
his emotions storm inside him. "Don't you believe me?" he asks in a voice that
is partially coarse and partially choked with tears. I then know that he's right:

his grandfather *is* buried beyond this house's fence. I feel the humiliation he has to endure, asking permission to enter to visit the grave and acknowledging the ownership of the person living there, and the anger that the graveyard has turned into someone's junkyard. "I believe you," I say.

We come down from the cemetery and walk under the Jerusalem–Tel Aviv highway's bridge to the other side of the demolished village. The "approaching work" signs are just beyond the curve. Did they see them, I ask. Yes, when they descended from Jerusalem to here. Nasser, the lawyer, asks me what I know about these works. They will choke Mevasseret, he tells me. Yes, I know. There will be just one entrance to the town when they finish the new highway. We'll become an enclave, somewhat like Biet Surik, I think. Then I tell him that the people of Mevasseret are already getting organized to "do something" about this monstrous plan—to appeal, demonstrate. Would he like to join us? No, he replies, these are fights of Jews against themselves, not his own business.

We emerge from the trail that goes underneath the highway, across the Soreq riverbed, which on the British map I brought them is called Wadi Qalunya. A police patrol car is standing on the shoulder of the highway. Seeing the police car, Taher tells me that while they waited for me to come today, at the parking lot near the school/café, a police car stopped by them and the police officers checked their papers and asked what they are doing there. He told them that he had come to visit his village, Qalunya. They had no idea what he was talking about and contacted their headquarters to check their ID numbers on the police computer. Nasser, his nephew, explained to them that they had come to see the *ruins* of their village, which had stood here, and only then did the policemen reluctantly let them be. "How can they forbid me to visit my village? They always give us trouble, the police," Taher exclaims when he tells me about the police examination/harassment (they did not examine other cars and people in the parking lot). His voice is angry. I think about the dissonance that he experiences knowing that while as a permanent resident of Jerusalem he is legally entitled to be here, he is also being told almost explicitly that he is not *welcome* here. Perhaps this is why he wanted me to come today, not only to exchange knowledge about Qalunya, not only to bear witness, to corroborate and acknowledge his family and communal history in this place, to claim his place here, but also to reach out and look for a respectful, perhaps even welcoming, acceptance.

Do I want to offer him the respect and acceptance that he is looking for, the acknowledgment that he seeks of his right to this place? Can I make a similar "Maklef offer" to him, and invite him to return here? Eventually, there is no escape from dealing with this question, I realize. And can I contain his evident anger, I wonder, as we make our way on a relatively broad and dusty trail in the valley of Motza/Qalunya. Half subconsciously and half knowingly, I mount the bike and start riding parallel to them, slowly, at their walking pace. On the bike, even at this slow pace, my anxiety and qualms about Taher's anger and need for recognition and recompense somehow dissipate. We thus make our way on the path toward a spring that is located at the foot of the hill east of the Husayni house—a spring, they say, they did not know from previous visits here.

Indeed, the spring is quite unknown. It is hidden among big fig trees, ailanthuses, and a thicket of bushes at the side of the path. I found it one day when I was looking for a trail that would cut through the slope of the Husayni house toward the Arazim Valley. Raspberry bushes at the edge of the trail told me that there is a water source, some wetness at least, there. Allured and almost enchanted by the promise of water, I kept riding slowly along the undergrowth, finally found a breach, and discovered this place. As opposed to the other springs of Qalunya, which were taken over by religious Jews as *mikvehs* (ritualistic purifying pools), this spring remained quite unknown. There is no Parks Authority sign that leads to this spring. It is also not marked on the current Israel Survey maps of the region, nor on the British ones I gave Isa earlier. I did not see it on Google Earth either. But a few months after I first came to it, someone else found the place too, and marked it on the Amud Anan (Pillar of Cloud) Geographical Information System (GIS) as Ein Maklef (Maklef's Spring).

Thinking about Ein Maklef inevitably leads me to recall the Amud Anan's Palestine Exploration Fund (PEF) "button"—a link that changes the display from the current map to the 1880 published map of the fund, the British Christian society that systematically mapped Palestine in the 1870s to corroborate the Bible. I'm not sure to what degree the Bible was authenticated by this mapping and surveying effort, but the PEF's maps became very instrumental in the British conquest of Palestine in 1917–18 (they were updated by means of aerial photographs). I have used the Amud Anan GIS for several years now, but had never wondered what the PEF button means—perhaps not even noticed it. Only eight or nine months ago, when I learned about the PEF, and was searching the Internet for a scanned PEF map, did I realize that this button could be what I was looking for. I clicked the button.

The result was amazing: in a click on a Web link, one is cartographically transported back in time to the 1870s. All the Israeli highways, interchanges, streams, towns, and villages disappear at once, and the demolished and forgotten Palestinian landscape, with its villages, wadis, hills, cliffs, caves, springs, and trails, reappears. The map is a "commemoration photo: it documented the scenery of the country precisely in the 'last moment' before the new Hebrew [*sic*] settlement caused considerable changes in the landscape."[13]

When I wandered off on the PEF digitized map from the familiar landmarks in my region, I quickly lost my way. It was like exploring a foreign country, which, in a sense, is what this map indeed depicts. Added to this feeling of loss of orientation was the artwork of the map: instead of the elaborate, computer-generated, multicolored Israeli map with the minute contour lines, there emerged a mostly brown and white, hand-drawn map, with the hills more rounded and gentle, the topography depicted somehow more artistically but no less accurately than on the current maps. Place-names and landmarks are written on the PEF map in handwriting, and the general look of the map reminds me of those maps at the beginning of fantasy books like *The Lord of the Rings*. Yet it is a scientific map, not a fantastic or even an orientalist one with drawings or illustrations of exotic persons and cities or sites on it (it just *reminds* me of fantasy book maps . . .). But it still gives an impression of innocence and bewilderment, unlike the current map, which is too realistic and familiar, as much as a map can be realistic and accurate, that is.

But the ironic thing in the PEF button application in the Amud Anan system is that the wanderer is not to be lost for long once he or she starts moving the computer's mouse on the screen: the map is strewn with little blue circles—placemarks that were pinned by users of the current Israeli map. On touching such a placemark with the mouse cursor, a comment, often accompanied by a picture, will open to depict the present-day location, but on the 1880 map. Thus, the present is retrospectively projected onto the past, as if the land was just waiting for the Israelis to know, name, and settle it.[14] Of course, the PEF map was made owing to British Protestant religious interest in the Holy Land, and the British War Office's need for a map of the region due to imperial considerations related to securing the road to India and the area of the Suez Canal.[15] It is definitely not a "genuine" or "native" Arab Palestinian map. Such a map, as far as I know, did not exist in the nineteenth and early twentieth centuries. Moreover, the most comprehensive Palestinian Arab mapping project of historic Palestine—Salman Abu Sitta's *The Atlas of Palestine, 1916–1966*—heavily relies on the British Survey of Palestine maps, which, in their turn, originated with the PEF map.

But even though the PEF map is an imperial map, and even though, like all maps, this one carves out a territory and makes it into a distinct "land" ("western Palestine"),[16] it still documents the native landscape of these hills and wadis at the "last moment." Yet the *digitized* PEF map in the Amud Anan system, with the blue placemarks, is perhaps the perfect Zionist map one can think of: even if inadvertently, it takes possession of the land even before "the new Hebrew settlement generated considerable changes in the landscape."

As Taher and his nephews and I enter through a breach in the thick shrubbery along the path and approach Ein Maklef, the hidden spring (here I already have to dismount the bike and walk it beside my Palestinian companions), I think, yes, Taher definitely deserves this respect and welcome from me, if only because he became a guest in his native village's landscape, coming here only in such "tours" as we conduct now. He wants to return to Qalunya, but is able only to *wander* in the village's *ruins*. He can only *visit* here, and that, too, mainly on Jewish and national Israeli holidays or Sabbaths (Saturdays), when he is not working (the Islamic weekly rest day is Friday). He found comfort in the British maps of the village that I brought today, but these are maps of the imperial conquerors, who scorned his grandfather and, eventually, enabled the Jews to conquer the land in their turn. I suddenly see the direct line that runs between the 1880 PEF map and the 2011 Amud Anan PEF application, and I wonder for how long these tours in Qalunya will still take place—Taher told me on the path that his nephews joined our tour today to learn about the village and to pass on the knowledge to the next generation once he is gone. Even if the Israelis cover almost everything here with concrete, roads, bridges, and interchanges, something of Qalunya will remain and emerge from within the cracks, so to speak, and they, he said, will find it and cling to it. Feeling somewhat threatened and awed by this perseverance, by this resolve to maintain the memory and the fantasy of the village so that "they" will be able to return to it one day, to reconstitute it—at the expense of "us"?—I also cannot but feel that if someone loves this place so much, I have to open my heart to him.

With these thoughts in my mind, we emerge on the other side of the undergrowth and come to the spring. It is flowing gently (in truth, I should have said "weakly flowing," but I love the place and therefore the "gently") from a narrow, twelve-meter-long cave, about the height and width of a person, dug in the limestone rock of the slope. An old almond tree grows on the outer walls of the cave, its roots straggling beautifully on the rock of the cave. I lean my bike on a gray-trunked and foliaceous tree that grows at the side of the spring's pool. Taher, Isa, and Nasser go to the other side of the pool to peer into the dark cave from which the spring flows. I call Isa, and throw to him my bicycle torch, which I take from my backpack, to illuminate the cave. He catches the torch, and they are now able to examine the cave. Nasser enters the cave, and comes back after a few moments. Taher and Isa wait for him, watching him advance in the cave until he reaches the bedrock, from which the spring flows.

Nasser comes out, the lower part of his pants wet. He says that he could not find the exact source of the flow (is there such a spot at all, I wonder). He looks disappointed. Isa turns his head back toward me to give me back the torch, and then he suddenly smiles and says, "Hey, your bike will have good luck now." "Why's that?" "Well, this is a Mëys tree [southern nettle tree]—it's a sacred tree in Islam. It frightens off all the evil genies and devils." "Wow," I respond, recalling my nightmare and not quite sure whether I am happy with the connection to the world of the genies and demons that the Mëys tree affects now on my bike . . . "Would the tree repel Jewish demons as well, or only Islamic ones?" I ask Isa, half jokingly and half seriously. "I think it works only on Islamic demons," he replies lightheartedly, and we laugh. The laughter is liberating. Only when we laugh do I realize how tense the situation was until now—both for me and for them.

We sit by the pool and talk for a while. "What's this place called in Hebrew?" asks Nasser. "Ein Maklef," I answer. Taher lifts his gaze from the pool at hearing the Maklef name. We now talk about our meeting on Nakba Day/Independence Day. The Nakba, says Isa, is still here for us, continuing every day. "1948 is not over. The occupation has many facets." I think I know what he's talking about, recalling my visits beyond the separation fence, my military service in Hebron, the situation in Sheikh Jarrah where Nabeela and Raja live, and even thinking about the coming destruction of this valley by the new highway bridge.

Isa keeps talking about "the occupation." He talks about the demolition of illegal houses in his East Jerusalem neighborhood of Jabel Mukabber (a place where, like many other Palestinian neighborhoods of East Jerusalem, a great many of the houses are considered illegal from the outset due to the lack of a project outline for the neighborhood). Every demolished house there, says Isa, connects again their large extended family, which lives in the neighborhood, to the trauma of the Nakba and the demolition of Qalunya. But as he speaks, I increasingly feel estranged from him. Not that I underestimate his experience or deny it. But when he keeps saying "the occupation," the word has a different sound—a different meaning?—than when "we" lefty-Israelis use it. Whose occupation is it, I think, and who is defined by it "more" than the other? "Can you imagine life here in this country after the occupation ends," I ask him, somewhat challengingly. "Can *you?*" he returns my question, in a very "Jewish" manner.[17] Realizing suddenly how the "occupation" is a part of me too, I chuckle bitterly.

We depart after a few more minutes. I lead them to the Soreq Road, from which they can easily walk to their car in the parking lot. When we emerge from the trail on the asphalt road, Taher says that this specific part of the village was his family's, "as well as the area near Sheikh Abdul Aziz. You know where that is, right?" I hesitate a bit, but then tell him that I know all too well where Sheik Abdul Aziz is, that in fact my street is very close to the place. There's a brief silence. Then he shakes my hand thoroughly and, I think, warmly, and says, "Thank you for coming today; we'll be in touch again." Nasser and Isa shake my hand in turn. We bid each other farewell and as they start descending the road toward their car, I begin the twenty-five-minute climb to Meron Street, where I live in my apartment, near Sheikh Abdul Aziz, on Taher's family land. As I climb toward Mevasseret, I think suddenly about Albert Camus's story "L'Hôte" ("The Guest" but also "The Host" in French). I am *l'hôte*, I understand. I'm not sure that my Palestinian companions on today's tour would have defined me in such a dualistic manner—for them, I am probably an invader, albeit an "enlightened" one (a useful idiot?), and not a welcome guest/host. But in practice, at least in today's tour, they were the guests and I the host, and vice versa. For both of us, it's a frustrating status, this indeterminate and involuntary condition of *l'hôte*, for sure. But it is real and very stable too. And there might be comfort in this duality, I realize as I enter Mevasseret's lower neighborhood. Perhaps even hope. Because once we *embrace*, not lament or deny, the duality of the guest/ host, the respect and consideration that the guest has to show toward the host, on the one hand, and the welcome and generosity that the host must display toward the guest, on the other hand, can hasten the end of the occupation, as a state of mind, by abolishing the no less dualistic and essentialist categories of invader/native.

Chapter Five

THE LAST RIDE
(FOR THE MEANWHILE)
IN THE ARAZIM VALLEY

July 26, 2011, 8:00 A.M: A Changing Landscape in the Arazim Valley

I am riding in the Arazim Valley on my way to Mt. Scopus for the last time this year—within two days I leave the country and fly to Vancouver Island for a year and a half of sabbatical leave. The ride today—I have to make some last arrangements on campus and say good-bye to some friends and colleagues—is also a farewell to my bike trail. From campus, I will ride to my mother's home in Jerusalem and store the bike in my childhood room. When I come back from Canada, in February 2013, the landscape in the valley will be very different: beyond the changing of the seasons (I leave in high summer, when everything is yellow, brown, and dusty, and will return in midwinter, when the almonds blossom white as snow), the construction of the railway track with its tunnels and bridges will have transformed the valley and its surroundings beyond recognition. The City of Jerusalem, in whose municipal jurisdiction the Arazim Valley is located, has also transformed the landscape: the development of the Jerusalem Park, an annular park that surrounds the city and extends into this valley too, entailed the paving of many of the dirt trails I used to ride here, thus making them into comfortable bike trails, accessible to many more riders, not only the "elite" mountain bikers. New trees were planted along the trail. A small grove of cedars—*arazim*—was planted in the valley, to correct the historical mistake of its naming (several old cypresses that grow at the entrance to the valley were mistakenly identified by Jewish settlers in the 1920s as cedars). But because cedars are not endemic species in this country and do not grow here without human support, a Jewish National Fund (JNF) water truck will come every week to water the seedlings, until they grow and provide "majestic shade," as the JNF's Palestinian Israeli worker told me once.[1] This is Zionism at its best and worst: no matter what, cedars *will* grow in the Arazim Valley. Not too far away from this grove, the national park Einot Telem, previously a relatively desolate location, underwent a renovation that made it more welcoming to hikers and visitors. Close to Einot Telem, the Israel Railway Company built a "deployment compound" for its trucks and excavation machinery. About ten mobile homes were brought there too, to serve as offices for the project's workers and supervisors. The place is reminiscent now of a military camp.

Due to the railway works, the old patrol roads in the valley were also paved with asphalt—the Parks Authority forced the railway company to do this, to reduce the production of dust by the truck traffic—and these roads now invite more people to visit Einot Telem and Jerusalem Park with their cars. In addition, more drivers found out about this route, and now use it to "cut" through traffic into or from Jerusalem during rush hour. Following these developments, a few *moshavim* (a type of Israeli cooperative agricultural community of individual farms) that own agricultural lands in the valley have started preparing to plant vineyards here. Plots of land that were wild and deserted for decades, full of thistles and rocks, are being leveled by tractors to prepare them for planting.

Deer, jackals, snakes, turtles, hyenas, and many species of birds and rodents lost their habitat in a matter of weeks. One of the Jerusalem Park's wardens told me that the *moshavim* are seeking to demonstrate their active ownership of the plots, and thus get financial compensation from the railway company and the City of Jerusalem for to the damage they have (supposedly) incurred because of the work in the valley. Of course, the damage will result from the very planting of the vineyards precisely during the high time of these development works— the plots stood deserted for decades . . .[2]

I feel full of anger at what seems to be the opportunistic destruction of the valley. Even though the Arazim Valley was never a space of pure nature or true wilderness, its frontier status—at the margins of Jerusalem, between the big city and Mevasseret, and along the Green Line—left it as a relatively desolate open space, not accessible to the great majority of Jerusalemites, in which rich fauna and flora thrived. True, the separation fence runs along the northeastern ridges of the valley, but "they" (Perhaps the landscape engineers of the fence? Does the fence have landscape engineers at all? I must check this someday) made good work in hiding it. And the Magav patrols were always here, chasing, on the rugged trails, the Palestinian "interlopers" who come from the village of Beit Iksa, which watches over the valley (this is the village that was left on the "Israeli side" of the fence). The 9/11 monument, in the middle of the valley, has loomed over the area too for two years now. And at the end of the valley, excavation of the government's nuclear bunker has been going on at least since 2002.

Therefore, I cannot say that I have ever known this space as an untouched outdoor environment. But for me, it was somewhat easier to contain the violent presence of the state in this space as long as the valley supported this rich and diverse wildlife habitat. The view of a deer galloping among the rocks or a snake eagle gliding over the valley, accompanying my ride from the sky, its shadow scampering over the rocks while I jump over them with the bike, was one of the things that allowed me to find, among the hard realities of coercion and conflict that are embedded in the valley, some innocence and joy.[3] Now, the animals are being driven out of the valley, and as it is becoming ever more "developed" for tourism, agriculture, and infrastructure, the state—in its narrowly and broadly defined terms—is claiming this landscape in a much more blatant way.[4]

Making my way on the moderate slope of the newly paved bike trail, Mevasseret and the (thankfully, still rugged and "natural") Halilim wadi behind me, I pass now a tractor that levels a plot of land full of rocks and thistles. The tractor operator waves a "hello" at me. He is a Palestinian Israeli from the nearby village of Abu Ghosh, and he, too, thinks, like the park's warden, that the excavation has additional motives besides growing grapes. I have seen him here every day now for the last three weeks or so, leveling the ground in preparation for planting. The plot he's working on now is the last refuge of a small herd of deer, which I used to see and admire every day on my way to campus during recent years. I stray off into the field he's leveling. The soil is soft and crushed, and my bike's wheels flutter in the dirt. I nonetheless continue riding toward the tractor. When I approach him, Sa'id, the operator, stops the tractor and comes down from the driver's seat, smiling at me. We shake hands, and I ask him if by any chance he can spare just this last piece of field for the deer. No, unfortunately, his instructions are strict. He has to uproot the thicket and level all the land. But, he adds, I shouldn't worry too much about the deer—once the vineyard is planted, they will come back and even have good grapes to feed on . . . I try to smile, to see the bright side in this situation.

I head back to the trail, and speed off. The feeling of riding on the paved trail is completely different from a few months ago when the trail was still rugged and dusty. The bike rolls easily and quickly, and there's hardly any resistance. I realize that despite the greater speed and comfort, I long for the trail's resistance, those bumps and jumps. This is too easy, too tempting to turn the ride into a practice of fast commuting again. Once they finish paving the whole trail, I might start contemplating buying a road bike—a faster and more efficient machine. What will become of my decommuting then?

More and more "invaders" appear in the valley. As I keep rolling on the comfortable paved trail, I notice on the other bank of the Soreq riverbed, on the railway trucks' service road, a group of railway company engineers, contractors, and some park wardens bending over the hood of a warden jeep, discussing and examining some big paper sheet that flutters in the wind. This is probably the plan of the railway bridge that is supposed to be erected here. One kilometer long, eighty meters above the valley, this will be "the largest railroad bridge in the Middle East," I can already hear Nissim, Ma'ayan's husband, telling our kids. I try to imagine the bridge above my head, and my heart breaks. Instead of all this destruction, they could have at least seriously considered adding a designated bus lane along Highway 1.[5]

A Magav jeep is standing next to the group, "securing" it. But there is hardly anyone to secure them from. The Palestinians from Beit Iksa who used to "infiltrate" through the Arazim Valley in the past no longer do it. Their village is blocked by the separation fence from behind, by Jewish neighborhoods and settlements on another flank, and by the Arazim Valley, which has turned into a huge work site, an opportunistic agricultural space, and a municipal park. The valley is now also under constant video and electronic surveillance. When the railway bridges here and in the nearby wadi Luz are finished, I am sure, there will be more "security" here to protect these "strategic infrastructures."

I recall the days when I used to see here the Ford Transit vans of the Palestinians, persistently navigating the rugged trails and muddy dirt roads from Beit Iksa, smuggling day workers into Jerusalem (for two or three shekels a ride . . .). A few years ago, somewhere close to here, on my way back home on a heavy rainy evening, after dark, my bike's chain was torn because the mud ground it down. The rain also ruined my flashlight, and I was making my way in almost complete darkness. "Suddenly," a Transit that was inching its way on the muddy path, stopped for me as I was walking the bike along the trail. At first, I thought the lights were those of a Magav jeep, but things turned out differently. I moved to the side of the path, and the Transit slowly stopped next to me. The Palestinian driver opened the window and offered to take me farther down the path, closer to Mevasseret. He was alone in the van, and I hesitated, but the rain was too heavy and I was soaked and shivering with cold, without the tools to fix my chain and without any light. Perhaps my stress from the storm and the darkness was greater than the fear of the Palestinian man, because finally I jumped in, after he helped me stow the bike in the trunk. But because of the heavy rain, he eventually decided to take me directly to my home, up in Mevasseret. He risked himself quite a bit by driving up there—some police patrol might have arrested him for being an "interloper." When we arrived, I offered to pay him—I had fifty shekels in my wallet—but he refused to accept any money, insisting that he just wanted to do a favor for a person in trouble. I invited him up for coffee, but he said he could not come. Perhaps he was afraid that some "vigilant" neighbor would report the obviously Arab-looking Transit to the police (besides being old and beat up, the van had a kaffiyeh, an Arab head scarf, on the dashboard and some Arab prints on the windows).

I have not seen the Transit driver since. Another missed opportunity, I think now, for the Ford Transits cannot come here anymore, as the valley is full of Magav jeeps, Jerusalem Park warden jeeps, and the railway company contractors' SUVs. All of these supposedly "all-terrain" vehicles, by the way, are new and shining, with hardly an speck of dust or mud on them, for they drive on the newly paved asphalt roads. All this engine power for nothing.

The paved bike trail now descends toward the dry riverbed, and crosses it on a low ford (an "Irish bridge"—the name is another vestige of the British Mandate in this country). After crossing, I decide to stray off the paved trail and ride up the hill to see the 9/11 monument. I could have continued on the paved road to there, but besides the fact that that path is longer, I really feel the need to ride what's left of the dirt trails. So I take a shortcut on a very rugged trail. After six or seven minutes of climbing, I reach the paved road that leads to the 9/11 monument. I stop for a moment and examine a border stone of the Green Line—a meter-high concrete pyramid base with a rectangular pillar that rises from it—and the village Beit Iksa at the top of the hill, two hundred meters from here. These border stones were very common along the Green Line before

1967, but now, my geographer friend Amiram Oren told me, there are only a few dozen of them left throughout the whole country. Most of them were removed or destroyed purposefully by the Israeli authorities, to blur the Green Line as part of the "creeping annexation" process/policy. This one here is, therefore, a historical relic. But somehow I don't feel as excited as Amiram was when we discovered this stone. Borders mean less to me now.

Petty Politics at the 9/11 Monument

I enter the paved road again, and start riding toward the 9/11 monument. It is still not visible, lying beyond a curve. But just ahead of me there is another work site of the railway company (the A3 tunnel portal). I take notice of the half-deleted graffiti in Arabic that covers the site's safety fence. "Palestine," "Hamas," "Fatah," "Muhammad," and "Allah," I manage to read. There is also a Nazi swastika. All the symbols and concepts that would enrage or destabilize many Israelis. The graffiti was probably sprayed by Khalil and Muhammad Dahuk, two Palestinian brothers (twenty-six and thirty-four years old) who on April 12 this year, at night, "illegally entered Israel" from Beit Iksa and painted the same graffiti on the encircling walls of the 9/11 monument. They also added several drawings of the Palestinian flag, spilled some oily material on the base of the monument, pulled out several plants and seedlings that had been planted in the monument's garden, and ripped off the metal railings of the staircase that leads to the place (they took the metal with them). They then tried to set fire to the pine grove at the upper entrance to the railway company's work site, but the fire was eventually extinguished by the guard there. Trying to run back to Beit Iksa, a police force in "hot pursuit" caught the Dahuk brothers (the brothers, running away on foot, probably were very hot and sweaty. The policemen, riding on ATVs, were probably less strained). Little did the brothers know that night-vision surveillance equipment makes the valley visible to women soldiers in a situation room somewhere in this "sector." I, on the other hand, learned all this after seeing the destruction myself soon after they committed it, and talking with the local police officer of Mevasseret, whom I met there collecting evidence.

After telling me about the wonders of the night-vision systems that cover the "sector" and comparing the all-terrain capabilities of the police ATVs with my mountain bike's, Inspector Gil (pseudonym) added, "The Americans gave a lot of money to build this monument; it should be protected." He was very kind and informative, and I could not but feel appreciation for his dedication to his forensic work and willingness to talk about what happened with me, who had just popped up there with a bike one morning. But I also felt pity for him, for doing his best to collect evidence that will incriminate these two Beit Iksans, whose village is surrounded by the separation fence, excavations of the railway track (the same track that confiscated some of the village's land in the nearby wadi Luz), the 9/11 monument (which is built on land that belonged to the village before 1948), and a network of surveillance cameras that monitor every movement to and from the village. I don't know what motivated the Dahuk brothers to do what they did. Inspector Gil said that the younger brother, Khalil, already had two previous convictions in military courts. Perhaps it was the suffocation of their village that caused them to try to set fire to the pine grove and railway company work site, and to vent their anger on the 9/11 monument. Perhaps they had other motives. At any rate, while I was not supportive of their vandalism, I also hardly felt any sorrow for the harm to this object, the memorial, which had suddenly appeared in the landscape almost two years ago.

I reach now the end of the hill and stand in front of the 9/11 commemoration site. I am dazzled by the whiteness of the whole compound, a round plaza of seven hundred square meters (seven thousand square feet), paved with chiseled white limestone. Half the plaza is surrounded by one-meter-high wall, at a sixty-degree inclination, creating (on purpose?) the impression of an impact crater. Around this wall, there are fourteen big copper plates, with the names of the thousands of victims of the 9/11 attacks cast on them. The other half of the plaza is encircled by stone tribunes that can seat around 250 people. A staircase descends from the "reflection concourse," where I stand now, into the main plaza. There, in the middle of the plaza, black and shimmering in the blazing sun, a nine-meter-high bronze statue stands. It has a conical base, from which a huge bronze flame-shaped US flag rises up to the sky.[6] When I stand in front of the statue, I strongly feel the emphasis given here to the state—the huge flaglike statue attracts the visitor's eye much more than the three thousand names of the individual victims, which are engraved so close to each other on the copper plates that there is hardly any space between them. With hardly any space for their individuality, the tightly engraved names create an image of the victims as a mass of people, not individual and unique human beings. Of course, on a certain level, these people were murdered, en masse, indiscriminately, in an act of terrorism committed against the *United States* as a state. But many of the victims were not American citizens (more than 300 persons, from ninety-two countries). There is no mention of this fact at the site, which is exclusively "American." Furthermore, by making the American national flag the center—literally—of the memorial, isn't this monument reiterating the terrorists' understanding and representation of "America" as a monolithic entity in itself?

There is no shade, and it is very difficult to stay at the site and ruminate or to honor the memory of the victims for more than a few minutes because of the heat and the shimmering brightness. Even on cooler days, the memorial does not invite a longer stay. Basically, this is a photo-op site: come, take a picture, and leave. Right now, there is no one here, but as the morning unfolds, an occasional tourist bus will arrive. On weekends, the site becomes busier, and in addition to the tourists, Israeli families, who visit the Arazim Valley, will come to see the monument. I often heard parents explain to their small children about 9/11. Is it necessary, I wonder now, that small children know that such horror is even possible? What a terrible emotional burden to put on a small child's shoulders. Why can't we preserve our children's innocence for a precious few more years? Why do families that come out for a Saturday bike ride on the new bike trail here in the valley have to confront this gigantic memorial site?

But the 9/11 monument cries out for attention and visibility. Initially, it was designed to be twelve meters high, not nine, but the JNF's landscape engineers objected to this height. Yet, even with the shortened American flamelike flag statue, the whiteness of the plaza is clearly seen even from the opposite Highway 1, above the Arazim Valley. But from this side of the valley, the dominant view is Jerusalem's enormous Har Hamenuchot cemetery. What a macabre view for a 9/11 monument, I think for the hundredth time. The macabre view *from* the monument is not something that the JNF, which built the memorial here, desired. But the high visibility of the site from Highway 1 was very much desired. The price of this high visibility is, unfortunately, that visitors cannot actually stay for long on the perimeter, to reflect about the various meanings of the 9/11 terror attacks and the consequent "war on terror." Perhaps this is for the better after all, I suddenly think, as I realize that the little children can't stay for long at the site due to the blaze and overbrightness.

I take a long sip from my "hydration system" (a nice name for a water bag with an elastic straw that comes out of it and rests on my shoulder during the ride, enabling me to drink without stopping). Then I ride through the wheel-

The 9/11 memorial at the Arazim Valley, the sun blazing on the reflection plaza. *At the background*, Jerusalem's central cemetery and the Jerusalem–Tel Aviv Highway Highway 1. (Photograph by Idit Wagner.)

chair track down to the bronze US flag, the main "attraction" here. The damage caused by the Dahuk brothers was fixed, but one can still see on the encircling white limestone-covered walls the faint remains of the graffiti. I suddenly smile cynically as I recall that only a few months ago, especially for Independence Day, the national water corporation, Mekorot, hired a restoration expert to restore the famous graffiti "Palmach, Baruch Jamili, PT,[7] 1948!" [פלמ"ח, ברוך ג'מילי, פ"ת, 1948!] on its Sha'ar HaGuy pumping station building along the Jerusalem–Tel Aviv highway. The now dead Palmach fighter Baruch Jamili (died 2004), wrote his name with tar, in large black letters on the concrete wall of the pumping station during the battles on the road to Jerusalem in 1948. Jamili said that he did this out of fear of dying there and becoming an anonymous casualty. "I wanted to make myself a memorial, for we did not know then who would live and who would die."[8]

The graffiti became an unofficial icon of the road to Jerusalem, and many copycats sprayed "Baruch Jamili" in hundreds of other places. In 1984, though, Mekorot deleted the graffiti, arguing that it marred the pumping station. Jamili appealed to a court of law, but his appeal was rejected. Now, however, with the surge of ultranationalism and the parallel/subsequent increase of collective existential anxieties in Israel, Mekorot and the National Heritage Project of the Prime Minister's Office (Prime Minister Netanyahu established this project in 2010), decided to restore the graffiti! Jamili's individual cry for meaning during war became a "national heritage" after his death. I wonder if, when there is peace one day, someone will pay a special restoration artist to restore any of the deleted graffiti here, at the 9/11 monument (probably not, if only because of the swastika . . .).

I ride around the bronze US flag/flame to its rear side. "A reminder of shared loss and a call for peace among nations," reads a stone plaque there, in three languages (Hebrew, Arabic, and English). Rich donors of the JNF from the United States gave money to this project. The plaza itself was donated by the Bronka Stavsky Rabin Weintraub Trust (a million-dollar donation to the JNF). The trust had a total sum of fifty million dollars to donate to various organizations, and the managers of the trust, a former high-ranking official of JNF Israel told me, stipulated that a donation to the JNF would be dependent on whether the organization might have some "attractive" project to offer. And it did—an "Israeli" 9/11 monument. The donation was secured.

The US flaming flag itself, the plaque says, was dedicated by Edward Blank (and several others of his family) from "New York, New York." Edward Blank is one the major donors to the US chapter of the JNF. He donated one million US dollars for this monument. The former high-ranking official of the Israeli branch of the JNF told me that the money the organization received from the Stavski Trust was enough for this project, and that the entrance of Blank into the project represented a "submission to the Americans" (that is, to the US chapter of the JNF).

Submission, but also flattery, to *the* Americans, not only those from the American JNF chapter, catches much of the essence of this place, I feel. Not surprisingly, the memorial has become a "must-see" site for many Jewish American "Taglit-Birthright Israel" youth/student groups.[9] which are brought in air-conditioned buses to the place to plant pine and cedar seedlings in the nearby grove or to help reconstruct, with JNF and Jerusalem Park guides, ancient stone terraces nearby. The terraces, they are told, were made by the "Jews" (actually, the right historical term in this context would be "Judahites"—the inhabitants of the ancient Kingdom of Judah) "three thousand years ago." Not a word is mentioned as to who else used—and maintained—the terraces after the Jews/ Judahites were supposedly exiled from the country in the first century CE.[10]

I recall how one evening, it was the day after Osama bin Laden was killed by the American military (May 2, 2011), when I returned from campus, I came to the 9/11 memorial and saw there a group of about twenty such American "kids" sitting by a bonfire in the nearby grove, singing, with their Israeli guide, "authentic" Israeli songs (songs that were popular in the youth movements in the 1970s, at most . . .). What brought me there that evening? Perhaps a desire to see if I would feel anything special about this successful end of a long hunt. Bin Laden, after all, was one of the "protagonists" of my book *Predators and Parasites*. Despite this, I did not feel anything special on the day he was killed. I was hoping that a visit to the memorial site would kindle some emotion in me regarding this, any kind of emotion, but it did not help. I remained quite indifferent. I did not pity bin Laden, but I was also not moved by the fact that they managed to kill him. Perhaps it was the monument itself that caused me to become so aloof, to be more aware of and worried about the local implications of the "war on terror" rather than simply rejoicing over the death of an archterrorist, abominable as he might be?

When I approached the Taglit kids, their Israeli guide was worried about me talking with them. She didn't know me—she was just generally overprotective, as if she were guarding the innocence of these youths, who came to *discover* Israel (*taglit*, in Hebrew, means "discovery"). She almost physically blocked my way to them, demanding to know exactly who I was and what precisely I wanted to say to the American kids (it turned out that there were two Australians and three Canadians among them).[11] I did not have anything specific to say to them, just wanted to reach out, and to hear what they thought about the monument and bin Laden's death. Most of them were really moved by the monument, especially on this particular day. I did not want to ruin their emotional elation with my skepticism, and after a while I bid them good-bye, riding home in the darkness.

I find a tiny piece of shade cast by the flag monument, and sit on the floor, laying the bike next to me. The shade's perimeter is small, just enough to protect me from the sun. I then think about the speeches in the official ceremonies that took place here in November 2009 (at the dedication ceremony) and on September 11, 2010 (I read the texts on the Internet—access to the memorial was allowed then only to VIPs). The US ambassador, former prime minister Ehud Olmert, and all kinds of other dignitaries said here much about the shared destiny and values of the United States and Israel, and about the similar nature of the "war on terror" that was imposed on both countries. National pathos poured like water, and wide shading sheets were stretched over the plaza, to cool the important guests, who flocked to this place in their expensive cars and choking suits and uniforms, the pictures and videos showed. When the ceremony was over, the shading sheets were dismantled. The dignitaries will return, though, soon, on September 11 this year too. And in the following years too. I look up at the statue. It suddenly looks like a bust of Caesar to be worshiped in the Province of Judea.[12] Yes, friendship among nations is something admirable and good, and identifying with the suffering of the American people after 9/11 is a noble motive. But beyond its bad aesthetics, this site also works, at least in effect if not in purpose, as a legitimizing machine for Israel's never-ending war on terror; it is a statement that the terror that hit the United States is of the same kind that hits Israel. Yet, there are innumerable differences between the two "terrorisms."

And in these ceremonies, there was a lot of talk about tolerance and the unity of humanity. At the site itself, too, a metal plaque at the entrance says, "Tolerance, Not Terrorism." But when I talked with one of the people who was directly involved in the planning and creating of the monument, he repeatedly emphasized his fear for the costly metal plaques and parts of the memorial, his fear that metal thieves (namely, Palestinians) might dismantle and steal them. I asked him about the seeming contradiction between the monument's message of tolerance, on the one hand, and the proximity of besieged Beit Iksa to the monument, on the other hand. He replied that the idea of the memorial is not something an ordinary Arab would understand. Then he told me about the historical hostility of the villagers of Beit Iksa to Israel.

"So, the memorial was built so close to Beit Iksa so the villagers would *not* steal or harm it?" I tried to joke with my interlocutor. He didn't laugh, but said that initially the memorial was supposed to be erected somewhere southeast of its current location, on top of the forested hill of Mitzpeh Naftoach, near the Jewish neighborhood of Ramot, at the edge of the Arazim Valley. There it was supposed to have enjoyed better visibility from Highway 1. The residents of Ramot, though, objected out of NIMBY (not in my backyard) considerations.

Finally, after many legal deliberations and negotiations, the current site was picked.

"But the whole purpose of placing the monument in this location in order to increase its visibility will be foiled in a few years, when the gigantic train bridge that will pass right above the memorial site and the Arazim Valley will actually dwarf it and hide it from the eyes of the drivers on Highway 1," a colleague who introduced me to some of the people who were involved in the planning and erection of the monument told me. Thus, without too much thinking, a literally shining memorial, designed for visibility, was put (although it is on the Israeli side of the Green Line) in immediate proximity to an occupied Palestinian village, whose residents have no civil rights. Now the memorial is almost waiting to be vandalized and in this way to "prove" the supposed innate tendency of the Palestinians to commit sabotage. In passing, it also corrupted a beautiful hill.

The heat is becoming intolerable, and the piece of shade starts to shrink. I begin to feel my head whirling beneath the helmet. I ride out of the memorial's plaza, and stop to watch it from above, on the hill, in the shade of a large pine tree. I think again about the Dahuk brothers, who defiled the place. Interestingly, they did not write any anti-American graffiti on the memorial, only words that can be seen as "anti-Israeli," and, of course, the swastika. Could it be that they would not have done what they did had the residents of Beit Iksa been allowed to access this monument, or been invited to the official ceremonies there? Or perhaps they would not have sprayed and defiled the memorial had it not been, in their eyes probably, a part of a *planned* (and not just stupidly incidental) policy of encircling their village. With all this talk about tolerance and good "interreligious" relations, the builders of the monument could have taken a closer look at the map or just stretched their necks and seen the neighboring villagers, even though they live two hundred meters beyond the deleted (that is, deleted for Israelis but not for Palestinians) Green Line. The organizers of the ceremonies here could have thought of inviting people from the close, so close, community. Perhaps if they had invited the *neighbors* from Beit Iksa, they wouldn't have had to worry so much about metal thieves afterward.

The Dahuk brothers will probably be convicted and sent to jail for their act. But perhaps their act, obnoxious as it was, provided an opportunity for the police, the JNF, and the Municipality of Jerusalem to demonstrate their *own* degree of forgiveness and tolerance. The more I think about this idea of my former student, Yonatan Fialkoff, with whom I had toured the Arazim Valley a few days before, the more I see the missed opportunity that was here.

In Yonatan's "thought experiment," such a conciliatory approach on the part of these Israeli authorities and organizations could have turned into a critical deconstruction of the concepts that constitute the conflict through an act of "face-value reading" of these notions. Couldn't such an interpretation of the vandalistic act drive it to a place of correction? By not defining the act automatically as a "crime" or "sabotage," the authorities could have looked at the case as an embodiment of the absurdity of the Israeli-Palestinian condition (a monument of tolerance at the doorstep of a suffocated and occupied village). If *all* the "actors" in this affair could have adopted an ironic perspective on the case, perhaps a new form of cooperation would have been born, wondered Yonatan? The Dahuk brothers would have apologized, cleaned up the graffiti, and fixed the other damage they caused (Perhaps with the help of friends from the village? Even better, they could have applied to some international aid agency to get funding for the work); the authorities would have apologized to the residents of Beit Iksa for not inviting them to the dedication and annual 9/11 ceremonies; if generous enough, the authorities could also have acknowledged that the land on which the memorial stands was Beit Iksa's before the 1948 war; the Beit Iksans could have been granted open access to the monument and the Jerusalem Park in the Arazim Valley (they could have used the new bike paths on a daily basis); and everyone could have sat together around the table to think about how we could combine forces in Mediterranean cunning to "milk" more money from the "patsy" Americans and Europeans for another "peace initiative."[13]

Yonatan, a religious Jerusalemite with "strong emotional, social, and familial connections to the settlement enterprise in Judea and Samaria," as he described himself to me once, wishes that one day the institution of the state will be freed from nationalism. He wants the state to be a "gray" institution, something like the municipality of a city. People, he says, don't hang the flag of their municipality or the picture of their mayor on their decks. "Yeah, but once they did, in city-states," I replied. "But we're beyond that today; the City is mainly seen now as a provider of garbage services, and all kinds of other mundane 'public goods.' No one will go to war for their cities," he said. In his effort to deconstruct nationalism, he is currently cowriting a script for a movie based on these ideas. In the tangled plot of this political satire, a childish Israeli film student who is on the run from the Mob joins forces with a small-scale Palestinian entrepreneur to produce a kitschy "peace" film for an eccentric German producer. Yonatan plans to cast a mix of Israeli and Palestinian actors and wishes to actually raise money for the production from European funds (that is, ones that have a good enough sense of humor . . .). This, he hopes, will be the first of many actions aimed at deconstructing the abstract and official concept of "peace." He offers to turn *peace*, a term that in his view unfortunately has become a leftist cliché, upside down into a long, patient, and cunning process, which will involve the joint "screwing" (he insists on the vulgarity, to expose the peace cliché) of "patsy" foreign donors—"mainly, Europeans trying to polish their postcolonial guilt"— through theatrically playing out our roles as enemies that look for new means of cooperation and who decide to openly play on the card of "conflict" to enrich themselves. Eventually, the performance of peace will develop into a genuine peace—one that is not a hollow "ideology" imposed by detached leaders but rather a mundane and down-to-earth fellowship of regular people. At first, I was uncomfortable with his idea of "screwing and enriching," as it reminded me of both Bibi Netanyahu's concept of "economic peace" (which, in my mind, is a guise to continue the occupation as a regime of segregation and inequality) and the tricks of the *moshavim* farmers down here in the valley, with their bid for compensation from the railway company and the Municipality of Jerusalem due to expected damages to their not-yet-planted vineyards. Moreover, is it moral to "screw" international donors just for the sake of sharing the revenues generated from their sincere good intentions? And wouldn't existing power politics be preserved or even aggravated in such a joint performance of conflict and peace? I thought about a movie that I'd seen recently, *Full Battle Rattle*. In the Mojave Desert in California, a whole fake Iraqi town was built in order to serve as background for training American forces on their way to Iraq. Iraqi refugees who recently became American citizens played many of the roles of "Iraqis" in the town, "Medina Wasl."[14] Was it a healing experience for them, to relive some of the experiences of the war in Iraq in this *faked* set, as American citizens, or were their emotional wounds opened again?

But the more I thought of Yonatan's ideas, I also understood that much of the current politics of the Israelis and Palestinians is based not only on avoiding healing wounds but also on keeping them open and reopening them time and again. Each side, of course, acknowledges and picks only at its own wounds. This never-ending process is motivated, at least partially, by the desire to extract various forms of international sympathy and material support as a resource within the conflict framework. This support—to the Palestinians and Israelis—often helps maintain the occupation, and so the cycle never ends. Various Israeli and Palestinian groups and elites have an interest in the status quo of the occupation: some Israelis believe that eventually there will be an opportunity to "get rid" of the Palestinians either through some cataclysmic war or, simply, by making their lives so miserable that many of them will "choose" to leave. Some Palestinians, on the other hand, believe in the "power of demography," that the womb of the Palestinian woman is the ultimate weapon in the conflict, and that one day the Palestinians will be able to claim a "one-state solution," based on demographic figures, and then many Jews will "choose" to emigrate. The occupation, thus, serves growing elements on both sides as a strategy of buying another day.

Of course, there is real victimhood, on both sides of the conflict, and we should do all we can to confront these issues and think about how to engage in practices of restorative justice and mutual acceptance and recognition of *our* traumas. But at the same time, it is also important to acknowledge that "the conflict" has become, effectively, a deep part of the self-identities of its parties and a strategic asset of certain elements within each party. Wouldn't it be better in some respects to expose this game and ironically work *together* to benefit both sides? After all, the boundaries between kitsch, authenticity, and performance are fluid. Moreover, if a considerable component of the conflict is a performative one, why not jointly charge the viewers for the tickets? At least in this way some of the victimhood mentality of people here could be changed, and people might develop some sense of self-irony. Irony can empower the weak too. Eventually, who knows, maybe Israelis and Palestinians will recognize the absurd elements in the conflict and grow up from it. I don't mean that the conflict as a whole is absurd or funny, but there are places and components in it that are such. Perhaps by treating these elements first, we will find new "solutions" (an absurd word in itself in this context) to the more tragic elements. At least the international "patsies" will get some real return on their money (and in that case, of course, they will not be patsies at all . . .).

Thinking about Yonatan's ideas, I give the memorial site a last look and ride on. Then I realize that the place actually tests *my own* tolerance too: can I be tolerant toward this absurd site? I know how much it means to some of the people who envisioned it. I can also assume that for many Americans it will become dear once they learn even about its mere existence. I do not underestimate or ridicule anyone's pain even for a minute. But I really find the place absurd in many ways (nationalistic imagery, artistic/architectural design, political effects on the ground, flattering "the Americans," and the use of it as a place to legitimize the never-ending Israeli "war on terror"). Can I be tolerant of all this? Can I be tolerant of Yonatan's ideas, which seem to me very sincere but also morally dangerous and challenging to my own identity and self-perception as a victim of this conflict system? After all, I have devoted so much time to exposing and being exposed to the pain of this land. Can I give this pain up for some ironic "milking" project a la Yonatan? The thoughts swirl in my mind while I race down the path, back to the Arazim Valley.

It is already getting close to 9:00 a.m. I am approaching the work site of the government's nuclear bunker "somewhere in the Arazim Valley."[15] The newly paved bike trail is slowly ascending between the hills. Beyond the next curve lies the work site. I cannot see it yet, but on the other side of the Soreq wadi I notice the pickup truck of the security team of the work site, patrolling. I wonder how they define the perimeter of their patrol, which extends a considerable distance from the bunker itself. Half a year ago, I once asked the guards about that, but they said that these were simply their directions. "But what is it actually that you're guarding here?" I asked. They did not answer, only quietly smiled, knowingly, as "insiders" or confidants will often do. I knew all too well what they were guarding there. Was I hoping to become an insider by getting an answer from them? To some extent, perhaps. But I also wanted to be the investigator, he who asks the questions, instead of the one who had been required by these guards—by the state, around whose secret temple I was sniffing—quite a few times by then to "present an ID." As I see the security vehicle now, I recall all these instances when the guards wanted to see my ID and I insisted first on seeing theirs, to authenticate *their* identity.

The bunker's work site, a huge scar on the landscape, is guarded 24/7 by the Shin Bet. The entrance to the bunker lies within the area of the Jerusalem Park, and is thus seen by many people who come to visit here. But it is discordant in the supposedly leisure and outdoor space of this area: it is surrounded by security fences and signs that prohibit photographing. Interestingly, there is no specification of who it is that actually prohibits photographing.[16] The park wardens told me that there is no communication between them and the Ministry of

Defense, whose construction unit is responsible for managing the works there. They simply refuse any communication with the park authorities, on the pretext of security reasons. And, apparently, there is nothing and nobody that can impose such communication on the Ministry of Defense.

With all this secrecy and security, the actual sight of the site is disappointing: behind the fences, there's just a very big quarrylike work site. Heavy drilling and mining machinery, bulldozers, piles of rocks that are being ground to dirt by a special machine. Trucks keep emerging from a large and wide hole in the hillside, loaded with dirt and rocks. All this can be clearly seen from a point on the bike trail—the part that is just behind the curve I'm approaching now. The landscape around the site is bathed in a thick layer of white limestone dust. White water, saturated with limestone silt, pours out of some place in the site, flowing into the Soreq riverbed and permeating the soil there. There is something bad or poisonous about the water: hardly anything grows along the small stream.

They have probably hit some underground water source there, I think. I wonder what this stream looks like inside the tunnel and bunker itself—they have been digging here for years, and have probably hollowed out the entire mountain. Judging by the huge amounts of dirt and rocks they keep taking out, perhaps they have even connected this tunnel to Zedekiah's Cave underneath the Old City of Jerusalem. There, in the coolness of the mythological escape tunnel (in fact, it is just an ancient quarry) of King Zedekiah, the last king of the Kingdom of Judah, drops of water trickle from the rock—the tears of the exiled king, who bemoans his slaughtered sons and destroyed kingdom by the Chaldean army of the Babylonians in 586 BCE.

As I think about King Zedekiah, I suddenly notice a deer in the middle of the trail, perhaps ten meters ahead. The animal stands with his back to me, very still. He is looking very attentively in the direction of the valley below. I know this deer quite well—he has only one horn, and this area here is his territory. The vineyard planting has not reached here yet. Something troubles the deer, I realize, and stop the bike. Despite the braking rustle, the deer remains focused on the valley. I look at the deer and think, "Zedekiah, he had a tunnel running from his house to the Prairies of Jericho, and he went out through the tunnel. What did the Almighty do? He brought a deer before the army of the Chaldeans, and the deer walked in front of them on the roof of the tunnel, and they pursued him. And when Zedekiah emerged from the tunnel at the Prairies of Jericho, they saw him and caught him."[17]

"Suddenly," both the deer and I are startled: a military helicopter appears in the air, no more than fifty meters above us. The sound of the rotors is extremely loud, and the wind the aircraft generates is very strong. The deer runs into the thicket, down in the dry riverbed. I stand, amazed, fighting the wind and watching the helicopter. I can clearly see the pilots. They are busy with what seem from down here to be the switches of their control panel. They don't appear to notice me. What is going on? A mixture of curiosity and alarm sweeps my body. I have been taken by complete surprise—what is this helicopter doing here? The helicopter then rises farther into the air and starts encircling the area. The wind subsides. It then goes down again, and I see it landing about two hundred meters away from me, in a clearing between the bike trail and the truck road. The helicopter touches the ground, and then goes up again. For the next ten minutes, the helicopter—an army "taxicab" for senior commanders and other VIPs, not a gunship—repeats the routine several times, at various locations in the valley in front of me. Perhaps they're rehearsing a quick escape from or entrance into the bunker, trying to look for an optimal landing point. Just a few weeks ago, the entire Cabinet "went down" into the bunker through this tunnel. I saw them passing in their limos and SUVs.[18] It was during the National Homefront Drill, a routine that began a few years ago, after the second Lebanon war, with the aim of preparing the nation for a missile attack on the home front. Part of the drill's purpose is, though, to maintain the state of emergency in the consciousness of every citizen *all the time*, as the Minister for the Defense of the Homefront said two years ago. Perhaps, in fact, this is the (*main*) aim not only of the drill but also of the bunker, which serves in this case as a theatrical backdrop for this maintenance of the state of emergency.

Finally, the helicopter takes off for the last time, and flies away from the Arazim Valley. As I watch it disappearing beyond the hills, I think, "They" will not be caught like King Zedekiah. The ministers, who practiced being evacuated into the bunker here, were awed by the shelter. Its sophisticated machinery and "futuristic" planning reminded them of the scenery of a science fiction movie.[19] I wonder how many of them actually know something about science fiction aside from naming a few popular Hollywood blockbusters. *A Canticle for Leibowitz* by Walter M. Miller, an apocalyptic history of the future that talks about the horrors and folly of nuclear war, is a book I would recommend that they read before they consider pushing the "red button" and taking shelter inside the supposedly impenetrable bunker. There's even a good translation to Hebrew. And perhaps they should also read Amos Kenan's *The Road to Ein Harod*.

There, in the final part of this very rare Hebrew-written science fiction novelette (namely, science fiction is a rare original genre in Hebrew—is it because Israelis are so absorbed in the past and find it difficult to think about the future?), the protagonist is locked inside a secret underground bunker with a mad IDF general, who plans to shoot from there vengeful missiles at the Jewish past, to target enemies such as Titus (the Roman destroyer of the Second Temple in 70 CE) or Khmelnytsky (the Cossack warlord who butchered tens of thousands of Jews in Poland and Lithuania in the seventeenth century). Eventually, the protagonist, who is a person running away from military-ruled Tel Aviv to Ein Harod, the last bastion of freedom in the country after a coup, manages to frustrate the general's scheme. It would not be so simple in "reality," I think—to frustrate the efforts of those inside this bunker to shoot missiles at the Jewish past.

As the helicopter leaves, I, too, continue riding on the path. Here, I pass the curve, and in front of me is revealed the work site in "all its majesty." It looks today much as it looked six years ago, when I started riding in this valley. Then, I thought it was some water installation—because of the continuous water flowing from the site, the digging of a tunnel (at that time, they were laying a major pipeline to Jerusalem through the Arazim Valley, and I thought that the hole in the hillside here was related to that). The yellow "security" signs seemed to me logical—to protect the water supply installation. Over the years, I realized the true nature of the place by gleaning information from the news media and the park's wardens. Yet all my efforts to find out something more concrete and authoritative about the place and the logic that brought about its construction were foiled—e-mails that I wrote to the Ministry of Defense, the Prime Minister's Office, and the National Security Council never received replies. Several former senior security officials—whose actual degree of involvement in this project I don't really know (they refused to elaborate)—were willing to talk and meet with me, after I was referred to them by some of my more trustworthy colleagues whom they knew personally. Yet all I learned from the people I was referred to was that the Israeli leadership, after employing for so many years the "strategy of decapitation" (*arifa*) against Palestinian and other enemy leaders, needs a safe place to manage the state from at times of war and emergency. And that the bunker is also a part of the broader deterrence policy of Israel—let the enemies of the state know that the Israeli leadership has a protected place, from which to order a "second strike" in case of a devastating attack on the country.

"But what if the enemies interpret the bunker, the existence of which has been widely covered in the Israeli and international media, as a 'machine' that enables the Israeli government to order an *aggressive* 'first strike,'" I pressed General (ret.) Shmuel Canaan (pseudonym), a very senior former security official who agreed to an interview should I not mention his real name in my book. We were sitting in his office in one of Tel Aviv's glass and steel towers, big windows facing the Mediterranean and models of various fighter jets and other airplanes on the table and glass shelves around us. Throughout the one-hour meeting, he sat with his profile facing me, never looking me straight in the eyes. He was extremely serious, hardly even smiling. War, security—this is serious stuff, I reminded myself. There are not too many amusing elements in war, so why was I expecting him to smile from time to time? Perhaps it was the little airplane models, those toys, in his office that made me think that something of the child remained in him. But of course, not all children are playful or willing to let strangers see the playful aspects of their personalities.

At my question, Canaan seemed confused for a moment. He then said, "Israel is not an aggressive state; it is only being dragged into employing policies that can be *interpreted* as aggressive." I felt his hesitation now, and "stormed" forward. "But does Israel have any organized conception of deterrence?" I then talked about Lieutenant General (ret.) Dan Halutz's seeming confusion when asked about this issue by the official Inquiry Committee on the second Lebanon war (2006). When asked by the committee about the absence of any document defining the concept of "deterrence," Halutz replied that deterrence was a "very complex concept," and he was doubtful that such a document would have been useful in defining war aims and security policy. He added, however, that he would have been happy if such a document existed.[20] Nonetheless, Halutz, as chief of staff, could have easily ordered the writing of such a document, I told Canaan, smiling in victory. Canaan was evidently displeased—perhaps he thought that I was a "smartass" academic who knows nothing about the real world of security. Perhaps I was indeed such a smartass—I felt that he had agreed to meet me more in order to see what *I* know about the bunker than to tell me anything regarding it. At any rate, watching the bunker's entrance now, in the heat of July, I wonder if there's anyone who actually knows anything certain about security issues. Perhaps we are all just blindmen groping in the darkness of war, trying to make it intelligible and to draw some self-confidence by convincing ourselves that we do know what war is and how to cope with it.[21]

Who will be invited or ordered into the bunker when *the* war starts, I wondered many times when I was riding here. I dreamed recently a strange dream: I am riding near the bunker, and I see Baruch Jamili standing at the entrance of the tunnel, with his IDF uniform and major ranks. He is welcoming a long line of people, entering silently into the hole. He hands each one a gas mask— just in case, even though the bunker is impenetrable (Jamili volunteered to distribute gas masks to the public during the 2003 Iraq war). "Suddenly," I notice Ma'ayan and Nissim, with their children, in the line. I wave and call to them, but they cannot hear me—perhaps I am too far away? The gate of the bunker then closes, and I remain outside.

But seriously, who will get in, the question keeps bugging me. Beyond the officials and politicians that are the obvious "suspects" in this case, is there any list of dignitaries or officials that have a reserved place? Will their families be allowed in too? What will they do with those who knock on the gates of the underground citadel and demand to be let in? How will they prove that they have a reserved place inside? Do they carry a special permit with them all the time? "If you really want to know who will be let in, you just have to find the list of those who were attending the state funeral of [assassinated] Prime Minister Yitzhak Rabin [in 1995]," I recall a friend telling me once. I indeed wrote to the Prime Minister's Office and the Foreign Office about this list, but, again, there were no responses. Well, one can assume that the pillars of the nation, people such as the famous writer Amos Oz, or the chief rabi, will have a reserved place, I think now as I try to retain some sense of irony in front of this doomsday location. I wonder about the place's aesthetics, and what the hundreds of people inside it will do in their spare time—they might be locked in for decades.[22] Do they have a library there? "Manuscripts don't burn," I recall the saying of the devil in Mikhail Bulgakov's *The Master and Margarita*. Manuscripts don't burn, but people do.[23]

Indeed, as I watch the dark hole of the escape tunnel, and see the trucks that keep emerging from it loaded with limestone rocks and dirt, I suddenly think to myself, could this be real, this whole place? Can there really be such an all-out war in this country, one that will force the government to entrench itself in such a formidable bunker? I know that "every modern country" has such a bunker, but Israel is, nonetheless, a "one-bomb state." Who, outside the shelter, will enjoy the "continuity of government" this bunker seems to promise? (This is a concept I learned after reading about bunkerology in the recent year).[24] The bunker "speaks to us of other elements, of terrific atmospheric pressure, of an unusual world in which science and technology have developed the possibility of final disintegration."[25] I realize that the bunker—and the high secrecy it is engulfed in—represents for me a deeply pessimistic, dystopian vision of the future, and, even more so, it sheds black light, so to speak, on my barely existing ability to influence this future—for who or what can penetrate the deep and fortified mountain shelter? "They" cannot even smile at my jokes. Perhaps I could have been one of those trustworthy professors who are fooled into believing that they are in the inner circle of decision making. But I can't fool *myself*—I will never be in this inner circle or even close to it. The bunker will always be, for me, a scar in the landscape, not a place where I belong.

I keep rolling down the path, finding some relief in the effortless movement, and now the trail intersects with the service road that emerges from the bunker, for the use of the trucks and other vehicles that operate there. To my right I see the security pickup truck, returning from one side of its patrol route, and preparing to continue to the other part. Inside the vehicle, two young Shin Bet guards sit. I wave at them; they smile and wave back. We already know each other well, have examined thoroughly each other's IDs, and I know their routines and scheduled patrols around the perimeter. We once talked about my bicycle, and ever since have we remained on friendly terms.

"Hey, Doc, what are you doing out here today?" one of the guards asks me. "It's a terrible *khamsin* [heat wave], 32 degrees [Celsius] already this morning, must be very hard on the bike," he adds, or provokes. I look at the pickup truck. Perhaps it would be a good idea to ask them for a ride to the top of the hill. The heat and dryness are intense, after all, and the dust from the digging is burning my throat. Then my glance drifts back to the gates of the bunker. Maybe under the influence of the heat, I suddenly envision these security guards on the "day of the bomb," jumping, as in a Hollywood "action" film, into the closing gates through a small space that is still left just before the tunnel shuts down for eternity. No, I change my mind. There is no point in asking for a ride; they will say it's against their instructions. I'll climb out of the valley myself. There is no problem with my bike, and I feel good, despite the heat. The radio in their truck, I hear, is playing a song of Meir Ariel and David Broza: "Hey, hey, it's all about drinking something cool in the middle of the desert . . ." (in Hebrew, היי, היי, כל העניין הוא לשתות משהו קר בלב מדבר).

We talk for a few more moments, and I tell them that I won't be riding here in the next year and a half. They wish me a happy journey, say good-bye, and continue their patrol. They close the car's window, comfortable again in the coolness of the air-conditioner. As they disappear in a cloud of dust, I continue singing Ariel and Broza's song.

> Look, look at these Gary Coopers,
> These smartass Clint Eastwoods, pretending to scorn the *khamsin*.
> It's about time that you pull your long tongue out of Western culture . . .

Looking ahead of me, I see the trail ascending from the Arazim Valley. I take a long breath, absorbing the *khamsin* into me, embracing it. I do not scorn it. It is a part of me. I go on with my ride.

Contradictions[1]

SOME CONCLUDING THOUGHTS
ABOUT *THE POLITICS OF THE TRAIL*

I wrote this book as an autoethnography of emotional and experiential exploration of a landscape of political violence and conflict in Israel and Palestine. True, the perspective of the book was mainly limited to the sights and experiences of the bike ride along a small portion of the frontier of Jerusalem (namely, along and beyond the northwestern parts of the route of the separation fence and the Green Line in the "Corridor of Jerusalem"). I investigated the landscape of past, current, and possible future violence along the bike trails I rode from home to campus, and became an expert in the history and current politics of the very close region near my home. Obviously, this exploration was quite arbitrary in terms of the issues and problems I dealt with, as these were mainly defined by the actual sights and experiences along the trails. Someone even told me that not only was the landscape I explored a landscape of violence but my very focus on this small region was a violent choice in itself, precisely due to my *insistence* on describing only what I saw or was exposed to in order to focus on certain pieces of a bigger reality.

Indeed, I focused mainly on the space I rode through. Yet I think it was important that after initially commuting to campus fast and in a relatively straight line (in the Halilim and Arazim valleys), I eventually started stopping along the path and also wandering off, decommuting, to other trails in the area, zigzagging in the hills (to wadi Luz, the ruins of Qalunya, Nabi Samwil, and along the fence near Beit Surik and Beit Iksa). I also rode in parts of East Jerusalem (for example, to Sheikh Jarrah to meet Nabeela and Raja from Qalunya and to the area of the Damascus Gate [to visit the nearby Zedekiah's Cave and get a sense of what it might be like deep underground in the nuclear bunker ...]). The sights and people I saw and met in these decommuting deviations led me to grasp many more realities and elements of the conflict, and to broaden my readings on it. Furthermore, as I mentioned in the introduction to this book, events and patterns that were "external" to my trail prompted me to look more closely around me: the second Lebanon war of 2006, the Gaza war of 2008–9, and the death of my father, for example. All of these events had broader political meanings that shed more light on the smaller manifestations of the conflict along my trails and helped connect these elementary particles to macrostructures.

True, even after grasping some of this "bigger picture," my account was surely not a comprehensive and objective political account and history, and others who might have ridden or walked the trails I rode would probably depict the realities I talked about here differently and would meet the physical and human landscape in a different manner. Yet, even if my stories are subjective and restricted in their historical and political purview, I don't think that my choice of issues and questions was violent or coercive. Incidental as these issues and questions were, they did touch, literally, in the bodily sense, on major open wounds and scars on this land (for example, the 1948 war, the 1967 war and the occupation regime that was constructed in its aftermath, the Israeli fear of existential threats, and Israeli-American politics). Upon touching these wounds and scars, I consciously tried to contain the violence and pain of the landscape and *transcend this violence, to see beyond it.* The physical and human landscape I encountered often invoked in me fear, anger, despair, bitterness, cynicism, and sadness. But I sought to make clear to myself why I feel this way and whether these feelings are necessary and/or unalterable, personally and politically. Not always did I manage to confront, transform, and overcome these feelings, or even answer my own questions about their necessity and/or fixity and durability. But at least I honestly began trying to think about these questions. And there were times when, among the painful realities I saw, there emerged moments of friendship and human connection. Thus, my stories tell about my confusion and doubts and expose the contradictions within me and the people I met. I struggled with essentialist and/or imposing and exigent identities and concepts (such as "Zionism," "Israelis," "Palestinians," "the conflict," "history," "the land," "borders," and "truth"), sometimes inattentively accepting their a priori validity regarding myself or other people and places and sometimes recognizing the arbitrariness, power politics, and absurdity these notions and perceptions entail, thus trying to shed them or see the humanity of other people through them.

Thus, perhaps my choices of subject matter, choices that were posed by the landscape, were not that coercive even if I did not provide the reader with a comprehensive narrative or the kind of coherent theory that political scientists often try to present. By exploring my qualms and contradictory emotions, I wanted to raise questions that will help readers think about their own personal political conditions, and thus ponder more about the certainties and truths, about the coherence, rigor, and comprehensiveness, that supposedly stand at the base of their own political subjectivity and political theorizing. The importance of the fortuitousness of my exploration lies in the fact that this haphazard investigation allowed me to lose traction and fall into the cracks and crevices of the world, and thus find and see things that otherwise I would have probably ignored or would not have been aware of. By adhering to a research program that was less disorganized methodologically, so to speak, I know that I would probably not have become aware of the political stories that are embedded in the hills and wadis I rode every day. I would have been tempted to continue hurrying to campus, to cut another minute or two from my total riding time, and thus miss many things that became visible to me only after I "tarried" along the path; I might have missed the connection between exploring issues such as the 1948 war and the post-1967 occupation regime simply because they seemed to me like two distinct problems, each of them complicated and extensive in itself. But on the trail, the Nakba and the occupation were joined in spatial geographic senses, and in human stories and encounters as they became, in effect, parts of a continuous daily experience for me.

The words of my former student Yontan Fialkoff, in a tour report he composed for me after he and I walked the trails (he, unfortunately, does not ride a bike ...), are very relevant in the context of the supposed fortuitousness of my methodology. I quote him at length here.

> I distinguish between a paradigmatic and syntagmatic axis along your trail. The syntagmatic one is a classical story of "to there and back" that depicts the riding on the trail itself: here it is jumpy and rugged, here it is paved and comfortable. Now the trail enters the bright light and heat of the sun, and now it is shaded. You look up to the sky and see a snake eagle, and then you carefully hop over a

beetle, to not run over it. But, your path is nonetheless interrupted by political and ideological bumps and obstacles that slow down or disrupt your ride. These are the wake of the paradigmatic meanings that refuse to disappear, refuse to be "cleared" by the maneuverability of the mountain bike and your "technical" skills. The landscape is never what it seems at first sight, and the trail can never have an end. Your home can never be a "real" home, because you discovered that Mevasseret is actually (a) Colonia (what an irony!)—it is built on Qalunya's land [recall the Roman origin of the name: Colonia]. Qalunya is in ruins, but its Palestinian refugees keep coming back to it. But the story does not end there: Qalunya of the Arabs is built on Colonia of the Roman legionnaires, who, in their turn, destroyed the Jewish Temple, which was built on the land of the Jebusites, etc., etc.[2]

Even though the paradigmatic axis is apparently more profound and scholarly appreciated (it is aware of the history of the things and the political circumstances that constituted them, and is cognizant of the correct order of the layers of history), it is not necessarily a more accurate depiction, historically, than the one provided by the syntagmatic axis. This is because the paradigmatic axis deletes or ignores most of the *daily* activity along the trail: the presence of the passersby, the life and struggle of the animals and plants. What will remain, in a paradigmatic depiction, of our encounters with people we saw today along the trail? From the long conversation you and I had? Almost nothing, perhaps only the tracks of your bike tires that were embedded in the [wet] concrete [of the newly paved bike trail—I walked the bike next to Yonatan . . .]. From a moral point of view, a paradigmatic depiction (even though it supposedly exposes power structures more systematically) is not necessarily truer, at least in the aspect of trying to solve the injustices.

Yonatan then wrote about developing a method of teasing and challenging dominant paradigms: acts of everyday constructive sabotage, not violent ones, but first and foremost acts that break the mental fixation on separation: visiting Beit Surik without inquiring first whether the village is "hostile" or not, sitting with a Palestinian family during a picnic, and, of course, his idea of joint Palestinian-Israeli milking of "patsy" international donors through sites such as the 9/11 memorial as part of a move to make the institution of the state in our country a "gray" one, like the municipality of a city.

Indeed, my "syntagmatic axis" of exploration was jerky and not very orderly, but without performing it I would have probably postponed or repressed some of the hardest "paradigmatic" questions I asked myself throughout this journey. And, on the other hand, the paradigmatic issues prompted me, in their turn, to zigzag along the syntagmatic axis. I thus hope that this disorganized inquiry of mine along the mountain bike trails will join the doubts raised by others before and after me, and perhaps one day the monoliths of the "state," the "nation," and the "conflict" will indeed crumble to make way for new trails that cannot be thought of and ridden today. Or, to be less dramatic (and one has always to maintain some self-irony), that these monoliths will become less shining and mind captivating, and more gray and beneficial to ordinary people, a la Yonatan.

But while trying to shed essentialist identities from myself and to crack and tarnish monoliths, I also realized how deep are the foundations of these identities and structures in my soul. I understood how, despite my efforts to emancipate myself, there are elements in my identity that are highly resistant to transformation: some of my fears, memories, and understandings of the Palestinian/Arab other remain "Israeli"/Israeli (with or without the quotation marks). Then again, I recognized that I am also a foreigner in this landscape and culture of conflict, an insider-outsider. As I said in the introduction, I have always retained an "immigrant" identity: the foreignness of my, at times, pushed-aside Hungarian-Jewish identity, and the foreignness of the scholar, who (wishes to believe that he) adheres to humanistic, universal liberal and enlightened values of freedom, equality, and justice.[3] So, in this sense, inasmuch as one can criticize my haphazard and jumpy "cross-country methodology of the trail," one can also wonder whether my text is indeed an "authentic" Israeli one, or whether this book is an autoethnography in the almost literal sense that Mary Louise Pratt writes about.

> [The terms] "autoethnography" or "autoethnographic expression" . . . refer to instances in which colonized subjects undertake to represent themselves in ways that engage with the colonizer's own terms. If ethnographic texts are a means by which Europeans represent to themselves their (usually subjugated) others, autoethnographic texts are those the others construct in response to or in dialogue with those metropolitan representations. . . . Autoethnographic texts are not, then, what are usually thought of as "authentic" or autochthonous forms of self-representation. . . . Rather, autoethnography involves partial collaboration

with and appropriation of the idioms of the conqueror. Often . . . the idioms appropriated and transformed are those of travel and exploration writing, merged or infiltrated to varying degrees with indigenous modes. Often . . . they are bilingual and dialogic. Autoethnographic texts are typically heterogeneous on the reception end as well, usually addressed both to metropolitan readers and to literate sectors of the speaker's own social group, and bound to be received very differently by each.[4]

Indeed, often in my rides and in this book I recalled and quoted from all kinds of (mainly English-written) cultural treasures such as *Tom Sawyer, The Lord of the Rings, Three Men in a Boat, Hamlet,* or *Winnie The Pooh.* These books are part of me in the sense that they accompanied my life as I read them repeatedly, in their Hebrew translations of course. Often the things that I witnessed in my decommuting in the hills reminded me of works of literature and poetry, as well as some films and TV shows. Perhaps by storying and fictionalizing these realities, I found it easier to deal with the anger, sadness, and feeling of suffocation the landscape generated in me.

But did I develop a habit of finding the right quote at the right moment and place also out of a need to appeal to the "metropolitan" audience of my book, an audience whose presence I felt even before I had a clear notion of what this book was written for and why. Frantz Fanon writes:

A handsome black man is introduced to a group of white French. If it is a group of intellectuals, rest assured the black man will try to assert himself. He is asking them to pay attention not to the color of his skin, but to his intellectual powers. Many twenty- or thirty-year olds in Martinique go to work on Montesquieu or Claudel for the sole purpose of being able to quote him. The reason is that they hope their blackness will be forgotten if they become experts in such writers.[5]

Thinking about Pratt's colonizer/colonized and Fanon's white/black dichotomies in this context, I also consider Hanna Arendt's concept of the Jew as pariah/parvenu—the outcast versus the successful and assimilated person in a "gentile" society.[6] I'd like to think about such concepts not as dichotomous notions but rather as signifying the ends of a continuum. In this sense, if I learned something about myself during this study, it is that I inhabit the space between the occupied and the occupier person, between the native and the settler, and between the Jew who is assimilated into Western culture and the Jew who remains an (internal) exile.

For even when I'm writing these words on Vancouver Island, far away from Israel, I am a participant, a very reluctant one, but still one who partakes of the regime of the occupation—broadly understood as a regime of ethnic segregation and privilege, as well as a regime of control over geographic space within Israel itself *and* in the Occupied Palestinian Territories/West Bank. For example, I hope that the separation fence and the occupation of 1967 will fall and end one day, that the refugees of Qalunya will be able to return to their village alongside Mevasseret or be free and welcome to live in Mevasseret itself (the occupation of 1948), yet am very afraid of that same day and prefer to abstractly ruminate about it than to actually prepare for it. I am enraged by the nuclear bunker, this Masada in reverse tunnel and cave inside the mountain, but avoided mentioning its exact location here, even though the exact location is very important historically and politically. I did this not only because of censorship laws but also because a retired Israeli senior security official implored me, in the name of a comradeship that I was never really a part of, not to do this, because should the enemy know this location, "they" might accurately target the place (there's a difference between an approximate and direct hit, he told me). Do I really need to carry on my conscience the deaths of some or all of the bunker's dwellers due to a direct hit that is the result of my disclosure, I often thought when I rode by the place and considered how and what to write about it. Of course, the thought is absurd—the intelligence apparatus of the "enemy" probably knows exactly where the bunker is, and if a nuclear missile hits the bunker, directly or just approximately, this means that I, outside the bunker, will probably no longer exist and will not have to face any conscientious dilemmas . . . But, still, this is a question of a moral principle   (-;   isn't it?

The bunker—it represents in many respects the fears of annihilation of the Israeli state, its sense of besiegement, and its conviction that there will never be a genuine, legitimate peace in this area—that Israel, as Moshe Dayan said, will ever need to live with the muzzle and the steel helmet (and with *our, only our,* nuclear weapons, the existence of which we only ambiguously admit and hardly discuss the rationale of among ourselves). That we will always be a generation of settlers. And by not disclosing its exact location, I realize, I participate myself in the occupation, in its meaning as an eternal pessimist state of mind and a conduct of conduct (ever preparing for some war, ever realizing that our hold on the land depends on the force of arms and "deterrence"),[7] a conviction that Israel is indeed a "villa in the jungle."[8]

Yet, besides being a critical occupier, I am also occupied by the occupation. It creeps into my dreams at night and wakes me up panting and shivering. It caused me to appear to Palestinian dayworkers who come to earn their bread in my town as an official who required seeing their "papers," perhaps because I really suspected that they had hostile intentions. The occupation invades and stains my memories of a passionate youthful love while a soldier in Hebron (of course, in another sense, it was me who invaded Hebron . . .), and it manifests itself in the form of an aggressive understanding of custodianship of land in the space where I feel I belong, so close to my home in Mevasseret. The occupation changes the landscape of the valleys and hills I love by "developing" them— passing massive and offhandedly planned train bridges in wadi Lauza and the Arazim Valley, leveling even the ruins of Qalunya—the Palestinian demolished village to which I came to feel such a strong connection. The occupation strews the hills with nationalistic monuments, whether in the form of memorial places like the 9/11 site or in the form of "sacred" objects such as the separation fence or the nuclear bunker, sites that beyond their function as machines of security, and beyond the fact that they simply block my ride and interrupt the "flow" of the trail, also become idols of the religion of security or Israel's "strategic relations with America."

Much of my political value-world comes from, is imported from, the metropolis—of Europe, and, even more, of the United States and Canada. (It is strange for Canadians, I know, to think about themselves as part of the world metropolis. But for a person from a province of Western culture, as Israel still is in many senses, Toronto and even Victoria, *British* Columbia, seem to me much closer to the cultural and political centers of the world . . .) Israel is, to some degree, a liberal democracy. But this democracy is much more procedural and formal than a stable and solid one, and even this condition is becoming ever more undermined. Increasingly, the lonely islands of liberal democracy in Israeli society are shrinking and attacked by the hegemony of the New Israeli Right.[9] As ultranationalism and religious fundamentalism in Israel deepen and widen, I find myself feeling like a minority and at odds with the dominant values of the society I am a part of. Perhaps, therefore, my insistence on telling only/mainly about the space of my bike rides?

Furthermore, as a scholar of international relations who has spent as a visiting scholar three and a half years in Canada,[10] this multicultural country, and who has traveled to many international conferences and workshops (mainly in the United States . . .), I am also much produced by the "international"—by the outside world. In this sense, my autoethnography is indeed informed by values and ideas from the outside and my text does seek to engage with metropolitan audiences, partially on their terms. This book is written, after all, in English.

This is not done in order to *flatter* these audiences or grovel before them, and thus attain material benefits (recall my discussion in the introduction about "shooting and crying") but because in certain ways I feel also a part of this "metropolis" and believe that approaching a wider audience, a metropolitan one included, is very important politically and scholarly. It is not that I gave up hope on my own domestic audience. I will teach this book in my classes at the *Hebrew* University (the university of the *Jewish* people, as it defines itself, not of the *Israeli* people (it was established in 1918, thirty years before the Israeli state), and its mission includes "broadening the frontiers of knowledge for the benefit of *all* humankind"—my italics). But increasingly, I also feel at home in English, or rather in my Bad English—the true international language. (-;   In this sense, the book represents my strong connection to and rootedness in the international, even if its subject matter is Israel-Palestine. I thus "live" both in Israel and in the international.[11]

This multilayered identity of mine will influence, I believe, the ways the book is received by domestic and international audiences. Generally, my experience is that the things I wrote and thought here will be accepted more critically, if not reproachfully, in Israel than abroad. My Israeli students have often been very angry over my depictions of the reality I face on my way to campus, and have remarked that my work might contribute to the increasing delegitimization of the State of Israel. Not a few of my colleagues who heard me in various talks and seminars have objected to my use of autoethnography as a legitimate social science method from the outset, and scholars of the Israeli-Palestinian conflict have often criticized me for my lack of systematic expert knowledge in this field (even though I maintain, as I said above, that I possess an *unsystematic* knowledge and scholarly authority regarding this conflict, which is also a valuable asset).

On the other hand, while on sabbatical in Canada, I presented parts of this book in several talks, seminars, and workshops at several universities (in Toronto's York, Ottawa's Carleton, Vancouver's Simon Fraser, Victoria's University of

Victoria and Royal Roads, and Nanaimo's Vancouver Island), and the responses of the audiences ranged from solidarity to indifference. Only in one case was I reprimanded by a Syrian Canadian for supposedly presenting propaganda of the Zionist regime, "which plans bombing Iran with nuclear weapons and murdering all the Palestinians at the same opportunity." Did I feel more at home in Canada due to this relatively welcoming reception of my work, this last response not included?[12] In many senses, of course, I did. It is nice to be appreciated and understood. Paradoxically, there was also something solacing in the indifference of some of the people who heard me—perhaps what I told them was not that terrible, perhaps I came not from such a crazy place, after all? But at the same time, I longed for the arguments with my Israeli students and colleagues—I felt that even if they were extremely against my work or even against me personally (and in this kind of work it is hard to distinguish between the author and the work ...), at least they cared much more about what I had to say than did my Canadian listeners, who would continue their daily business after hearing me.

I also felt that I appreciated much more the positive or accepting responses that a few people in Israel did offer than the similar and more frequent accepting responses in Canada. I felt that I, due to my tenured position in the Hebrew University,[13] bear some responsibility to protect and nurture those students who opened up to my narrative in classes. Could I really protect them in the ever-deteriorating democratic climate in Israel? Would they benefit from my protection or support? These questions are still left unanswered for me while I write this final part of the book. Yet the sabbatical on Vancouver Island taught me that I belong in many places at once: in the larger, macro-, political context of Israel, and in the micropolitical enterprise of deconstruction along my trail. I belong in the internationally oriented and liberal Hebrew University ("for the benefit of *all* humankind") and, at the same time, in the closed-minded and national institution that it is in other respects. I feel that I, too, belong in Jewish culture and history, and in the Western tradition. And while I found my place on the dusty trails of the Halilim and Lauza wadis and Arazim Valley, I also feel at home in the rain forests and Pacific beaches of Vancouver Island.

Beautiful Vancouver Island. Two days after arriving here, on July 30, 2011, I bought a mountain bicycle. My "Israeli" bike (an American-designed machine, manufactured in Taiwan) I left at my mother's home and later sold to a friend of a friend. I loved that bicycle. Like any previous bicycles I have owned, I used to think of it as the best bike I have had so far. It was a 29er trail/cross-country machine—full suspension aluminum frame equipped with twenty-nine-inch wheels (instead of the "standard" twenty-six inches). It was a companion on many good rides in the hills and wadis. I treated it with much care and love. My "Canadian" bike (also an American-designed 29er machine, made in Taiwan but sold in a special "edition" for the Canadian market only), is even better. This bike will return with me from Canada to Israel, even if only to bring with it some of the good memories of my stay here. One day I will sell this bike too and buy another one—will it be another "Israeli" bike or a "Canadian"? Probably an "Israeli" . . . But the bicycle, eventually, is an idea: an idea of freedom and unrestricted mobility, of self-sufficiency and control, of physical challenge and connectivity with the terrain and the outdoors.

In Israel, I started riding the bike from Mevasseret to campus, from home to university, mainly in order to *disengage* from the local political conditions, which pressed themselves hard on me in the form of exploding busses. In practice, what happened was the opposite, as I turned my riding into a practice of decommuting that involved exposure to and of the violent landscape along the trails from home to campus. On Vancouver Island, on the other hand, I ride not to decommute to work. I am on a sabbatical leave, and live too far from the campus of the University of Victoria, the university with which I am affiliated. We live about sixty kilometers away from Victoria, in the Cowichan Valley, probably the warmest place in Canada.[14] We came here because Cowichan has the only Waldorf School on the island and we wanted our kids to have continuity in this regard. And I felt I needed to get as far away from Israel as possible in order to write this book, a mission that in the space between Mevasseret and Mt. Scopus was too onerous for me to complete. My rides in the Cowichan Valley are mainly to keep in shape and to recreate in the outdoors. But for good or bad, I also continue "riding" on my Mevasseret-Jerusalem trails while on the island: my thoughts wander to *those* trails all the time as I write this book far away from Jerusalem. This keeps me, for a while, from exposing the politics of the Cowichan trails.

At first the woods of Vancouver Island seem to me very dark and dense, real pristine forests. The Douglas firs, spruces, and western red cedars looked immense, tall and almost reaching the sky. The arbutuses are huge compared to the few I see in the hills of Jerusalem. The trees appear so old and deep rooted too, unlike the fragile and thin pines around Jerusalem. Climbing Mt. Tzouhalem or Cobble Hill Mountain, the forest is like the woods that I read about in James

Fenimore Cooper's books or Robin Hood's Sherwood:[15] the thick trunks and stumps, covered with moss, the ferns that grow among the trees, the soil that is always wet or muddy, the steeper and more rugged and curving trails that flow almost endlessly without leading to any separation fence, the water that runs freely on the slopes, the ocean that can be seen from the summits of the mountains. In the shadows, the eyes of black bears and cougars. Busy with thoughts about the Jerusalem trails, while admiring the old trees and fearing the wild animals, I pay no attention to the politics of the trail here.

And then comes the winter, which in Canadian terms is very mild at this time, but in Israeli notions is not, to say the least. I keep riding in the winter, too, and with the right riding clothes I eventually did not miss a ride even when it snowed (mildly, of course). It took me several months to get used to the new landscape, climate, and light (the light was much softer), and then I fell in love with this island. The woods no longer seemed menacing, and the soil became more stable under my tires, even though I could not stop thinking about the vast Pacific Ocean that this island "floats" upon. I started drinking water from the running creeks in the woods, and opened up to meet other riders along the trails. They told me that these are, in fact, "second-growth" woods, only sixty to eighty years old. The real old forests of the island have mostly been logged by now.

Daniel, a high school teacher and mountain biker who was born and raised in Cowichan, in a family that has its origins among the first British settlers, told me about his internal struggles with his cherishing of his own family's engagement in the logging industry, on the one hand, and his love of the woods and the secret paths in them, paths that he gladly shared with me, on the other hand. He took me to see the ruins of his grandparents' logging cabin in the Koksilah River Park. Deep inside the regenerating forest, the only remains of the cabin are some bricks from the fireplace, a few pieces of kitchenware that survived the decades, and the iron door of a cookstove. I told Daniel about the ruins of Qalunya, about the ruins of the mufti's house. We then talked about *Eichmann in Jerusalem* and the Holocaust. After that he asked me to tell him, if possible, "what it means to me to be Jewish." "I'm much better at telling what it means to live in Israel," I responded.[16]

The months passed, and I became aware of the colonial and postcolonial situation of the Canadian state and of the crimes committed against the First Nations there. I learned about the residential schools that shattered the family structure and aboriginal culture, and about the devouring of the ancient rain forests by the logging companies.[17] Yet I also visited and loved the University of Victoria's "First People's House,"[18] was a guest in a (white) family's home where they kept totem poles of First Nations tribes out of genuine respect for the former "custodians of this land" (at first I was sure that this was just petit bourgeois interior design, but it really wasn't), and met a Jewish Canadian, a former American who had relinquished his American citizenship when he moved to this island in the 1970s, who, among his many deeds in life, had worked as a "pencil sharpener" for a First Nations organization (a code name for the job of being a "spy" and "agent" inside the white Canadian government . . .). I was moved deeply by the ability of the people here to contain and embrace so many identities within themselves and to try to come to terms with the crimes of the past. Of course, the big picture, the larger context, is very different from Israel's: here most of the indigenous people died because of various European diseases and alcohol use. And the country, Canada, is so large, territorially—Vancouver Island alone is larger than Israel. It is easier, under such conditions, to be "generous to the natives" and to face the past. But still I could not overlook the fact that coming to terms with the past is socially legitimate here, very different from what I was used to in Israel.

Countless times on Vancouver Island, English-speaking Canadians had difficulty pronouncing my name, Oded. Some pronounced it "Odet," others "Odeed," and on several occasions I was called "Obed." When I lamented this to Idit, and told her that just because of this I sometimes felt I would like to return to Israel right now, she said, "Yes, they have difficulty in pronouncing your name [and hers too], but at least they earnestly try." When she said that, and when her words seeped into my mind, I realized how much I love and feel connected to this island too, how I can see myself living here beyond this sabbatical, even if many people here will never be able to say my name correctly. I thought of Meron Benvenisti, who knows where in Jerusalem he was born and where he will be buried.[19] I know where I was born in Jerusalem, but don't know where I will be buried—whether it will be in Jerusalem or even somewhere else in Israel, for that matter. This does not mean, though, that I am less a native than Benvenisti. Perhaps being a native also entails the ability to leave the country you love, being confident in the love you have for this land, but also loving another country. Or perhaps nativity also entails the realization that even from "abroad" one can still work, and even work better than from "within," to deconstruct a culture of conflict and violence. I will surely continue to think about these questions when I return to the trails of the northwestern frontier of Jerusalem within a few months.

Oded Löwenheim
Mevasseret Zion, the hills and wadis of northwestern Jerusalem,
and Mt. Scopus, Jerusalem, Israel, May 2010–July 2011
Cowichan Bay, Vancouver Island, British Colombia, August 2011–January 2013

NOTES

Prologue

1. Although *wadi* is an Arabic word, it is very much in Hebrew usage. Even though the Israelis and the Palestinians, as national collectives, are in conflict, many Hebrew and Arabic words were assimilated in each other's language.

2. For where is the international physically located? At the airport? On the border? At the foreign office? At another country's embassy? At the United Nations (UN) or World Trade Organization offices and buildings? At the battlefield? Of course, it is in all these places and others like them, and, at the same time, it is nowhere. All these places and others like them are physical locations or spaces in the territory of certain countries that are invested with international status or imagined international status through a specific practice performed in them. And if the state itself is an imagined community, then interstate relations are imagination of the second order?

3. The Hebrew University has four campuses. Mt. Scopus was the first one, and in it the university was inaugurated in 1925. After the 1948 Arab-Israeli war, Mt. Scopus became an Israeli enclave within Jordanian-ruled East Jerusalem. The faculties of the university were moved to Giva't Ram in West Jerusalem. In 1981 the humanistic faculties (Humanities, Social Sciences, Law, Social Work, and Education) returned to Mt. Scopus, to a new campus. Natural Sciences and Mathematics remained in Giva't Ram, which is an open-space garden campus, sharply distinct from the closeness of Mt. Scopus.

4. Large portions of the "official" Masada story told to Israeli schoolchildren and youths are exaggerated and mythical. For example, the Sicarii were not freedom zealots in the current meaning of the term but rather religious fanatics who terrorized Jerusalem and the Jewish villages of the desert. In addition, there is hardly any archaeological evidence for the story of the mass suicide. On the construction of the Masada myth as part of the state-building process of Israel, see Nachman Ben Yehuda, *The Masada Myth: Collective Memory and Mythmaking in Israel* (Madison: University of Wisconsin Press, 1985).

5. Often Israeli Jews find it difficult, if not despicable, to use the word *Palestinian*. They would rather use *Arab*.

6. The term *Arab Houses* refers to old, large, and usually luxurious houses that were built and owned by Palestinian "aristocrats," mainly in former Palestinian neighborhoods

in Jerusalem, before 1948. Their prices are usually very high to rent or buy. See, in this context, Prof. George Bisharat's account of his visit to his family house, Villa Harun ar-Rashid, in the former Palestinian neighborhood of Talbiyeh in Jerusalem, "The Family Never Lived Here," *Haaretz*, English ed., January 2, 2004, accessed August 10, 2011, http://www.haaretz.com/the-family-never-lived-here-1.60698.

7. *Chizbats* are fantastic, half-comic, half-thriller "stories" told by the bonfire. They were very common among the members of the Palmach, the Jewish elite militia during the pre-state era (before 1948) and often involved fictive Arab characters and "folklore." See Elliot Oring, *Jokes and Their Relations* (New Brunswick, NJ: Transaction Books, 2010), 55–62.

8. Such stubble is often "securitized" in Israel as a suspicious sign or mark, giving one the appearance of an "Arab."

9. "This is a well-folded letter of recommendation from my father: / He is, nonetheless, a good boy, full of love." Yehuda Amichai, "A Letter of Recommendation," in *Behind All This, a Great Happiness Is Hiding* (Tel Aviv: Schoken, 1985), 41–42 (in Hebrew).

10. Michel Foucault, "The Subject and the Power," in *Michel Foucault: Beyond Structuralism and Hermeneutics*, ed. Hubert Dreyfus and Paul Rabinow (Brighton: Harvester, 1982), 220–21.

11. See the picture on the Palestine Remembered" website, accessed August 11, 2011, http//www.palestineremembered.com/Jerusalem/Qalunya/Picture73291.html.

12. See the picture on the Palestine Remembered website, accessed August 11, 2011, http://www.palestineremembered.com/Jerusalem/Qalunya/Picture25562.html.

13. The "Prime Directive" in the *Star Trek* "universe" refers to the Federation of Planets' "prohibition against interfering in the internal development of alien civilizations."

Introduction

1. Even though Israel considers Jerusalem its capital, almost no other state recognizes this claim due to the contested status of the city within the Israeli-Palestinian conflict. Some countries do not even acknowledge that Jerusalem, including its western part, is "in" Israel. Such contradictions between Israeli and international conceptualizations and perceptions generate a constant state of ambiguity and tension in Israeli politics that permeates many aspects of the daily lives of Israelis and Palestinians. On this innate ambiguity, see Lev Louis Grinberg, "Speechlessness: In Search of Language to Resist the Israeli Thing without a Name,'" *International Journal of Politics, Culture, and Society* 22 (2009).

2. Most of the trail I ride on runs parallel to the Green Line—the 1949 armistice agreement line between Israel and Jordan that demarcated the space usually called thereafter the "West Bank." Since the 1967 war, the West Bank has also been known as the largest part of the Occupied Palestinian Territories. Although Israel does its best to blur and even delete the political significance and relevance of the Green Line, the line still remains in many parts of it, like the one I ride along, a frontier zone in the sense of being an area of mutual penetration (interpenetration) by Israelis and Palestinians (though hardly on an

equal and egalitarian basis). On the definition of the frontier as a zone of interpenetration, see Howard Lamar and Leonard Thompson, *The Frontier in History: North America and Southern Africa Compared* (New Haven: Yale University Press, 1981), 7.

3. In this sense, this book is a "microscopic" investigation, in Clifford Geertz's notion. See his *The Interpretation of Cultures* (New York: Basic Books, 1973), 21.

4. Claude Lévi-Strauss, *Tristes Tropiques* (New York: Penguin, 2012), 1; Kim Soochul, "Moving around Seoul," *Cultural Studies <=> Critical Methodologies* (2010): 7.

5. The literature on the Israeli-Palestinian and Arab-Israeli conflicts is vast. However, as general introduction texts I would recommend these two books: Benny Morris, *Righteous Victims: A History of the Zionist-Arab Conflict, 1881–2001* (New York: Vintage Books, 2001); and Rashid Khalidi, *The Iron Cage: The Story of the Palestinian Struggle for Statehood* (Boston: Beacon Press, 2006).

6. Obviously, my perspective is that of an Israeli, although one could say that a similar or parallel culture imbues the Palestinian being too.

7. On this aspect of ethnographic work see Geertz, *The Interpretation of Cultures*, 25–30.

8. See, for example, Morgan Brigg and Roland Bleiker, "Autoethnographic International Relations: Exploring the Self as a Source of Knowledge," *Review of International Studies* 36 (2010); Elizabeth Dauphinee, "The Ethics of Autoethnography," *Review of International Studies* 36 (2010); and Oded Löwenheim, "The 'I' in IR: An Autoethnographic Account," *Review of International Studies* 36 (2010). See also Naeem Inayatullah, ed., *Autobiographical International Relations* (London: Routledge, 2011); and Daniel A. Bell and Avner de Shalit, *The Spirit of Cities: Why the Identity of a City Matters in a Global Age* (Princeton: Princeton University Press, 2011). In geography see Pamela Moss, ed., *Placing Autobiography in Geography* (Syracuse: Syracuse University Press, 2001); and Henry Hunker, *Columbus, Ohio: A Personal Geography* (Columbus: Ohio State University Press, 2000). In business see Mark Learmonth and Michael Humphreys, "Autoethnography and Academic Identity: Glimpsing Business School Doppelgängers," *Organization* 19 (2012).

9. Carolyn Ellis, *The Ethnographic I: A Methodological Novel about Autoethnography* (Walnut Creek, CA: AltaMira Press, 2004), 37.

10. See Laurel Richardson, *Fields of Play: Constructing an Academic Life* (New Brunswick, NJ: Rutgers University Press, 1997).

11. See Nicholas L. Holt, "Representation, Legitimation, and Autoethnography: An Autoethnographic Writing Story," *International Journal of Qualitative Methods* 2 (2003), 2.

12. See Leon Anderson, "Analytic Autoethnography," *Journal of Contemporary Ethnography* 35 (2006), 390.

13. Eric Mykhalovskiy, "Reconsidering Table Talk: Critical Thoughts on the Relationship between Sociology, Autobiography, and Self-Indulgence," *Qualitative Sociology* 19 (1996), 140, 141. See also Anthony Giddens, *Modernity and Self-Identity: Self and Society in the Late Modern Age* (Stanford: Stanford University Press, 1991), 12.

14. See Pamela Moss, "Writing One's Life," in *Placing Autobiography in Geography*, ed. Pamela Moss (Syracuse: Syracuse University Press, 2001), 3.

15. Hannah Arendt, *The Human Condition* (Chicago: University of Chicago Press, 1958), 184.

16. Dauphinee, "The Ethics of Autoethnography," 802.

17. Two recent very good ethnographic works on the conflict are Juliana Ochs's *Security and Suspicion: An Ethnography of Everyday Life in Israel* (Philadelphia: University of Pennsylvania Press, 2011); and Rochelle A. Davis's *Palestinian Village Histories: Geographies of the Displaced* (Stanford, CA: Stanford University Press, 2010). Ochs's text analyzes the Israeli culture of conflict by examining daily practices such as the work of security guards in public locations (cafés, malls, etc.), volunteering in the Civic Guard, daily commuting within Jerusalem, and tours along the separation wall (as she names the structure). Davis collected more than one hundred books written by Palestinian refugees about their demolished and/or depopulated villages and through reading these books, interviewing their writers, and conducting ethnographic work in Palestinian communities in Israel, the West Bank, Syria, Jordan, and Lebanon ponders questions of how history is written and how memory plays a role in contemporary life. But both these authors are not explicit about their motives for writing these books (a stance which is a legitimate academic practice) and they also hardly reveal what the writing of these books has done to them. Both Ochs and Davis sound in their respective texts as omniscient narrators, and we are not being told much about their doubts and personal processes of transformation, which, I argue, are essentially part of the depicted reality too. My book aims precisely at providing the reader the element of "felt news." It seeks to describe the personal dimensions and emotional upheavals and costs that are entailed in being a "participant" in my own ethnography, and, in so doing, to provide a richer and thicker description of the culture of conflict.

18. This is, in some senses, paradoxical. I already experienced the secluding outcomes of sharing the burden, but I want to continue sharing it. I cannot deny that there is a paradox here, but I hope that in the long run the paradox will vanish as my readership becomes broader and more diverse.

19. I am thankful to Elizabeth Dauphinee for this observation.

20. "But why in English, so that the 'gentiles' will know?!" exclaimed a senior professor in my department after hearing my talk on this book. His response is not anti-Semitism in reverse but a manifestation of Israel's ghetto syndrome—suspicion of everything that is foreign and external (with the exception, perhaps, of neoliberal economic methods and systems . . .).

21. For a very vivid example of how the state system's norms instill shame and fear in the individual "illegal immigrant" see Shahram Khosravi, "The 'Illegal' Traveler: An Autoethnography of Borders," *Social Anthropology* 15 (2007).

22. See Roxanne Lynn Doty, "Maladies of Our Souls: Identity and Voice in the Writing of Academic International Relations," *Cambridge Review of International Affairs* 17 (2004).

23. Brent J. Steele, though, argues that irony could be useful in allowing scholars a "critical distance" from their subject of study *without* requiring them to abandon their emotions. See his "Irony, Emotions, and Critical Distance," *Millennium: Journal of International Studies* 39 (2010).

24. Moss, "Writing One's Life," 9.

25. This is a project of unearthing the demolished and deliberately hidden and forgotten Palestinian landscape and presence, an effort of demolition and concealment taken relentlessly by the Israeli state since the 1948 war.

26. Meron Benvenisti, *Sacred Landscape: The Buried History of the Holy Land since 1948* (Berkeley: University of California Press, 2000), 336. Yet Benvenisti implies (or do I want to read him like that?) that Israel's conduct during and after the 1948 war, in relation to the destruction of the Palestinian landscape, could not have been different in the specific historical context; he writes that had the Palestinians won the 1948 war, "they would have destroyed *our* landscape." But eventually, "the sword had decided" in favor of Israel (3, italics added). Does this comfort Benvenisti? And me? Do I find in this alternate history path a justification for what Israel has done in actual reality?

27. Meron Benvenisti, *Son of the Cypresses: Memories, Reflections, and Regrets from a Political Life* (Berkeley: University of California Press, 2007), 232–33.

28. Ibid., 233.

29. Ibid., 230.

30. Benvenisti, *Scared Landscape*, 1.

31. Benvenisti, *Son of the Cypresses*, 230.

32. That is, it was the capital politically and culturally, even if not legally according to international law.

33. Benvenisti himself uses "Arabs" and "Palestinians" interchangeably. See note 5 in the prologue.

34. Noga Kadman writes at the beginning of her *The Depopulated Palestinian Villages of 1948 in the Israeli Discourse* (Jerusalem: November Books, 2008), 11 (in Hebrew), "During my childhood in Jerusalem, I participated in many school and youth movement trips to Lifta, the empty and half-ruined Arab village near the city, in which a spring runs its water into a pool. These tours left in me the vague impression that Lifta is such an ancient place, that its essence is in being a 'ruin,' as if it always stood desolate, somewhat mysterious, somewhat beautiful and threatening, with its silence and the narrow lanes between the houses and the heavy walls." I can attest to very similar experiences and memories, both in Lifta itself and in other places as well.

35. The city of Jerusalem was divided in the 1948 war between Israel and Jordan. In the 1967 war, Israel conquered the eastern, Jordanian-ruled, and Palestinian inhabited part of the city and imposed its sovereignty over it, as well as over many surrounding villages and towns that were never considered a part of Jerusalem but now were included in the municipal borders of the city. Benvenisti played a major role in determining these bound-

aries, as Mayor Teddy Kollek's aide. Jerusalem, though, was never really united, as the stark differences in the quality and quantity of municipal services, among many other factors and phenomena, between east and west demonstrate. See more on this on the website of Ir Amim (City of Peoples), a civil society group that "seeks to render Jerusalem a more viable and equitable city for the Israelis and Palestinians who share it" (accessed January 9, 2012, http://eng.ir-amim.org.il/).

36. Rachel Aldred argues that cycling involves "a more or less conscious non-consumption." Indeed, cycling consumes no petrol, and hardly any parking space and road space. See her "'On the Outside': Constructing Cycling Citizenship," *Social and Cultural Geography* 11 (2010): 36. Yet cycling, and especially mountain biking, often involves consumption of many gadgets and accessories. It is also often characterized by frequent replacements of the bicycle itself, which keeps "developing" and "improving." In this context, bike technological development becomes a manifestation of postmodern consumerism. See Paul Rosen, "The Social Construction of Mountain Bikes: Technology and Postmodernity in the Cycle Industry," *Social Studies of Science* 23 (1993).

37. Ochs, in *Security and Suspicion* (92), underestimates and downplays, I believe, the subjective sense of fear of riding a bus during the high days of the second Intifada. Indeed, the great majority of bus rides in Israel at that time did not end in a suicide bombing. And suspicion and fear of bus passengers were politically and socially constructed more than based on "real" considerations and factors. But the fear and suspicion were nonetheless very much present, and they had very concrete influences on people's daily lives not only at the level of behavioral practice, as Ochs shows, but, more important, at the inner, emotional, and psychological level. Interestingly, Ochs does not tell us about her own feelings: in the page from her book that I referred to above, she says nothing about how *she* felt during the bus ride in which she observed other passengers' fear and suspicion.

38. On cycling and exercise in the biopower context, see Aldred, "On the Outside." On page 36 she writes, "Regimes of bio-power construct the responsible citizen-subject who maintains his or her body, with stigmatized signs of failure including obesity. Cycling as a body practice could thus be seen as a means of displaying one's identity as a healthy, low-carbon subject."

39. See Nicholas Oddy, "The Flaneur on Wheels?" in *Cycling and Society*, ed., P. Rosen, Peter Cox, and David Horton (Burlington, Surrey: Ashgate, 2007), 101.

40. Justin Spinney, "Cycling the City: Non-place and the Sensory Construction of Meaning in a Mobile Practice," in, *Cycling and Society*, ed., P. Rosen, Peter Cox, and David Horton (Burlington, Surrey: Ashgate, 2007), 29.

41. I am thankful to my friend and colleague Oren Barak for this term.

42. See, in this context, these words of Max Weber in his essay "Science as a Vocation": "Ideas occur to us when they please, not when it pleases us. The best ideas do indeed occur to one's mind in the way in which Ihering describes it: when smoking a cigar on the sofa; or as Helmholtz states of himself with scientific exactitude: when taking a walk on a slowly

ascending street; or in a similar way. In any case, ideas come when we do not expect them, and not when we are brooding and searching at our desks. Yet ideas would certainly not come to mind had we not brooded at our desks and searched for answers with passionate devotion." Available at the University of Minnesota website, accessed January 12, 2012, http://tems.umn.edu/pdf/WeberScienceVocation.pdf, 6. I am thankful to Brent J. Steele for this quote.

43. In the 2010 science fiction movie *Inception*, there is a nice depiction of different layers of dreaming within one dream, or of a dream within a dream within a dream.

44. On the importance of the sensual experience in anthropological research, see Paul Stoller, *The Taste of Ethnographic Things: The Senses in Anthropology* (Philadelphia: University of Pennsylvania Press, 1989).

45. Tim Ingold, *The Perception of the Environment: Essays on Livelihood, Dwelling, and Skill* (London: Routledge, 2000), 192.

46. This tendency comes to the extreme in the case of integral Global Positioning System (GPS) navigation screens in cars, which "release" the driver from the need to actively look for the way to the destination (the device simply directs you—"turn right," "turn left," etc.—turning locations and driving itself into a form of simulation), or in the case of digital video disc (DVD) players installed in the car, which move attention from what happens outside to the content shown on the screen.

47. Jack Katz found that drivers experience cars as an extension of their bodies. This experience often leads to rage when other motorists "cut" in front in one's lane, for example. See his *How Emotions Work* (Chicago: University of Chicago Press, 2000), chap. 1.

48. Spinney, "Cycling the City," 29.

49. Sovereignty in premodern times was much constrained and limited by topography and the difficulty of projecting power, which was essentially manpower, into hilly or rugged terrain. See James C. Scott, *The Art of Not Being Governed: An Anarchist History of Upland Southeast Asia* (New Haven: Yale University Press, 2009). Scott suggests that in order to better understand the various power dynamics between states and nonstate populations and actors in premodern Southeast Asia, which were much determined by the rugged geography and constraining climate, "we would have to devise an entirely different metric for mapmaking: a metric that corrected for the friction of terrain. . . . The result for those accustomed to standard, as-the-crow-flies maps would look like the reflection of a fairground funhouse mirror. Navigable rivers, coastlines, and flat plains would be massively shrunken to reflect the ease of travel. Difficult-to-traverse mountains, swamps, marshes, and forests would be, by contrast, be massively enlarged to reflect travel times, even though the distances, as the crow flies, might be quite small" (47).

50. Nigel Thrift, "Driving in the City," *Theory, Culture & Society* 12 (2004), 47. Interestingly in this context, there's no "rush hour" for biking—so one never has to be strategic about timing. (I thank Mira Sucharov for this insight).

51. On similar aspects in the practice of walking in the city and hiking in the country,

see John Urry, *Sociology beyond Societies: Mobilities for the Twenty-First Century* (London: Routledge, 2000), 51–55.

52. Janice G. Stein, *The Cult of Efficiency* (Toronto: The House of Ananasi, 2002).

53. The two most notable, influential, and now "classic" examples in this context are Kenneth Waltz, *Theory of International Politics* (Reading, MA: Addison-Wesley, 1979); and Alexander Wendt, *Social Theory of International Politics* (Cambridge: Cambridge University Press, 1999).

54. For a primary discussion of these aspects, which influenced my thinking on these issues, see my PhD supervisor's book, Benjamin Miller, *States, Nations, and the Great Powers: The Sources of Regional War and Peace* (Cambridge: Cambridge University Press, 2007).

55. This saying is attributed to Abba Eban, former Israeli foreign minister.

56. During and after the 2006 Lebanon war, notable Israeli politicians and spokespersons bragged about how Hassan Nassrallah, the leader of Hizb'allah, had to constantly hide in a bunker, while they conducted themselves freely. None of them mentioned in this context the project of the nuclear bunker for the Israeli government. Former Israeli prime minister Ehud Olmert even said in December 2007, "We will not shield ourselves to insanity" (my free translation). He was referring to his cabinet approval to fund the construction of only a limited number of shelters and fortified buildings for civilians in Sederot, a town on the border of the Gaza enclave, which constantly suffers from Palestinian rockets and missiles. On the other hand, he spared no budget in building the bunker for the government, which in many senses is much more insane a project than simply protecting the lives of the residents of Sederot. During conversations I had with former security officials who in this or that way were involved in the project of the bunker, the mention of the fear of "beheading" of the Israeli leadership—due to Israel's own use of this strategy against the enemy leadership—was made again and again.

57. The article in which he took most pride is Avigdor Löwenheim, "Zsidók és a párbaj" [Jews and the duel], *Múlt és Jövő*, new ser., 3 (1992). This is an article about the participation of Hungarian Jews in duels at the end of the nineteenth century and the beginning of the twentieth. The duel was seen then as a mechanism for social mobility, and Jews had to prove their "worthiness" even to participate in the practice. I believe that this article, as well as his other writings about Hungarian Jewry, stemmed from the basic quest in his life: to come to terms with his identity as a Jewish Hungarian who had to leave his country but always longed for it. I did not think about it when my father was still alive, but now, when writing this book, I noticed that he used his Hebrew name (Avigdor) even when he published in Hungarian academic journals (his Hungarian name was László). In Israel, Avigdor was my father's "formal" name—he used it at his workplace at the Hebrew University's central library, at the bank and other "official" institutions, in correspondence with my schoolteachers (unfortunately, there were many such occasions when he had to excuse my "problematic" behavior . . .), and so on. However, in our family and among his Hungarian and Hungarian Israeli friends, he called himself László, or Lászi. After 1982, my

father traveled several times to Hungary, for his doctoral research and to meet his childhood friends. I once asked him if people there noticed that he was not from Hungary. "Of course," he replied. "After more than thirty years in Israel, I already have a Hebrew accent in my Hungarian." My father's Hebrew had traces of a Hungarian accent in it too, so he was always suspended between these two worlds, between being Lászi and being Avigdor, between being Hungarian and being Israeli. Whenever I think of emigrating from Israel, I am reminded of my father's dual life in Budapest/Jerusalem. Will I become an immigrant/refugee like him one day?

58. Jenny Edkins's book *Missing: Persons and Politics* (Ithaca: Cornell University Press, 2011), was prompted, she says, "by an anger at the way prevalent forms of political or biopolitical governance both objectify and instrumentalize the person. Contemporary systems of political management are based on the administration of populations; they treat persons as objects to be governed. . . . Contemporary politics does not see the person-as-such, only the person as object" (viii). Perhaps this tendency is at its worst in the health care system.

59. W. J. T. Mitchell, in his article "Holy Landscape: Israel, Palestine, and the American Wilderness," in *Landscape and Power*, ed. W. J. T. Mitchell (Chicago: University of Chicago Press, 2002), 262, says that he is concerned with "representations and stereotypes of the landscape that, while often demonstrably false and superficial, nevertheless have considerable power to mobilize political passions." In my case, my investigations led me to a conclusion similar to Mitchell's. The more I came to know the landscape of my ride, the more I saw the dimensions of superficiality and falseness that Mitchell talks about. But I also felt the passions that those images create in people I talked with about my research as well as feeling my own passion and attachment to the landscape, even when I became aware of the superficiality of its images.

60. This quote from the Danish author Isak Dinesen is the preamble to chapter 5 in Arendt's *The Human Condition*.

61. A major force in this context is the rightist student movement Im Tirzu, which "monitors" and publishes quasi-academic reports on "anti and post-Zionism bias" in Israeli academia. It considers the discussion of the Palestinian narrative by Israeli scholars as motivated by the desire for "scholarships, awards or tenure." See Erez Tadmor and Erel Segal, "Nakba—Nonsense: The Booklet That Fights for the Truth," accessed March 5, 2013, http://www.imti.org.il/Upload/NakbaNonsense.pdf, 18. See also Ofira Seliktar's article "'Tenured Radicals' in Israel: From New Zionism to Political Activism," *Israel Affairs* 11 (2005): 731: "Middle East Centres and women studies programmes in elite universities provide visiting opportunities for Israeli critical scholars, beyond what their rather modest academic output would have normally warranted. The United States Institute for Peace is another venue which showcases critical [Israeli] scholars." Not unrelated to the siege on free thinking I mentioned above is also the recommendation of an international evaluation committee (in fact, three of the seven members of the committee were Israeli professors) to

close the Department of Politics and Government in Ben Gurion University should it not implement various academic reforms and changes, among them to become less "political," and "that the Department [make] an effort that the program is perceived as balanced by the community concerned." Committee for the Evaluation of Political Science and International Relations Programs, "Ben Gurion University Department of Politics and Government Evaluation Report," September 2011, 15, accessed March 5, 2013, http://che.org.il/wp-content/uploads/2012/05/Ben-Gurion-Report.pdf. For more about the causes of the siege on Israeli academia, see Itzhak Galnoor, "Academic Freedom under Political Duress: Israel," *Social Research* 76 (2009).

62. See Uri Cohen, *The Mountain and the Hill: The Hebrew University of Jerusalem during the Pre-independence Period and Early Years of the State of Israel* (Tel Aviv: Am Oved, 2006), 49 (in Hebrew).

63. Yet Sternhell once expressed the view, in the op-ed pages of *Haaretz*, that the Palestinians would have been more rational had they directed their violence only against the settlers and not against Israelis within the boundaries of the Green Line. Ben Gurion University's Dr. Eyal Nir reportedly called upon the world to "break the necks" of rightist activists in Jerusalem. See Tomer Zarchin and Talila Nesher, "Israeli Professor Faces Criminal Charges over Facebook Status," *Haaretz*, October 27, 2011, accessed March 5, 2013, http://www.haaretz.com/news/national/israeli-professor-faces-criminal-charges-over-facebook-status-1.392342.

64. Letter from Professor Zvi Hacohen to the faculty of Ben Gurion University, September 5, 2010.

65. *Hasbarah*, in Hebrew, literally means "an act of explanation." *Hasbarah* entails an assumption that Israel should not lie about its policies in old-fashioned despotic propaganda, but rather should rationally "explain" itself to the world, and thus its justice would become evident.

66. See, for example, *Haaretz* columnist Gideon Levy's characterization of the Israeli-produced and Oscar-nominated animated movie "*Waltz with Bashir*, which critically deals with the 1982 Israeli invasion of Lebanon, as a pretense. "'Antiwar' Film *Waltz with Bashir* Is Nothing but a Charade," *Haaretz*, February 21, 2009, accessed March 5, 2013, http://www.haaretz.com/gideon-levy-antiwar-film-waltz-with-bashir-is-nothing-but-charade-1.270528.

67. Yehuda Shenhav's criticism of the Zionist Left is along these lines. See his *In the Trap of the Green Line: A Jewish Political Mass* (Tel Aviv: Am Oved, 2010) (in Hebrew).

68. On such an addiction to conflict in Israel/Palestine, see Jennifer Mitzen, "Ontological Security in World Politics: State Identity and the Security Dilemma," *European Journal of International Affairs* 12 (2006).

69. This vision comes from a seminar paper written by three graduate students at the Technion of Haifa—Alon Weingarten, Dan Berkovitch, and Michal Dor. The paper won the "outstanding planning project" prize of the Israeli Planners Association's 2012 annual convention.

70. Karl Kraus wrote in 1917, "At first, war is the hope that one will be better off; Then the expectation that the other will be worse off; Then the satisfaction that the other is not better off; Finally, the surprise that everyone is worse off." Quoted in Oren Barak, *The Lebanese Army: A National Institution in a Divided Society* (Albany: SUNY Press, 2009), 151.

71. W. J. T. Mitchell, "Imperial Landscape," in *Landscape and Power*, ed. W. J. T. Mitchell (Chicago: University of Chicago Press, 2002), 29.

72. Saint Augustine, *The Confessions*, trans. Henry Chadwick (Oxford: Oxford University Press, 1991), 180.

73. Dauphinee, "The Ethics of Autoethnography," 813.

74. Ibid.

75. Carolyn Ellis, "Creating Criteria: An Ethnographic Short Story," *Qualitative Inquiry* 6 (2000): 273.

76. Ibid., 275. See also Michael Quinn Patton, *Qualitative Research and Evaluation Methods* (Thousand Oaks, CA: Sage, 2002), 87; and Kristina Medford, "Caught with a Fake ID: Ethical Questions about Slippage in Autoethnography," *Qualitative Inquiry* 12 (2006).

77. See G. Thomas Couser, *Vulnerable Subjects: Ethics and Life Writing* (Ithaca: Cornell University Press, 2004), x. See also Carolyn Ellis, "Telling Secrets, Revealing Lives: Relational Ethics in Research with Intimate Others," *Qualitative Inquiry* 13 (2007): 5.

78. Ellis, "Telling Secrets, Revealing Lives," 26.

79. See Richardson, *Fields of Play*, 9–10.

80. See Paul Spicker, "Ethical Covert Research," *Sociology* 45 (2011).

81. See Ochs, *Security and Suspicion*, chap. 7.

82. See, for example, Sasha Polakow-Suransky, *The Unspoken Alliance: Israel's Secret Relationship with Apartheid South Africa* (New York: Random House, 2010), prologue and chap. 1.

83. Robert Musil, *The Man without Qualities*, vol. 1 (New York: Vintage Books, 1996), 13.

84. Mitchell, "Holy Landscape," 264.

Chapter One

1. *Shabachim* is the plural of *Shabach*. The latter is, in fact, an acronym of, literally, a person who stays illegally. While in previous years police spokespersons and many media outlets used to refer to Palestinians as "members of minority groups," since the second Palestinian intifada and the consequent erection of the separation fence with its complex regime of entry permits, Palestinians are increasingly referred to as Shabachim, often regardless of whether they do or don't have entry permits.

2. On Tegart forts, see Yigal Eyal and Amiram Oren, "Tegart Forts: Government and Security," *Cathedra* 104 (2002) (in Hebrew).

3. His two most recent books Amiram Oren, *"Drafted Territories": The Creation of Israeli Army Hegemony over the State's Land and Its Expanses during Its Early Years (1948–1956)* (Jerusalem: Madaf Publishing, 2009) (in Hebrew); and Amiram Oren and Raffi

Regev, *A Country in Khaki: Land and Security in Israel* (Jerusalem: Carmel, 2010) (in Hebrew).

4. Ami, my mentor in the field of the security landscape, also sent me to read this article: Nurit Kliot, "Afforestation for Security Purposes: Spatial Geographic Aspects," in *Studies in Eretz Yisrael: Aviel Ron Book*, ed. Y. Bar Gal, Nurit Kliot, and A. Peled (Haifa: Department of Geography, University of Haifa, 2004) (in Hebrew).

5. See Adi Hashmonai, "The Honey Is Enlisted: Trees against Rockets," *NRG Maariv*, March 20, 2011, accessed March 5, 2013, http://www.nrg.co.il/online/1/ART2/223/708.html?hp=1&cat=459 (in Hebrew).

6. See Saul E. Cohen, *The Politics of Planting: Israeli-Palestinian Competition for Control of Land in the Jerusalem Periphery* (Chicago: University of Chicago Press, 1993); and Carol Bardenstein, "Trees, Forests, and the Shaping of Palestinian and Israeli Collective Memory," in *Acts of Memory: Cultural Recall in the Present*, ed. Mieke Bal, Jonathan V. Crewe, and Leo Spitzer (Lebanon, NH: Dartmouth College Press, 1998).

7. Magav soldiers are actually, officially, policemen. But they are equipped with military weapons and they wear dark green uniforms, only slightly different from the olive-green/khaki-colored uniforms of IDF soldiers.

8. The Corridor of Jerusalem is the area that surrounds the highway from Tel Aviv to Jerusalem.

9. Ain Nakuba is among the handful of cases I know of a new Palestinian village built *legally* in the State of Israel (there are many illegal expansions of existing villages). Most of the other thirty Arab localities built legally since the establishment of Israel are towns in the Negev Desert, which were founded to funnel the nomadic Bedouin tribes into permanent locations, and thus take control of their traditional grazing lands. Ironically, the IDF itself built a large Arab mock village in its Tze'elim training facility in the Negev. See the photograph taken by Shai Kremer at http://www.shaikremer.com/il19.html (accessed March 5, 2013). The US Army also built such mock Arab towns at its Fort Irwin training base in the United States, the largest "town" called Medina Wasl. The Israeli Arab village is a ghost town—with no permanent "residents" in it. But the American-built town had actors, mostly Iraqi refugees, who played the roles of the inhabitants. These images and representations of the Arab other are a fascinating case for further research!

Chapter Two

1. In 1994, Jordan and Israel signed a formal peace treaty. Munir Ibn Hassan was one of the high-ranking Jordanian representatives at the peace talks. Even though the two militaries had maintained "good working relations" for many decades before this treaty, it is interesting to see that one of the first places Ibn Hassan visited in Israel after the peace treaty was signed was the place where he fought in 1967.

2. At the foot of the Mt. Scopus campus, there is a British war cemetery from the first world war. I pass it everyday when I ascend to campus; it is just on the side of the road.

In addition to the thousands of graves of Australian, British, and New Zealander soldiers who were killed in the 1917–18 battles in Palestine between the British and the Ottomans, there are five tombs of Italian soldiers in this cemetery. During that war, Italy was an ally of Britain. But when these soldiers were actually buried in the cemetery, in the early 1920s, Italy was already ruled by the fascists. On their tombstones, the Fascio—the bundle of rods, the symbol of Italian fascism—is engraved. Thus, they were made fascists in retrospect. Perhaps this is an opposite case from that of the Jordanian-Palestinian soldiers.

3. See Nachum Bruchi, *Har'el Armored Brigade (10) in the Six Days War* (Jerusalem: Ariel Publishing House, 2010) (in Hebrew).

4. This image is much related to the fact that in the 1948 war the Jordanian Arab Legion fought "professionally" against the Jewish forces, namely, that on top of its high level of military organization and performance (especially in comparison with the other Arab armies that invaded Palestine on May 15, 1948), the legion did not commit any atrocities against Jewish civilians or soldiers, and treated the Jewish captives with respect and fairness.

5. Once when I used this term in a conversation with my son, he said, "But crows don't fly straight, dad, they wind their way in the sky!" Perhaps, then, a better metaphor in the Israeli context, which indeed is often used in the public discourse in the country, would be "within bowshot." This case is a nice example of the "lost in translation" problem, and it also raised in me questions as to where I "live" mentally: in Hebrew or in English?

6. The fate of Beit Iksa is constantly debated in the Israeli government. There were conflicting governmental decisions about the route of the fence in the area—some resulted in including the village in the area that is "west of the fence" (i.e., on the Israeli side) and others concluded that the village should be "east of the fence" (i.e., disconnected and without access to Israel). See Amos Harel, "Flying in Face of Previous Government's Decision: Temporary Route of West Bank Fence Puts Beit Iksa on 'Wrong Side,'" *Haaretz*, July 29, 2009, accessed March 5, 2013, http://www.haaretz.com/print-edition/news/flying-in-face-of-previous-government-s-decision-temporary-route-of-west-bank-fence-puts-beit-iksa-on-wrong-side-1.280905. It is interesting to note, in this context, that the Israeli discourse usually considers the relevant village (for there are other similar cases) as an object that can be "put" on this or that side of the fence, and not vice versa (i.e., the fence can be "put" on this or that side of the village).

7. The Green Line was never acknowledged by Israel or Jordan as a final borderline, only as an armistice line after the 1948 war. Yet, de facto, the international community treats this line as the border between Israel and the future Palestinian state. Israel, for its part, has intentionally blurred the line in various ways and meanings (e.g., building settlements beyond it, deleting it from official and schoolbook maps, building highways that crisscross the line, and erecting the separation fence not in congruence with the line).

8. See Raja Shehadeh, *Palestinian Walks: Notes on a Vanishing Landscape* (London: Profile Books, 2010), 8.

9. Ibid., 15.

10. The term *minority* exemplifies how Israel managed to divide the Palestinians into five distinct groups, with varying political statuses and rights: the "Arab Israelis," with Israeli citizenship; the residents of "East Jerusalem," who have permanent residency rights but not citizenship; and the Palestinians of the West Bank, who live in three distinct administrative areas—A, B, and C—under the Palestinian Authority's rule (A) and the Israeli Civil Administration (C). "B" Palestinians live under Israeli military rule and Palestinian Authority's civil administration. In Gaza, the Palestinians live supposedly under their own independent rule, but, in fact, Israel controls the aerial and maritime spaces of the "strip" and most of the land entry points. Thus, even though the number of Palestinians in the space of Mandatory Palestine, which Israel rules in various degrees and forms, equals or slightly exceeds the number of Jewish Israelis, they can still be referred to as "minorities" due to these divide-and-rule techniques.

11. Reportedly these are the words of the Israeli author Amos Kenan, quoted in Nurit Gertz, *Unrepentant: Four Chapters in the Life of Amos Kenan* (Tel Aviv: Am Oved, 2008), 177 (in Hebrew).

12. On these supposedly comical prints, see Uri Blau, "IDF Raps Soldiers for Images of Dead Palestinian Babies on T-shirts," *Haaretz*, April 1, 2009, accessed March 5, 2013, http://www.haaretz.com/print-edition/news/idf-raps-soldiers-for-images-of-dead-palestinian-babies-on-t-shirts-1.273270.

13. Combatant soldiers in the IDF take their personal rifles home when they are on leave. In basic training, commanders instill in the new recruits the saying "Your rifle is like your wife—you should never take it off." In addition, a hierarchy of weapons indicates the seniority and "combativeness degree" of the weapon's owner: the lighter and shorter the rifle, the better.

14. On the social and political implications of the increasing number of knitted skullcaps in the fighting units of the IDF, see Yagil Levy, "The Clash between Feminism and Religion in the Israeli Military: A Multilayered Analysis," *Social Politics* 17 (2010).

15. After riding from there, I recalled my father's article on the duel and the Jews in Hungary. At the turn of the nineteenth century, Hungarian modern Jews, Israelites as they called themselves, were ashamed of their alleged blood and religious connections to "eastern" Jews from Poland and Russia, who escaped from the pogroms there and immigrated to Hungary. The Israelites did their best to distinguish between themselves and the Ost Juden, and taking part in duels was meant to underline this difference.

16. And perhaps this is rightly so if I accept Arendt's interpretation of Eichmann the person as an idiot who followed orders and strove to excel, in almost a machinelike state of mind, at his "job" of sending people to their deaths . . .

17. During the following months, and after I had returned to this place several times, I discovered a whole literature about the Crusaders in the Holy Land, and about the Zionist-Crusaders analogy. Evidently, Palestinian and Arab nationalists often compared

the Zionist movement and the State of Israel to the Crusaders' fallen "Kingdom of Jerusalem," arguing that due to its foreign, extraregional, and colonizing nature, Israel will "disappear" from the region, much like the Crusaders did. On the other hand, Israeli Zionist intellectuals often invoked the analogy as a warning sign and historical lesson that Zionism should learn, and highlighted the fact that Zionism is the opposite of the crusading project. See Ronnie Ellenblum, *Crusader Castles and Modern Histories* (Cambridge: Cambridge University Press, 2007), 54–60. For me, the important point about this debate between Zionism and Palestinian Arab nationalism is not necessarily who is "right" in it but rather that it actually exists: it is depressing to discover that the place I live in, the polity I am a part of, is the subject of such a debate. Moreover, eventually, for the Israelis, "the Crusaders ceased to be hostile and violent foreigners who had conquered the land by force of arms, slaughtering Jews who happened to cross their path, and plundering ancient civilizations. They were transformed simply into another group of inhabitants of the country, part of its history—or at least part of the Israeli nation. The fact that the Crusaders fought the Muslims made this conceptual transformation all the easier" (60). What is more depressing, then: to be aware that Israel, and me within it, is the subject of a debate about whether it is a Crusader state or not or to realize that the brutal Crusaders were made part of the Israeli national history merely because they killed Muslims?

18. *The Chamber Quintet* (*Ha-Hamishiya HaKamerit*) was a satirical Israeli TV show that was produced and broadcast in the early to mid-1990s. Many of the skits criticized Zionist and Jewish myths and ethos. After the murder of Prime Minister Yitzhak Rabin in 1995, the Quintet became more political and its satire more bitter.

19. See this YouTube video, accessed March 5, 2013, at http://www.youtube.com/watch?v=Tagi-Klh8dg.

20. On the military use of bicycles in the Swiss army, see Rainer Hülsse, "I, the Double Soldier: An Autobiographic Case Study on the Pitfalls of Dual Citizenship," in *Autobiographical International Relations*, ed. Naeem Inayatullah (London: Routledge, 2011).

21. Ariella Azoulay and Adi Ophir, *This Regime Which Is Not One: Occupation and Democracy between the Sea and the River, 1967–* (Tel Aviv: Resling, 2008) (in Hebrew).

22. Ramot is, in most of its parts, built on land that was occupied in the 1967 war. As such, it is considered by the Palestinians and many in the international community as an illegal settlement. But there are hardly any Israelis who see it as a settlement, mainly because it is a "part" of Jerusalem.

23. I learned this while talking with a warden of the Parks Authority at the place. Later I gathered additional information from the Internet. See this YouTube video, for example, in which the military and Magav come to prohibit the planting of olive seedlings on Palestinian "Land Day" 2011, accessed March 5, 2013: http://www.youtube.com/watch?v=bQn0 GUOmRWs&feature=related.

24. See this YouTube video, accessed March 5, 2013: http://www.youtube.com/watch?v=WQVJoDa6iZI.

25. I tried to inquire about them at the Jordanian embassy in Tel Aviv, but officials there did not reply to my e-mails.

26. In Jordan, as I found out, there is no developed and deep-rooted culture of military commemoration as in Israel. There is no national day of remembrance for the war dead (while there is a commemoration of the supposedly heroic Karameh battle of 1968), and the commemoration of dead soldiers is not individually oriented but rather reflects a communal culture. Furthermore, there are no military cemeteries. Dead soldiers are buried in civilian graveyards, not in uniform military tombs as in Israel. More recently, though, on March 21, 2012, King Abdullah instructed the government to declare a special veterans day. See the Independent Media Review Analysis website, accessed March 5, 2013, http://www.imra.org.il/story.php3?id=56151. See also Assaf David, "The Revolt of Jordan's Military Veterans," *Foreign Policy*, June 16, 2010, accessed March 5, 2013, http://mideast.foreignpolicy.com/articles/2010/06/15/the_revolt_of_jordans_military_veterans.

27. See George L. Mosse, *Fallen Soldiers: Reshaping the Memory of the World Wars* (New York: Oxford University Press, 1990).

28. Indeed, along the Gaza Strip, Palestinian militants and terrorists routinely shoot missiles and rockets toward Israeli towns, transcending the separation fence there. These attacks come sometimes as retaliation for Israeli strikes, and sometimes the Palestinians shoot first. It is often hard to really tell "who started it." But, compared to the suicide-bombing attacks, these rockets cause only very few casualties in Israel. In addition, since 2011 the IDF has deployed batteries of rocket-intercepting missiles, which demonstrate sometimes a success rate of 85 percent in intercepting incoming Palestinian rockets.

29. High Court of Justice Ruling 2056/04, accessed March 5, 2013, http://www.btselem.org/hebrew/Legal_Documents/HC2056_04_Beit_Surik_Barrier_Ruling.pdf (in Hebrew).

30. See Ghazi-Walid Falah, "The Geopolitics of 'Enclavisation' and the Demise of a Two-State Solution to the Israeli-Palestinian Conflict," *Third World Quarterly* 26 (2005): 1362ff. See also George Gavrilis, "Sharon's Endgame for the West Bank Barrier," *Washington Quarterly* 27 (2004); and Uri Ben Eliezer and Yuval Feinstein, "'The Battle over Our Homes': Reconstructing/Deconstructing Sovereign Practices around Israel's Separation Barrier on the West Bank," *Israel Studies* 12 (2007): 178.

31. High Court of Justice Ruling 2056/04, 11.

32. Ibid., 49.

33. On the other hand, another group of residents from Mevasseret argued before the court during the Beit Surik appeal that the fence should *not* follow the Green Line because in this manner there would be an increased risk to Mevasseret and the schools in it. Their representative, Efrayim Halevy, mentioned that in the (unspecified) past there had been "terrorist activity" in the Beit Surik region (ibid., 14). As far as I know, historically Beit Surik was more a source of criminal activities such as robberies and theft than a source of terrorism. See Benny Morris, *Israel's Border Wars, 1949–1956: Arab Infiltration, Israeli*

Retaliation, and the Countdown to the Suez War (Oxford: Oxford University Press, 1997), 56. Theft (mainly car theft) and burglaries continued until the erection of the fence, but I did not find any cases of terrorist violence (murder, arson, bombing, etc.).

The threat of terrorism was mentioned again in 2006, when a group of Mevasseret residents, represented by the former head of the Local Council, Dani Azriel, appealed to the HCJ in a demand that the IDF redirect the fence's already redirected route farther into the territory of the Palestinian village (the court rejected this appeal). See High Court of Justice 11409/05 (in Hebrew).

34. One of the crucial points during the deliberations of the court was when the appellants presented elaborate three-dimensional models, made of plaster, of the region and the various possible routes of the fence. The models, designed by the NGO Bimkom— Planners for Planning Rights, cost several tens of thousands of shekels to prepare. This money was obtained from the New Israel Foundation by another key figure from the Mevasseret group—Hagai Agmon-Snir. The models were required in order to demonstrate vividly to the judges the spatial meanings of the fence. The judges did not leave the court to tour the relevant area, and therefore the models had a dramatic effect—they were very large and elaborate. The military, too, brought its own models to the court, but they were shabby in comparison with the Bimkom-designed models. The models contained small houses, and agricultural lands were painted in green (e-mail correspondence with Hagai Agmon-Snir, October 4, 2010).

I rode to Bimkom's offices, at Rechaviya in Jewish Jerusalem. The staff showed me the models, which were stored in an unused bathtub in the cellar of the building. The manager of Bimkom suggested that I take the models into my possession, if I were interested. They had no need for them anymore. I took some elaborate pictures of the models, but politely refused to take them—the models were too large for me to store. But to be honest, at this stage of my research, I also felt that the models represented the ingratitude of the Beit Surikians, and I did not want their *presence* in my home.

35. See this picture of Beit Surikians watching the construction of the separation fence west of their village, between Mevasseret and Har Adar. There are two interesting talkbacks below the picture. Talkback #40454 says, "My heart breaks." Talkback #128675 says, "What was taken by force can be restored only by force": accessed March 5, 2013, http://www.palestineremembered.com/GeoPoints/Bayt_Surik_887/Picture_28416.html.

36. Mustafa Joubran (pseudonym), interview at his house, September 23, 2010. From the point of view of the Israeli state, though, there is a no special suspicion of Beit Surik but rather a general suspicion of all Palestinians and a desire to make the fence continuous without any "holes" to prevent the entry of "interlopers" and terrorists from other regions. Indeed, in the region of the Israeli town of Beit Shemesh, the fence was not complete as of 2012, and many "illegal stayers"/interlopers from various areas in the West Bank use the "hole" in the fence to enter Israel for work. In 2010 terrorists from a village near Hebron murdered two Israeli women who hiked in this region, on the Israeli side of the Green Line.

37. Rotem Mor, meeting at his home in Mevasseret, September 29, 2010.

38. See this interview with self-proclaimed "disillusioned" professor Benny Morris, whose early works challenged the traditional Zionist historiography of the conflict: Ari Shavit, "Survival of the Fittest," *Haaretz*, January 8, 2004, accessed March 5, 2013, http://www.haaretz.com/survival-of-the-fittest-1.61345.

39. Suicide bombings in the Israeli-Palestinian conflict did not start in the 2000s. There were fourteen such attacks during the mid-1990s, when the Oslo process still had not gone aground. But there was no precedent for the intensity and number of attacks after 2001. Partially, this intensification resulted from the sharp discrepancy in the "balance" of casualties between the Israelis and the Palestinians in the first period of the uprising—suicide bombings turned into a "strategic weapon" for the Palestinians in their struggle to close the gap of causalities. The outburst of the uprising in October 2000 was answered with a harsh response by the IDF. In the first two weeks of the second intifada, the IDF shot one million bullets at Palestinian rioters and demonstrators. One of the IDF's central command officers reportedly joked that this figure stands for a "bullet for each [Palestinian] child." See Ben Caspit, "Rosh HaShana, 2002: Two Years to the Intifada," *NRG News*, September 5, 2002, accessed March 5, 2013, http://www.nrg.co.il/online/archive/ART/344/233.html (in Hebrew). The military was determined to "overwhelm" the Palestinians in an unequivocal manner, so as not to repeat previous "ties" or "standoffs" as in the case of the first Palestinian uprising (1987–93) or the 1996 Western Wall Tunnel's riots. See the testimonies in Israel's Channel 8 film *Million Bullets in October* (produced by Assaf Amir and Rut Lev Ari and directed by Moysh Goldeberg in 2007), in which senior and "mainstream" Israeli ex-officials and journalists discuss the events of the first months of the second intifada, accessed March 5, 2013, http://www.youtube.com/watch?v=NQr7MDWNuPE&feature=relmfu (in Hebrew). I became aware of these facts and testimonies only while writing this book and researching the separation fence. I believe that a great majority of Israelis is not familiar with the complex reality of the outburst of the second intifada, which resulted, among other things, in the construction of the fence.

Chapter Three

1. See Yair Bar-El et al., "Jerusalem Syndrome," *British Journal of Psychiatry* 176 (2000).

2. Benny Morris, *The Birth of the Palestinian Refugee Problem Revisited* (Cambridge: Cambridge University Press, 2004), 239–40.

3. Ibid., 239.

4. See, for example, Michal and David Carmon, "Halilim Cave: A Bedouin Love Song," *Ynet News*, April 28, 2005, accessed March 6, 2013, http://www.ynet.co.il/articles/1,7340,L-3072603,00.html.

5. See Victor Guerin, *Description Geographique, Historique, et Archeologique de la Palestine*, vol. 1 (Paris: L'Imprimerie Impériale, 1868), 262. Guerin visited the region personally and depicted it very accurately, in terms of both the landscape and the time required

to walk from site to site. For another identification of the place as wadi a-Zananir, see Salman Abu Sitta, *Atlas of Palestine, 1948: Reconstructing Palestine* (London: Palestine Land Society, 2004), 282. See also a survey map of plots and agricultural lands of Qaluniya available on the Palestine Remembered website, accessed March 6, 2013, http://www.palestine remembered.com/Jerusalem/Qalunya/Picture14743.html.

6. Zeev Vilnay, *Ariel: An Encyclopedia of Eretz Yisrael*, vol. 3 (Tel Aviv: Am Oved, 1977), 2387 (in Hebrew).

7. Meeting of the Governmental Names Committee, January 4, 1955. The State of Israel Archives, file no. 46698/4, 43.26/4-4 (in Hebrew).

8. See Yossef Ben Baruch, "Zeev Vilnay and the Legends of Eretz Yisrael," in *The Book of Zeev Vilnay*, ed. Eli Shiller, vol. 1 (Jerusalem: Ariel Press, 1984).

9. An interesting point in this regard relates to the admiration of the Palmach for the image of the "Arab." Especially, one of the Palmach's units, the Mistarabim (those who "turn" Arab) used to dress up in Arab clothes, "adopting Arab speech and ways." See Haim Watzman, "Translator's Note," in Oz Almog, *The Sabra: The Creation of the New Jew* (Berkeley: University of California Press, 2000), xv. See also Yael Zerubavel, "Memory, the Rebirth of the Native, and the 'Hebrew Bedouin' Identity," *Social Research* 75 (2008): 325–26.

10. "The time is out of joint:—O cursed spite / That ever I was born to set it right!" (Shakespeare, *Hamlet*, act 1, scene 5). I used this quotation in a previous study of mine that dealt with the American-led "war on terror," to indicate the desire of the United States to set time right after the trauma of 9/11. But I thought about this quote when I watched David truing my bike's wheel because I first got to know *Hamlet* in Hebrew, not in English. In the wonderful Hebrew translation of Avraham Shlonsky, the line goes like this (I literally translate the Hebrew translation back into English): "The wheel of time was dislocated from its pedestal; ah me, that I have to reinstall it." (It sounds much, much better in Hebrew itself . . .) Shlonsky, in fact, translated Shakespeare from Russian and French, for he did not command English.

11. Search the Web for Hakim Bey's "TAZ: The Temporary Autonomous Zone, Ontological Anarchy, Poetic Terrorism."

12. I know that the phrasing should be "with which," but in the original text in Hebrew, the term is "with whom"—pointing to a perception of the village as a unified, single community.

13. "Castel/Nachshon," at the website of the Haganah, the main Jewish militia during the British Mandate in Palestine, accessed January 8, 2012, http://www.hagana.co.il/show_item.asp?levelId=59798&itemId=48048&itemType=3.

14. See Morris, *The Birth of the Palestinian Refugee Problem Revisited*, 235.

15. See Noga Kadman, *The Depopulated Palestinian Villages of 1948 in the Israeli Discourse* (Jerusalem: November Press, 2008), 31 (in Hebrew). The quotes are from an official letter from Yaacov Yanai, of the Israeli Ministry of Tourism, to the JNF.

16. Although the English translation of the title is as cited in note 15 (the book itself is only in Hebrew).

17. Zvi Grinhot, "Motsa and Jerusalem during the Iron Age II: Chronological, Agricultural, and Administrative Aspects" Israel Antiquities Authority, accessed March 6, 2013, http://www.antiquities.org.il/article_Item_ido.asp?sec_id=17&sub_subj_id=477&id=923#as (in Hebrew).

18. See Ilan Pappé, *The Aristocracy of the Land: The Husayni Family, a Political Biography* (Jerusalem: Bialik Institute, 2002), 132–33 (in Hebrew).

19. A news report in the Hebrew daily *Maariv*, January 12, 1949, states, "The ruins of an ancient fort were discovered" and "The ruins of a fort that King Herod built to guard the road to Jerusalem were revealed recently during archaeological research in the village of Qalunya, near Motsa.... [I]t has been known for a while that there was a Herodian fort here, but an important part of this fort was discovered only now due to the explosion of [Palestinian] houses in the place. Meanwhile, the work of removing the debris [of the demolished houses] was halted, *in order not to damage the antiquities*" (my emphasis).

20. See Lana Kamleh's interview and tour with refugees from Qalunya, minute 4:46, accessed, March 6, 2013, http://www.youtube.com/watch?v=8wscunMvFaI&feature=related (in Arabic). See also Meir Broza and Tsori Broza, *Motza: On the Road to Jerusalem, 1860–1994* (Jerusalem: Cana, 1994), 223 (in Hebrew); and Ruth Kark and Michal Oren-Nordheim, *Jerusalem and Its Environs: Quarters, Neighborhoods, Villages, 1800–1948* (Detroit: Wayne State University Press, 2001), 225. Kark and Oren-Nordheim quote Edith Larson, who argues that the Husaynis allowed the people of the American-Swedish colony in Jerusalem to use their country house, located "near the village spring." (225). Indeed, the house I identify as the Husayni one is located very close to the main spring of the village.

21. Ilan Pappé, though, portrays the Mufti as a prudent person, who did all he could to avoid this eruption of violence. See Ilan Pappé, "Haj Amin and the Buraq Revolt," *Jerusalem Quarterly File* 6 (2003).

22. On the number of saved Jews in Hebron, see Oded Avishar, ed., *The Hebron Book* (Jerusalem: Keter Publishing House, 1970), 424–26 (in Hebrew). Palestinians saved and warned Jews beforehand of attacks during the 1929 Riots in several other locations, yet many of them were branded collaborators and traitors by the Palestinian national leadership. See Hillel Cohen, *Army of Shadows: Palestinian Collaboration with Zionism, 1917–1948* (Berkeley: University of California Press, 2008), 62.

23. See the testimony of Aliza Schmalz-Ha'Ivri, a resident of the Emek Ha'arazim settlement in Shmuel Eben Or, "To the History of the Arazim Valley [Emek Ha'arazim]," in *The Book of Zeev Vilnay*, ed. Eli Shiller, vol. 1 (Jerusalem: Ariel Press, 1984), 359–60.

24. Yisrael Amikam, *The Attack on the Jewish Yishuv in Eretz Yisrael in 1929* (Haifa: Zarodinsky Bros. Publishers, unknown date), 35 (in Hebrew).

25. This is according to Ghalib Muhammad Sumrayn's *My Village, Qalunya* (Amman: Matba'at al-Tawfiq, 1993), chap. 4 (in Arabic). Sumrayn, a refugee from Qalunya (he is

a seventh-generation native of the village), is the son of one of the twelve Qalunya residents who were indicted in the British court in Jerusalem in the murders committed at the Maklef house. According to the testimony of Hayim Maklef, the twenty-one-year-old son of the family, who survived the attack, Muhammad Sumrayn, Ghalib's father, stabbed his mother, Batya Maklef, with his sword, and while doing this he cried, "Slaughter the dogs!" While in January 1930, the court found all twelve Qalunya defendants not guilty of the murder, there is strong reason to believe that the decision was politically motivated, in order not to further aggravate the Palestinians in the wake of the British suppression of their uprising. Ghalib Sumrayn, though, in his book, notes that his father participated in the attack on the Maklef house, carrying a short sword in his hand (as described by Hayim Maklef). He also takes pride in the fact that his father killed four Jews who supposedly insulted the Qalunya villagers in 1936, when they passed by the village in a truck (178). All references to Sumrayn's book are from Hillel Cohen's *1929: Blood, Sanctity, History* (Jerusalem: Keter, forthcoming) (in Hebrew). Further information on Sumrayn and his book (though without reference to Sumrayn father's involvement in the 1929 riots) can be found in Rochelle A. Davis, *Palestinian Village Histories: Geographies of the Displaced* (Stanford: Stanford University Press, 2010).

26. Sumrayn's *My Village, Qalunya,* quoted in Cohen, *1929* (my italics).

27. See Cohen, *1929.*

28. On the political and religious background of these riots, see Avraham Sela, "The 'Wailing Wall' Riots (1929) as a Watershed in the Palestine Conflict," *The Muslim World* 84 (1994).

29. Baruch Katinka, *Ever Since Then* (Jerusalem: Kiryat Seffer, 1961), 262 (in Hebrew).

30. Meron Benvenisti, *Sacred Landscape: The Buried History of the Holy Land since 1948* (Berkeley: University of California Press, 2000), 251–52.

31. Whalid Khalidi, ed., *All That Remains: The Palestinian Villages Occupied and Depopulated by Israel in 1948* (London: Institute for Palestine Studies, 1992).

32. See the picture of Qalunya, taken by the Australian soldiers who conquered the Jerusalem area from the Ottomans in December 1917 (imperial periodization again . . .), in which the slope and the valley are meticulously attended, and there is no sign for any ailanthus, in Kark and Oren-Nordheim, *Jerusalem and Its Environs,* 214. See also this painting by Siona Tagger, *Village on the Way to Jerusalem,* 1930, on Sionah Tagger's website, accessed March 6, 2013, http://www.tagger-siona.co.il/showPic.php?pic_name=fullsize/46.jpg&pic_str=45.

33. In the "documentation file" submitted to the Municipality of Jerusalem on behalf of a Jewish settler society that purchased the mufti's house in Sheikh Jarrah in East Jerusalem, and plans to build there a Jewish neighborhood, the architect Giora Solar writes, "The house has top educational importance, inasmuch as it is important to preserve concentration camps, prisons, and gallows. He does not recommend demolishing the house, mainly due to its architectural value. But he recommends that it be turned into an "education

center" (within the proposed Jewish neighborhood) that will deal with "the 1929 and 1936 riots, as well as highlight the connection between the mufti and the Nazis. These subjects have not found a suitable place yet. One can imagine a site that deals with the anti-Jewish propaganda that is published in Arab states in Muslim society." Giora Solar, "A Preliminary Documentation File [submitted to the City of Jerusalem]—the Sheppard Hotel and the Mufti's House, Jerusalem," 2011 (no specific publication date, in Hebrew).

34. See Richard Breitman and Norman J. W. Goda, *Hitler's Shadow: Nazi War Criminals, US Intelligence, and the Cold War*, report published by the US National Archives, December 2010, 19, accessed March 6, 2013, http://www.archives.gov/iwg/reports/hitlers-shadow.pdf. See also Peter Wien, "Coming to Terms with the Past: German Academia and Historical Relations between the Arab Lands and Nazi Germany," *International Journal of Middle East Studies* 42 (2010): 314–16.

35. Quoted in Philip Mattar, *The Mufti of Jerusalem: Al-Hajj Amin Al-Husayni and the Palestinian National Movement* (New York: Columbia University Press. 1992), 105.

36. See Idith Zertal, *Israel's Holocaust and the Politics of Nationhood* (Cambridge: Cambridge University Press, 2005), 102–3. See also Mattar, *The Mufti of Jerusalem*, chap. 8.

37. See, for example, Roni Stauber, "'Realpolitik' and the Burden of the Past: Israeli Diplomacy and the 'Other Germany,'" *Israel Studies* 8 (2003). See also Shraga Elam and Dennis Whitehead, "In the Service of the Jewish State," *Haaretz*, March 29, 2007, accessed March 6, 2013, http://www.haaretz.com/weekend/magazine/in-the-service-of-the-jewish-state-1.216923; and Sasha Polakow-Suransky, *The Unspoken Alliance: Israel's Secret Relationship with Apartheid South Africa* (New York: Random House, 2010), prologue and chap. 1.

38. Edward Said, "Bases for Coexistence," in his *The End of the Peace Process: Oslo and After* (New York: Vintage Books, 2001), 208. Said refers also to the Palestinian instrumental attitude to the Holocaust, that involves denial, silence, or underestimation, due to the fear that recognition of the Jewish tragedy will serve Israeli interests.

39. See Ilan Gur-Ze'ev and Ilan Pappé, "Beyond the Destruction of the Other's Collective Memory: Blueprints for a Palestinian/Israeli Dialogue," *Theory, Culture & Society* 20 (2003).

40. Avraham Sela, "Arab and Jewish Civilians in the 1948 Palestine War," in *Caught in Crossfire: Civilians in Conflict in the Middle East*, ed. P. R. Kumaraswamy (Reading, UK: Ithaca Press, 2008), 25–26.

41. Morris, *The Birth of the Palestinian Refugee Problem Revisited*, 97.

42. This is the standard explanation of the name in many geographic and historical sources I read. But among the Palestinians some believe the name originated from the good scent of the various fruit trees and flower bushes they grew in the village—Qaluniya in the sense of eau de cologne. See Lana Kamleh's interview with Bassam al Ralizi, a descendant of refugees from Qaluniya, who says that his great-uncle and grandfather explained to him the meaning of the name in this manner. YouTube video, minute 5:40, accessed March 6,

2013, http://www.youtube.com/watch?v=1k87-oo_Nmk&NR=1 (in Arabic). I like this explanation much more than the one dealing with the Roman Colonia . . .

43. See the science fiction novel of Michael Chabon, *The Yiddish Policemen's Union* (New York: Harper Collins, 2007). In this novel, which takes place in an alternate history in which Jewish autonomy was established in Alaska after the Jews were defeated in Palestine in 1948, there are frictions between the Jewish settlers and the Tlingit Alaskan natives too . . .

44. Harry Levin, *Jerusalem Embattled: A Diary of the City under Siege, March 25, 1948 to July 18, 1948* (London: Victor Gollancz, 1950), 67.

45. For me, the issue of the ownership of the land boils down to this: as a secular person, I cannot accept religious rights and justifications. And if one bases ownership on historical grounds, then why do the historical rights of one people prevail over those of others? It is true that there was never an independent Palestinian state in this country, but the last historical occurrence of Jewish sovereignty was during the Hasmonean kingdom, which ended in the year 37 BCE—quite an ancient period on which to base current ownership rights. Yet beyond such historical claims, Israel has always based its legitimacy on various declarations and partition plans for Palestine by different international bodies such as the League of Nations, the Anglo-American Committee, and the UN. Israelis traditionally argue that while the Jews were pragmatic and accepted the 1947 UN partition plan, the Palestinians rejected it and initiated the 1948 war. Therefore, they can only blame themselves for the refugee problem and the conquest of large parts of Mandatory Palestine by the Jewish forces in 1948, places that were not initially designated as part of the Jewish state by the UN plan.

Beyond the various historical problems of such a simple interpretation of the events, then, there is a greater risk in this argument: it implies that under certain conditions, the "right of conquest" still applies. The constant reliance on, discursive return to, and even *celebration* of the right of conquest, this moment of constitutive violence, may justify (at least for the Israelis) the current structure of the political regime and the geographic division of space in this land. But at the same time it also drops the ground from under the chance to achieve lasting peace and true security. By insisting on the absolute justness of our use of force against the Palestinians, and by being unwilling to recognize the 1948 war as a tragedy for *both* peoples, we, Israelis, maintain our identity as conquerors and keep fanning the flames of rage and desire for revenge of the Palestinians. True, the majority of the Palestinians never welcomed the Zionists/Israelis in this land, and, at most, were/are willing to accept the Israeli Zionist presence in this land as a compromise. But Israelis have treated the Palestinians the same way throughout the conflict. Naive as this may sound, true security for both peoples will be achieved only once there begins a process of deep introspection and withdrawal from the discourse of violence. This, of course, entails facing difficult identity challenges and questions of political and spatial organization, but I believe that we, Israelis and Palestinians, must start the process of disengaging from violence in the emotional sense, hard as the process might be. We should learn history, not mythology, and turn our faces to the future, not just the past. Perhaps then we'll be able to see the humanity of each other.

46. See Ariella Azoulay, "Declaring the State of Israel: Declaring a State of War," *Critical Inquiry* 37 (2011).

Chapter Four

1. I thought about the artwork *Magav in Weimar* by Ronen Eidelman. Eidelman placed a cardboard print of the profile of a Magav jeep in almost real size on a supermarket cart and "patrolled" the streets of Weimar, to provide himself if not real security then at least a facade of security. See Eidelman's website, accessed March 7, 2013, http://roneneidelman.com/?p=9145. See also Ronen Eidelman, "Personal Security," *Mafteakh* 3 (2011), accessed March 7, 2013, http://mafteakh.tau.ac.il/wp-content/uploads/2011/03/mafteakh03.pdf (in Hebrew).

2. The state's planning committee allowed the railway company to breach the West Bank due to the excuse that the railway track will also serve the Palestinian cities of Gaza and Ramallah one day, when a branch of the track is built there. In this way, the track is supposedly not violating the Geneva Convention articles on the management of occupied territories, which prohibit an occupier from exploiting the territory without benefiting the local inhabitants. See Coalition of Women for Peace, "Crossing the Line: The Tel Aviv–Jerusalem Fast Train" Tel Aviv, 2010, 8, accessed March 7, 2013, http://www.whoprofits.org/sites/default/files/Train%20A1.pdf (in Hebrew).

3. See HCJ file 281/11, *Head of the Council of Beit Iksa and Others v. Minister of Defense and Others*, February 16, 2011 (in Hebrew).

4. Sayed Kashua, perhaps the best-known Israeli Palestinian journalist and scriptwriter, deals with the myth/reality of Arabs who speak loudly on his hit TV show *Arab Labor*, episode 8 of season 3 (in Hebrew and Arabic). See the Mako VOD website, accessed March 7, 2013, http://www.mako.co.il/mako-vod-keshet/Arabic-work-s3/VOD-b98eb-1c686a2631006.htm.

5. Until the early 1990s, Subaru was one of the very few Japanese-made car brands imported into Israel, mainly due to the Arab boycott on the state of Israel that led most Japanese car manufacturers to opt out of that market. The Oslo peace process, which began in 1993, caused many international and transnational corporations to start selling in Israel. I remember how joyful we were to drink for the first time Pepsi-Cola or see Mitsubishi and Toyota cars . . .

6. An interesting—and telling?—point about transliteration: Arab names have various transliterations to roman letters. While Benvenisti transliterates الحسيني to al Husseini, Ilan Pappé chooses al Husayni. Both speak and read Arabic well, and, I guess, have their reasons for the different transliterations. On the other hand, a great number of Israeli (Ashkenazi) surnames are more uniformly transliterated into roman letters, for they are European in origin. This applies to my name too . . .

7. Yehuda Amichai, "God Has Pity on Kindergarten Children," in Chana Bloch and Stephen Mitchell, trans., *The Selected Poetry of Yehuda Amichai* (Berkeley: University of California Press, 1996), 1.

8. See Nili Sharf Gold, *Yehuda Amichai: The Making of Israel's National Poet* (Lebanon, NH: Brandeis University Press, 2008), chap. 11.

9. "In the Trial of the Murderers of Maklef family," *Davar*, January 10, 1930, quoted in Cohen, *1929*.

10. Cohen, *1929*.

11. In another meeting with Taher, I found out that he owns and has read Ghalib Muhammad Sumrayn's *My Village, Qalunya* (Amman: Matba'at al-Tawfiq, 1993) (in Arabic). There, in chapter 4, the author relates how his father and other residents of Qalunya, not Bedouin outsiders, attacked Motsa and killed the Maklefs. Did Taher not read this part? Again, I felt that he was hiding something from me or was not telling me the (whole) truth. But, I had to remind myself, Taher is not a student of mine, one that I examine and grade for his "reading comprehension" or historical knowledge. Perhaps he did not read this part of Sumrayn's book, perhaps he forgot it, or perhaps he simply believes his grandfather's "version" more than Sumrayn's. Or maybe he knowingly chose to tell an untruth to me about the 1929 murders because he felt that this would stand in contradiction to the "Maklef offer" to return to Qalunya.

12. See Oren Yiftahcel, *Ethnocracy: Land and Identity Politics in Israel/Palestine* (Philadelphia: University of Pennsylvania Press, 2006).

13. Yehuda Ziv, "The 'Zionist' Map of the British Military (1917–1918)," *Cathedra* 123 (2007), 124 (in Hebrew). Interestingly, while during the Yishuv pre-state period the word *Hebrew* (*Ivri* עברי) was often used to describe the Zionist project in Palestine, after the establishment of the state in 1948, the word *Jewish* (*Yehudi* יהודי) became much more prevalent. Currently, *Hebrew* (*Ivri*) would be considered an anachronism. Indeed, the author of the article I quote from here is a member of the generation of the Yishuv.

14. The blue placemarks can be removed by unchecking them in the "layers" option of the system. But this is not the default condition of the map.

15. John James Moscrop, *Measuring Jerusalem: The Palestine Exploration Fund and British Interests in the Holy Land* (London: Leicester University Press, 2000).

16. Actually, the PEF map does not include the southern region of Israel—the Negev desert. The map surveyed the region roughly between "Dan" (in today's southern Lebanon) and Beersheba—the supposed boundaries of the Biblical Patriarchs' possessions in the land.

17. There is a famous joke that Jews always answer a question by raising another question . . .

Chapter Five

1. The cedar has a very special meaning in Jewish folklore/mythology/history, mainly signifying royal architecture. King Solomon's Temple in Jerusalem was built, according to

the Bible, from cedars the Hebrew king received from Hiram, the Phoenician king of Tyre. At the entrance to the Giv'at Ram campus of Hebrew University, three tall and impressive cedars grow (they were able to grow so high because they are regularly watered). A small metal plaque near the trees mentions the story of the cedars of Solomon's Temple and then says, "Growing here at the campus entrance, this tree symbolizes the university as a 'temple' of modern learning."

2. In the occupied territories, on the other hand, Israeli authorities use an Ottoman decree (Article 78) to take control of "deserted" Palestinian land. Article 78 originally was meant to create ownership over territory if one could prove that he had cultivated the land and bettered it. This served the Ottoman interest of enlarging the taxpayer base. However, Israel turned Article 78 upside down: for several decades now, the *lack* of cultivation (for a period of ten years or more) signifies denunciation of ownership, which enables the state to take control of previously private land. Of course, often the lack of cultivation comes from the inability of Palestinian farmers to access their lands due to the various obstacles created by the occupation regime. See Irus Braverman, "'The Tree Is the Enemy Soldier': A Sociolegal Making of War Landscapes in the Occupied West Bank," *Law and Society Review* 42 (2008).

3. Interestingly, one of the single places in Jerusalem in which the various populations of the city—secular Jews, religious and ultrareligious Jews, and Palestinian Arabs from East Jerusalem—meet on friendly terms in a relatively relaxed atmosphere is the Jerusalem Biblical Zoo. In this beautiful and large zoo, Jerusalemites of "all stripes" and ages become more relaxed and tolerant of each other. People smile at each other, and kids get a chance to play together in the playground.

4. On people's efforts to evade the state's coercive power by escaping or moving into desolate or difficult to access regions, see James C. Scott, *The Art of Not Being Governed: An Anarchist History of Upland Southeast Asia* (New Haven: Yale University Press, 2009).

5. See in this regard the "Protocol of the Discussion of the Subcommittee for Principal Planning Issues [ולנ"ת]))," no. 396, September 9, 2009, 40, accessed March 7, 2013, http://www.yitla.com/r/1/4.pdf (in Hebrew).

6. Interestingly, this flame design of the statute is highly reminiscent—if not a duplication—of another work of its designer/sculptor, Eliezer Weishoff: the cover of the 1973 war booklet he designed in 1974 for the Command of the Hebrew Youth Battalions (acronym GADNA in Hebrew), in which the names of the fallen Israeli soldiers appear. See the image of this cover at this Wikipedia page, accessed March 7, 2013: http://he.wikipedia.org/wiki/%D7%A7%D7%95%D7%91%D7%A5:Yom-kipur-war.jpg.

7. PT stands for Petach Tikvah, an Israeli town near Tel Aviv.

8. See Meirav Yodilovich, "Baruch Jamili Dies at the Age of 81," *Ynet News*, December 29, 2004, accessed March 7, 2013, http://www.ynet.co.il/articles/0,7340,L-3025370,00.html#n (in Hebrew).

9. Taglit-Birthright Israel is an educational enterprise that brings groups of Jewish youths (ages eighteen to twenty-six) to Israel for their first (organized) ten-day visit.

About 80 percent of the participants are from the North America. The aim is to strengthen Jewish identity and the connections between young "Diaspora Jews" and Israel by showing them the positive facets of the state. Funding comes from the government of Israel, various Jewish community organizations, and private donors. Showing these young Jews the positive aspects of Israel is especially important for the organizers of Taglit due to the increasing numbers of young Jews in North America who distance themselves politically and religiously from Israel, do not consider it as part of their identity, and even see it as a burden.

10. Interview with a Jerusalem Park guide, May 29, 2011.

11. Later I discovered that she was just following the organization's security procedures: "Participants stay with their group the entire duration of the trip and are not allowed to explore or visit with Israelis on their own." This sounded to me somewhat North Korean. See Taglit, "Our Safety Guidelines," accessed March 7, 2013, http://www.birthrightisrael. com/VisitingIsrael/Pages/Safety-and-Security.aspx.

12. The Province of Judea—Provincia Judea—is the Roman name given to the country after the Roman occupation during the first century CE.

13. In this sense, his idea reminds me of the need of Aboriginal Australians to almost theatrically perform their local traditions in order to substantiate a native title or land claim: "[I]ndigenous performances of cultural difference must conform generally to the [Australian] imaginary of Aboriginal traditions." Elizabeth A. Povinelli, "The State of Shame: Australian Multiculturalism and the Crisis of Indigenous Citizenship," *Critical Inquiry* 24 (1998): 590.

14. See *Full Battle Rattle*, produced and directed by Tony Gerber and Jesse Moss, Mile End Films, 2008, accessed March 7, 2013, http://www.fullbattlerattlemovie.com/.

15. I am prohibited by Israeli censorship laws to specify its exact location. Yet the existence of the installation in this area has been widely published by Israeli and international media.

16. The signs are in three languages (in this order): "A Security Installation—No Photographing," in Hebrew (מתקן בטחוני. אסור לצלם); "RESTRICTED AREA— PHOTOGRAPHING IS PROHIBITED" (in English, capitalized letters); and only "No Photographing" in Arabic (ممنوع التصوير). The signs, thus, represent a hierarchy of information for various groups according to the language they're supposed to read. But what about someone who can read all three languages?

17. This is the Torah scholar Rashi's interpretation of Ezekiel 12:13: "My net also will I spread upon him, and he shall be taken in my snare: and I will bring him to Babylon to the land of the Chaldeans; yet shall he not see it, though he shall die there."

18. You could actually see the ministers' cars enter the place that morning on a video (skip to the twentieth second): "Ministers about the Bunker: 'Looks Like Science Fiction Movies,'" Nana10 News, accessed March 7, 2013, http://news.nana10.co.il/ Article/?ArticleID=809864 (in Hebrew).

19. Ibid.

20. Testimony of Lieutenant General Dan Halutz before the Winograd Committee, 69–70 (available at the website of the Winograd Committee for the Investigation of the Events of the Campaign in Lebanon, 2006, http://www.vaadatwino.gov.il [accessed October 7, 2013]).

21. See, in this context, Carol Cohn, "Nuclear Language and How We Learned to Pat the Bomb," *Signs: Journal of Women in Culture and Society* 12 (1987).

22. In Germany, they built somewhere in the Schwarzwald an underground shelter to preserve the treasures of German culture, history, and science in case of an atomic holocaust or other major catastrophe: a *Kulturbunker*. See Ofer Aderet, "The Time Capsule," *Haaretz*, May 20, 2010, accessed March 7, 2013, http://www.haaretz.com/weekend/mag azine/the-time-capsule-1.291282 (in English).

23. *Yediot Acharonot*, the country's largest daily newspaper, wrote in on August 27, 2007, about the immensity of the underground compound inside the mountain. Ofer Petersburg, the newspaper's real-estate reporter, was allowed into the tunnel that leads to the bunker within the mountain. He wrote, "Things like these can be seen only in movies and TV. In this place, you walk with a sense of awe. *From here, they will command a burning state*" (my italics).

24. The most interesting book in this regard was Paul Virilio, *Bunker Archeology* (Princeton: Princeton Architectural Press, 2008).

25. Ibid., 39.

Contradictions

1. *Contradiction* is the opposite of *introduction*, according to Owl, "who is very good at long words," in A. A. Milne, *The House at Pooh Corner* (Toronto and Montreal: McClelland and Stewart, 1957), 153.

2. For a very graphic depiction of the never-ending cycle of conquest and reconquest in this land, see Nina Paley's video *This Land Is Mine*, accessed March 7, 2013, http://blog. ninapaley.com/2012/10/01/this-land-is-mine/.

3. Yet I must admit that I have not yet reflected seriously on the liberal and multicultural value world that is so ingrained in me and drives much of my writing. For a call to reflexive scholars to examine their own value world, see Inanna Hamati-Ataya, "Reflectivity, Reflexivity, Reflexivism: IR's 'Reflexive Turn'—and Beyond," *European Journal of International Relations*, forthcoming.

4. Mary Louise Pratt, *Imperial Eyes: Travel Writing and Transculturation* (London: Routledge, 1992), 7.

5. Frantz Fanon, *Black Skin, White Masks* (New York: Grove Press, 2008), 170.

6. Hannah Arendt, *The Origins of Totalitarianism* (Orlando, FL: Harcourt, 1973), 56–68.

7. On deterrence as a culture, see Amir Lupovici, "The Emerging Fourth Wave of Deterrence Theory: Toward a New Research Agenda," *International Studies Quarterly* 54 (2010).

8. This idiom is ascribed to Ehud Barak, former Israeli prime minister and defense minister. See Akiva Ekdar, "The Price of a Villa in the Jungle," *Haaretz*, January 30, 2006, accessed March 7, 2013, http://www.haaretz.com/print-edition/opinion/the-price-of-a-villa-in-the-jungle-1.178800.

9. On this Right, see Shuki J. Cohen, "When Unconscious Wishes Become Laws: Policing Memory and Identity in Israel and Palestine," *International Journal of Applied Psychoanalytic Studies* 10, no. 2 (June 2013): 152–73.

10. I spent two years at Toronto during 2001–3 and a year and a half on Vancouver Island during 2011–13.

11. Perhaps then, in postscript, I can be more accepting toward the 9/11 monument in the Arazim Valley—yes, there is in it a strong element of flattering and submitting to "the Americans," and it does function to legitimize and idolize an Israeli war on terror that is not always just and necessary. Yet it also represents true emotions of empathy and connectedness between Israelis and Americans. On sympathy in international politics, see Todd Hall, "Sympathetic States: Explaining the Russian and Chinese Responses to September 11," *Political Science Quarterly* 127 (2012).

12. To own up to the truth, I was appalled by this response, especially at a time when the Syrian regime butchers its own citizens.

13. "A tenured professor is like a nail hammered so deep into a concrete wall, that it cannot be pulled out without breaking the wall itself," a retired colleague from my department told me when I received tenure in early 2010. But in September and October 2012, it turned out that indeed the new hegemony of the Right in Israel is willing to demolish the "concrete wall" of the Department of Politics at Ben-Gurion University of the Negev—to shut down the entire department in order to silence the voices of its more critical faculty. See Talila Nesher, "Israeli Academics Sign Petition against Closing Ben-Gurion University's Politics Department," *Haaretz*, September 23, 2010, accessed March 7, 2013, http://www.haaretz.com/news/national/israeli-academics-sign-petition-against-closing-ben-gurion-university-s-politics-department.premium-1.466402; and, Matthew Kalman, "Fate of Controversial Political-Science Department in Israel May Be Decided Soon," *Chronicle of Higher Education*, September 30, 2012, accessed March 7, 2013, http://chronicle.com/article/Fate-of-Controversial/134782/. As of March 2013, the international campaign against closing the department helped, and the unit continues to exist.

14. Cowichan is the English distortion of the Hul'q'umi'num First Nations name Quw'utsun, meaning "the warm lands." See the Cowichan Tribe's website, accessed March 7, 2013, http://www.cowichantribes.com/.

15. See my good friend Oren Barak's, "The Modern Sherwood Forest: Why the International Community Cannot Let States Fail," paper presented at the annual meeting of the International Studies Association, Honolulu, Hawaii, March 5, 2005.

16. On the growing rift between many young, liberal North American Jews and Israel

because of the entrenchment of the occupation and the political deliberalization of Israel, see Peter Beinart, *The Crisis of Zionism* (New York: Times Books, 2012).

17. See Warren Magnusson and Karena Shaw, eds., *A Political Space: Reading the Global through Clayoquot Sound* (Minneapolis: University of Minnesota Press, 2003).

18. See the University of Victoria's First People's House website, accessed March 7, 2013, http://web.uvic.ca/fphouse/.

19. Meron Benvenisti, *Son of the Cypresses: Memories, Reflections, and Regrets from a Political Life* (Berkeley: University of California Press, 2007), 233.

BIBLIOGRAPHY

Abu Sitta, Salman. *Atlas of Palestine, 1948: Reconstructing Palestine*. London: Palestine Land Society, 2004.

Aldred, Rachel. "'On the Outside': Constructing Cycling Citizenship." *Social and Cultural Geography* 11 (2010): 35–52.

Almog, Oz. *The Sabra: The Creation of the New Jew*. Berkeley: University of California Press, 2000.

Amikam, Yisrael. *The Attack on the Jewish Yishuv in Eretz Yisrael in 1929*. Haifa: Zarodinsky Bros. Publishers, unknown date. In Hebrew.

Anderson, Leon. "Analytic Autoethnography." *Journal of Contemporary Ethnography* 35 (2006): 373–95.

Arendt, Hannah. *The Human Condition*. Chicago: University of Chicago Press, 1958.

Arendt, Hannah. *The Origins of Totalitarianism*. Orlando, FL: Harcourt, 1973.

Augustine. *The Confessions*. Trans. Henry Chadwick. Oxford: Oxford University Press, 1991.

Avishar, Oded, ed. *The Hebron Book*. Jerusalem: Keter Publishing House, 1970. In Hebrew.

Azoulay, Ariella. "Declaring the State of Israel: Declaring a State of War." *Critical Inquiry* 37 (2011): 265–85.

Azoulay, Ariella, and Adi Ophir. *This Regime Which Is Not One: Occupation and Democracy between the Sea and the River, 1967–*. Tel Aviv: Resling: 2008. In Hebrew.

Barak, Oren. *The Lebanese Army: A National Institution in a Divided Society*. Albany: SUNY Press, 2009.

Barak, Oren. "The Modern Sherwood Forest: Why the International Community Cannot Let States Fail." Paper presented at the annual meeting of the International Studies Association, Honolulu, Hawaii, March 5, 2005.

Bardenstein, Carol. "Trees, Forests, and the Shaping of Palestinian and Israeli Collective Memory." In *Acts of Memory: Cultural Recall in the Present*, ed. Mieke Bal, Jonathan V. Crewe, and Leo Spitzer, 148–70. Lebanon, NH: Dartmouth College Press, 1998.

Bar-El, Yair, Rimona Durst, Gregory Katz, Josef Zislin, Ziva Strauss, and Haim Knobler. "Jerusalem Syndrome." *British Journal of Psychiatry* 176 (2000): 86–90.

Beinart, Peter. *The Crisis of Zionism*. New York: Times Books, 2012.

Bell, Daniel A., and Avner de Shalit. *The Spirit of Cities: Why the Identity of a City Matters in a Global Age.* Princeton: Princeton University Press, 2011.

Ben Eliezer, Uri, and Yuval Feinstein. "'The Battle over Our Homes': Reconstructing/ Deconstructing Sovereign Practices around Israel's Separation Barrier on the West Bank." *Israel Studies* 12 (2007): 171–92.

Ben Yehuda, Nachman. *The Masada Myth: Collective Memory and Mythmaking in Israel.* Madison: University of Wisconsin Press, 1985.

Ben-Baruch, Yossef. "Zeev Vilnay and the Legends of Eretz Yisrael." In *The Book of Zeev Vilnay,* ed. Eli Shiller, vol. 1, 30–35. Jerusalem: Ariel Press, 1984. In Hebrew.

Benvenisti, Meron. *Sacred Landscape: The Buried History of the Holy Land since 1948.* Berkeley: University of California Press, 2000.

Benvenisti, Meron. *Son of the Cypresses: Memories, Reflections, and Regrets from a Political Life.* Berkeley: University of California Press, 2007.

Bisharat, George. "The Family Never Lived Here." *Haaretz,* English ed., January 2, 2004. Accessed August 10, 2011. http://www.haaretz.com/the-family-never-lived-here-1.60698.

Bloch, Chana, and Stephen Mitchell, trans. *The Selected Poetry of Yehuda Amichai.* Berkeley: University of California Press, 1996.

Braverman, Irus. "'The Tree Is the Enemy Soldier': A Sociolegal Making of War Landscapes in the Occupied West Bank." *Law and Society Review* 42 (2008): 449–82.

Breitman, Richard, and Norman J. W. Goda. *Hitler's Shadow: Nazi War Criminals, US Intelligence, and the Cold War.* Report published by the US National Archives, December 2010. Accessed May 17, 2012. http://www.archives.gov/iwg/reports/hitlers-shadow.pdf.

Brigg, Morgan, and Roland Bleiker. "Autoethnographic International Relations: Exploring the Self as a Source of Knowledge." *Review of International Studies* 36 (2010): 779–98.

Broza, Meir, and Tsori Broza. *Motza: On the Road to Jerusalem, 1860–1994.* Jerusalem: Cana, 1994. In Hebrew.

Bruchi, Nachum. *Har'el Armored Brigade (10) in the Six Days War.* Jerusalem: Ariel Publishing House, 2010. In Hebrew.

Caspit, Ben. "Rosh HaShana, 2002: Two Years to the Intifada." *NRG News,* September 5, 2002. Accessed March 5, 2013. http://www.nrg.co.il/online/archive/ART/344/233.html. In Hebrew.

Chabon, Michael. *The Yiddish Policemen's Union.* New York: Harper Collins, 2007.

Cohen, Hillel. *Army of Shadows: Palestinian Collaboration with Zionism, 1917–1948.* Berkeley: University of California Press, 2008.

Cohen, Hillel. *1929: Blood, Sanctity, History.* Jerusalem: Keter, 2013. In Hebrew.

Cohen, Saul E. *The Politics of Planting: Israeli-Palestinian Competition for Control of Land in the Jerusalem Periphery.* Chicago: University of Chicago Press, 1993.

Cohen, Shuki J. "When Unconscious Wishes Become Laws: Policing Memory and Identity in Israel and Palestine." *International Journal of Applied Psychoanalytic Studies* 10, no. 2 (June 2013): 152–73.

Cohen, Uri. *The Mountain and the Hill: The Hebrew University of Jerusalem during the Pre-independence Period and Early Years of the State of Israel.* Tel Aviv: Am Oved, 2006. In Hebrew.

Cohn, Carol. "Nuclear Language and How We Learned to Pat the Bomb." *Signs: Journal of Women in Culture and Society* 12 (1987): 687–718.

Couser, Thomas. *Vulnerable Subjects: Ethics and Life Writing.* Ithaca: Cornell University Press, 2004.

Dauphinee, Elizabeth. "The Ethics of Autoethnography." *Review of International Studies* 36 (2010): 799–818.

Davis, Rochelle A. *Palestinian Village Histories: Geographies of the Displaced.* Stanford: Stanford University Press, 2010.

Doty, Roxanne Lynn. "Maladies of Our Souls: Identity and Voice in the Writing of Academic International Relations." *Cambridge Review of International Affairs* 17 (2004): 377–92.

Edkins, Jenny. *Missing: Persons and Politics.* Ithaca: Cornell University Press, 2011.

Eidelman, Ronen. "Personal Security." *Mafteakh* 3 (2011): 105–16. Accessed March 7, 2013. http://mafteakh.tau.ac.il/wp-content/uploads/2011/03/mafteakh03.pdf. In Hebrew.

Ellenblum, Ronnie. *Crusader Castles and Modern Histories.* Cambridge: Cambridge University Press, 2007.

Ellis, Carolyn. "Creating Criteria: An Ethnographic Short Story." *Qualitative Inquiry* 6 (2000): 273–77.

Ellis, Carolyn. *The Ethnographic I: A Methodological Novel about Autoethnography.* Walnut Creek, CA: AltaMira Press, 2004.

Ellis, Carolyn. "Telling Secrets, Revealing Lives: Relational Ethics in Research with Intimate Others." *Qualitative Inquiry* 13 (2007): 3–29.

Eyal, Yigal, and Amiram Oren. "Tegart Forts: Government and Security." *Cathedra* 104 (2002): 95–126. In Hebrew.

Falah, Ghazi-Walid. "The Geopolitics of 'Enclavisation' and the Demise of a Two-State Solution to the Israeli-Palestinian Conflict." *Third World Quarterly* 26 (2005): 1341–72.

Fanon, Frantz. *Black Skin, White Masks.* New York: Grove Press, 2008.

Foucault, Michel. "The Subject and the Power." In *Michel Foucault: Beyond Structuralism and Hermeneutics,* ed. Hubert Dreyfus and Paul Rabinow, 208–26. Brighton: Harvester, 1982.

Galnoor, Itzhak. "Academic Freedom under Political Duress: Israel." *Social Research* 76 (2009): 541–60.

Gavrilis, George. "Sharon's Endgame for the West Bank Barrier." *Washington Quarterly* 27 (2004): 7–20.

Geertz, Clifford. *The Interpretation of Cultures.* New York: Basic Books, 1973.

Gertz, Nurit. *Unrepentant: Four Chapters in the Life of Amos Kenan.* Tel Aviv: Am Oved, 2008. In Hebrew.

Giddens, Anthony. *Modernity and Self-Identity: Self and Society in the Late Modern Age.* Stanford: Stanford University Press, 1991.

Guerin, Victor. *Description Geographique, Historique, et Archeologique de la Palestine, vol. 1.* Paris: L'Imprimerie Impériale, 1868.

Gur-Ze'ev, Ilan, and Ilan Pappé. "Beyond the Destruction of the Other's Collective Memory: Blueprints for a Palestinian/Israeli Dialogue." *Theory, Culture & Society* 20 (2003): 93–108.

Hall, Todd. "Sympathetic States: Explaining the Russian and Chinese Responses to September 11." *Political Science Quarterly* 127 (2012): 369–400.

Hamati-Ataya, Inanna. "Reflectivity, Reflexivity, Reflexivism: IR's 'Reflexive Turn'—and Beyond." *European Journal of International Relations*, forthcoming.

Holt, Nicholas L. "Representation, Legitimation, and Autoethnography: An Autoethnographic Writing Story." *International Journal of Qualitative Methods* 2 (2003). Accessed March 7, 2013. http://www.ualberta.ca/~iiqm/backissues/2_1/pdf/holt.pdf.

Hülsse, Rainer. "I, the Double Soldier: An Autobiographic Case Study on the Pitfalls of Dual Citizenship." In *Autobiographical International Relations,* ed. Naeem Inayatullah, 56–64. London: Routledge, 2011.

Hunker, Henry. *Columbus, Ohio: A Personal Geography.* Columbus: Ohio State University Press, 2000.

Inayatullah, Naeem, ed. *Autobiographical International Relations.* London: Routledge, 2011.

Ingold, Tim. *The Perception of the Environment: Essays on Livelihood, Dwelling, and Skill.* London: Routledge, 2000.

Kadman, Noga. *The Depopulated Palestinian Villages of 1948 in the Israeli Discourse.* Jerusalem: November Books, 2008. In Hebrew.

Kark, Ruth, and Michal Oren-Nordheim. *Jerusalem and Its Environs: Quarters, Neighborhoods, Villages, 1800–1948.* Detroit: Wayne State University Press, 2001.

Katinka, Baruch. *Ever Since Then.* Jerusalem: Kiryat Seffer, 1961. In Hebrew.

Katz, Jack. *How Emotions Work.* Chicago: University of Chicago Press, 2000.

Khalidi, Rashid. *The Iron Cage: The Story of the Palestinian Struggle for Statehood.* Boston: Beacon Press, 2006.

Khalidi, Whalid, ed. *All That Remains: The Palestinian Villages Occupied and Depopulated by Israel in 1948.* London: Institute for Palestine Studies, 1992.

Khosravi, Shahram. "The 'Illegal' Traveler: An Auto-ethnography of Borders." *Social Anthropology* 15 (2007): 321–34.

Kliot, Nurit. "Afforestation for Security Purposes: Spatial Geographical Aspects." In *Studies in Eretz Yisrael: Aviel Ron Book,* ed. Y. Bar Gal, Nurit Kliot, and A. Peled, 205–19. Haifa: Department of Geography, University of Haifa, 2004. In Hebrew.

Lamar, Howard, and Leonard Thompson. *The Frontier in History: North America and Southern Africa Compared.* New Haven: Yale University Press, 1981.

Learmonth, Mark, and Michael Humphreys. "Autoethnography and Academic Identity: Glimpsing Business School Doppelgängers." *Organization* 19 (2012): 99–117.

Levin, Harry. *Jerusalem Embattled: A Diary of the City under Siege, March 25, 1948 to July 18, 1948.* London: Victor Gollancz, 1950.

Lévi-Strauss, Claude. *Tristes Tropiques.* New York: Penguin, 2012.

Levy, Yagil. "The Clash between Feminism and Religion in the Israeli Military: A Multilayered Analysis." *Social Politics* 17 (2010): 185–209.

Louis Grinberg, Lev. "Speechlessness: In Search of Language to Resist the Israeli 'Thing without a Name.'" *International Journal of Politics, Culture, and Society* 22 (2009): 105–16.

Löwenheim, Avigdor. "Zsidók és a párbaj" [Jews and the duel]. *Múlt és Jövő*, new ser., 3 (1992): 83–94.

Löwenheim, Oded. *Predators and Parasites: Persistent Agents of Transnational Harm and Great Power Authority.* Ann Arbor: University of Michigan Press, 2007.

Löwenheim, Oded. "The 'I' in IR: An Autoethnographic Account." *Review of International Studies* 36 (2010): 1023–45.

Löwenheim, Oded, and Gadi Heimann. "Revenge in International Politics." *Security Studies* 17 (2008–9): 685–724.

Lupovici, Amir. "The Emerging Fourth Wave of Deterrence Theory: Toward a New Research Agenda." *International Studies Quarterly* 54 (2010): 705–32.

Magnusson, Warren, and Karena Shaw, eds. *A Political Space: Reading the Global through Clayoquot Sound.* Minneapolis: University of Minnesota Press, 2003.

Mattar, Philip. *The Mufti of Jerusalem: Al-Hajj Amin Al-Husayni and the Palestinian National Movement.* New York: Columbia University Press. 1992.

Medford, Kristina. "Caught with a Fake ID: Ethical Questions about Slippage in Autoethnography." *Qualitative Inquiry* 12 (2006): 853–64.

Miller, Benjamin. *States, Nations, and the Great Powers: The Sources of Regional War and Peace.* Cambridge: Cambridge University Press, 2007.

Milne, A. A. *The House at Pooh Corner.* Toronto and Montreal: McClelland and Stewart, 1957.

Mitchell, W. J. T. "Holy Landscape: Israel, Palestine, and the American Wilderness." In *Landscape and Power,* ed. W. J. T. Mitchell, 261–90. Chicago: University of Chicago Press, 2002.

Mitchell, W. J. T. "Imperial Landscape." In *Landscape and Power,* ed. W. J. T. Mitchell, 5–34. Chicago: University of Chicago Press, 2002.

Mitzen, Jennifer. "Ontological Security in World Politics: State Identity and the Security Dilemma." *European Journal of International Affairs* 12 (2006): 341–70.

Morris, Benny. *The Birth of the Palestinian Refugee Problem Revisited.* Cambridge: Cambridge University Press, 2004.

Morris, Benny. *Israel's Border Wars, 1949–1956: Arab Infiltration, Israeli Retaliation, and the Countdown to the Suez War.* Oxford: Oxford University Press, 1997.

Morris, Benny. *Righteous Victims: A History of the Zionist-Arab Conflict, 1881–2001.* New York: Vintage Books, 2001.

Moscrop, James. *Measuring Jerusalem: The Palestine Exploration Fund and British Interests in the Holy Land.* London: Leicester University Press, 2000.

Moss, Pamela. "Writing One's Life." In *Placing Autobiography in Geography,* ed. Pamela Moss, 1–21. Syracuse, NY: Syracuse University Press, 2001.

Mosse, George L. *Fallen Soldiers: Reshaping the Memory of the World Wars.* New York: Oxford University Press, 1990.

Musil, Robert. *The Man without Qualities,* vol. 1. New York: Vintage Books, 1996.

Mykhalovskiy, Eric. "Reconsidering Table Talk: Critical Thoughts on the Relationship between Sociology, Autobiography, and Self-Indulgence." *Qualitative Sociology* 19 (1996): 131–51.

Ochs, Juliana. *Security and Suspicion: An Ethnography of Everyday Life in Israel.* Philadelphia: University of Pennsylvania Press, 2011.

Oddy, Nicholas. "The Flaneur on Wheels?" In *Cycling and Society,* ed. P. Rosen, Peter Cox, and David Horton, 97–112. Burlington, Surrey: Ashgate, 2007.

Oren, Amiram. *"Drafted Territories": The Creation of Israeli Army Hegemony over the State's Land and Its Expanses during Its Early Years (1948–1956).* Jerusalem: Madaf Publishing, 2009. In Hebrew.

Oren, Amiram, and Raffi Regev. *A Country in Khaki: Land and Security in Israel.* Jerusalem: Carmel, 2010. In Hebrew.

Oring, Elliot. *Jokes and Their Relations.* New Brunswick, NJ: Transaction Books, 2010.

Pappé, Ilan. *The Aristocracy of the Land: The Husayni Family, a Political Biography.* Jerusalem: Bialik Institute, 2002. In Hebrew.

Pappé, Ilan. "Haj Amin and the Buraq Revolt." *Jerusalem Quarterly File* 6 (2003): 6–16.

Polakow-Suransky, Sasha. *The Unspoken Alliance: Israel's Secret Relationship with Apartheid South Africa.* New York: Random House, 2010.

Povinelli, Elizabeth A. "The State of Shame: Australian Multiculturalism and the Crisis of Indigenous Citizenship." *Critical Inquiry* 24 (1998): 575–610.

Pratt, Mary Louise. *Imperial Eyes: Travel Writing and Transculturation.* (London: Routledge, 1992.

Quinn Patton, Michael. *Qualitative Research and Evaluation Methods.* Thousand Oaks, CA: Sage, 2002.

Richardson, Laurel. *Fields of Play: Constructing an Academic Life.* New Brunswick, NJ: Rutgers University Press, 1997.

Rosen, Paul. "The Social Construction of Mountain Bikes: Technology and Postmodernity in the Cycle Industry." *Social Studies of Science* 23 (1993): 479–513.

Said, Edward. *The End of the Peace Process: Oslo and After.* New York: Vintage Books, 2001.

Scott, James C. *The Art of Not Being Governed: An Anarchist History of Upland Southeast Asia.* New Haven: Yale University Press, 2009.

Sela, Avraham. "Arab and Jewish Civilians in the 1948 Palestine War." In *Caught in Crossfire: Civilians in Conflict in the Middle East,* ed. P. R. Kumaraswamy, 1–30. Reading, UK: Ithaca Press, 2008.

Sela, Avraham. "The 'Wailing Wall' Riots (1929) as a Watershed in the Palestine Conflict." *The Muslim World* 84 (1994): 60–94.

Seliktar, Ofira. "'Tenured Radicals' in Israel: From New Zionism to Political Activism." *Israel Affairs* 11 (2005): 717–36.

Shcarf Gold, Nili. *Yehuda Amichai: The Making of Israel's National Poet.* Lebanon, NH: Brandeis University Press, 2008.

Shehadeh, Raja. *Palestinian Walks: Notes on a Vanishing Landscape.* London: Profile Books, 2010.

Shenhav, Yehuda. *In the Trap of the Green Line: A Jewish Political Mass.* Tel Aviv: Am Oved, 2010. In Hebrew.

Soochul, Kim. "Moving around Seoul." *Cultural Studies <=> Critical Methodologies* 10 (2010): 199–207.

Spicker, Paul. "Ethical Covert Research." *Sociology* 45 (2011): 118–33.

Spinney, Justin. "Cycling the City: Non-place and the Sensory Construction of Meaning in a Mobile Practice." In *Cycling and Society,* ed., P. Rosen, Peter Cox, and David Horton, 25–46. Burlington, Surrey: Ashgate, 2007.

Stauber, Roni. "'Realpolitik' and the Burden of the Past: Israeli Diplomacy and the 'Other Germany.'" *Israel Studies* 8 (2003): 100–122.

Steele, Brent J. "Irony, Emotions, and Critical Distance." *Millennium: Journal of International Studies* 39 (2010): 89–107.

Stein, Janice G. *The Cult of Efficiency.* Toronto: House of Ananasi, 2002.

Stoller, Paul. *The Taste of Ethnographic Things: The Senses in Anthropology.* Philadelphia: University of Pennsylvania Press, 1989.

Sumrayn, Ghalib Muhammad. *My Village, Qalunya.* Amman, Jordan: Matba'at al-Tawfiq, 1993. In Arabic.

Thrift, Nigel. "Driving in the City." *Theory, Culture & Society* 12 (2004): 41–59.

Urry, John. *Sociology beyond Societies: Mobilities for the Twenty-First Century.* London: Routledge, 2000.

Vilnay, Zeev. *Ariel: An Encyclopedia of Eretz Yisrael,* vol. 3. Tel Aviv: Am Oved, 1977. In Hebrew.

Virilio, Paul. *Bunker Archeology.* Princeton: Princeton Architectural Press, 2008.

Waltz, Kenneth. *Theory of International Politics.* Reading, MA: Addison-Wesley, 1979.

Wendt, Alexander. *Social Theory of International Politics.* Cambridge: Cambridge University Press, 1999.

Wien, Peter. "Coming to Terms with the Past: German Academia and Historical Relations between the Arab Lands and Nazi Germany." *International Journal of Middle East Studies* 42 (2010): 311–21.

Yiftachel, Oren. *Ethnocracy: Land and Identity Politics in Israel/Palestine.* Philadelphia: University of Pennsylvania Press, 2006.

Zertal, Idith. *Israel's Holocaust and the Politics of Nationhood.* Cambridge: Cambridge University Press, 2005.

Zerubavel, Yael. "Memory, the Rebirth of the Native, and the 'Hebrew Bedouin' Identity."
    Social Research 75 (2008): 315–52.
Ziv, Yehuda. "The 'Zionist' Map of the British Military (1917–1918)." *Cathedra* 123 (2007):
    93–124.

INDEX